when quitting is
Not
an option

My Road to Cycling, a Guinness World Record and Making a Difference

Arvid Loewen with Paul Loewen
Foreword by David Balzer

GWR - July 2020
Farthest Distance cycled
in one month.

Arvid Loewen.

CASTLE QUAY BOOKS

When Quitting Is Not An Option: My Road to Cycling, a Guinness World Record and Making a Difference

Copyright ©2014 Arvid Loewen and Paul Loewen
All rights reserved
Printed in Canada
International Standard Book Number: 978-1-927355-48-0
ISBN 978-1-927355- 49-7 EPUB

Published by:
Castle Quay Books
Pickering, Ontario, L1W 1A5
Tel: (416) 573-3249
E-mail: info@castlequaybooks.com   www.castlequaybooks.com

Edited by Marina Hofman Willard
Cover design by Burst Impressions
Printed at Essence Publishing, Belleville, Ontario

Library and Archives Canada Cataloguing in Publication

Loewen, Arvid, 1956 Nov. 25-
    When Quitting Is Not An Option: My Road to Cycling, a Guinness World Record, and Making a Difference/ foreword by David Balzer ; Arvid Loewen and Paul Loewen..
Also issued in electronic format.

ISBN 978-1-927355-48-0

CASTLE QUAY BOOKS

Endorsements

I have known Grandpa Arvid since we were teenagers 40 years ago. We share a common past and country of origin. We were at times teammates on a volleyball team or competed for a spot on the university soccer team. Arvid won. What I remember most is Arvid's tenacity to overcome the toughest odds. Today he is directing that tenacity to beat the odds of those less privileged, the homeless and the fatherless. If you envision a grandpa's life in a hammock on a sunny beach, find another book to read. If you want to be inspired to a greater purpose, read Arvid's story.

Ben Sawatzky
CEO, Spruceland Millworks Ltd.

I was with Arvid at his low point in Death Valley and at his highest in Halifax with a Guinness World Record. His cycling feats are legendary. But for me, his personal sacrifice and the love he has for the Mully children are his greatest accomplishments.

Frank DeFehr
Friend of Arvid

Arvid is a brilliant example of what can happen when passion for a cause becomes priority number one. His book vividly describes the journey he has taken to use his gifts to help "the least of these." The true story of his transformation from business to full-time philanthropy is remarkable and is an example to all of us. I recommend the book, and I know you will be challenged to rethink your priorities and your personal response to the poverty that confronts each one of us.

Herb Buller
Chairman and president, Buller Foundation

I was moved by Arvid Loewen's account of what can be accomplished with strong faith and determination. An inspirational read—I recommend anyone to explore these stories of failure, success and hope. Arvid offers a reminder that, despite life's impressive accomplishments, one's faith is the most important of all.

Joy Smith
Member of Parliament, Kildonan-St. Paul, Canada
Chair, National Standing Committee on Health

Arvid, as a grandpa, has accomplished feats on a bike that most of us would not even dream of, let alone dare to tackle. Dedicated to living for Christ and helping those in need, his message is an inspiration, clearly demonstrating that age is no barrier when it comes to being the hands and feet of Jesus.

Cindy Klassen
Six-time Canadian Olympic medallist

Every now and then you hear of someone who goes to great lengths, even superhuman, to follow their passion and calling. They use their God-given athletic ability, extreme mental fortitude and extraordinary determination to accomplish their goals. Very few of us can say we have tested ourselves to such a degree. Even fewer of us can say we have done it for a cause outside of our own or family need. Arvid Loewen, grandpa and extreme cyclist, epitomizes such "extraordinariness" for a cause, destitute children in Kenya who live in extraordinary life-threatening situations.

David Unruh
Former international coach, athlete, realtor

We are honored to be able to render our insight in the journey of Arvid Loewen. We, too, have raced alongside Arvid as race officials during some of these endeavours. About 1,700 miles into the race, we found Arvid sitting in a chair beside the car, eating a sandwich. We stopped to inquire about how he was doing. Instead of telling us about the fatigue he was experiencing, Arvid lit up with enthusiasm as he told us of his family that was meeting him on the course. We were blessed with descriptions of them and his ministry to help homeless children. It became apparent that Arvid's goal was not to just do this event but to use it as a springboard to spread his love for family, children and God. Arvid, you are winning that race! Ride on my friend.

Guy and Stephanie Wells
RAAM 2005–2013

An inspiring story of what Christ can do in a life surrendered to Him. I had the privilege of journeying with Arvid and seeing his compassion firsthand. His son Paul gives us an incredible opportunity to discover what it is that drives Arvid.

Paul H. Boge
Author of *Father to the Fatherless: The Charles Mulli Story*,
Hope for the Hopeless: The Charles Mulli Mission

I am grateful to the Almighty God for giving me and my family Arvid's dear friendship. Arvid is a source of inspiration to us at Mully Children's Family and to many around the world. We have been challenged by his incredible commitment to ride his bike through tough circumstances and over incredible distances for MCF. Whenever I have visited him I have been blessed by his determined, prayerful and focused attitude. We are thankful for the privilege of joining with him on some of his races and his special focus on the alleviation of poverty among the needy children of Africa. We cannot forget his beautiful wife, Ruth, for sharing Arvid with our large family. Those of us here at MCF would like to thank Arvid and Ruth and their entire family for their support. We encourage you to read this book—may it challenge you to give yourself for the sake of others!

Dr. Charles M. Mulli (PhD, HSC)
Founder and CEO, Mully Children's Family

This book is the wonderful story of a man who has been moved to the core of his soul to join in with what he sees God can do in a powerful way through the work of others.

Murray Taylor
President and CEO, Investors Group

Every once in a while there's a story of someone who does something amazing, something few people would even attempt—let alone accomplish. This is that kind of story. A successful man and a proud grandpa lays it all on the line to change the lives of the poorest of the poor. As someone who's been on a support crew for Arvid when he accomplished what we all thought was impossible—I can say this story is going to grip your heart and mind and encourage you to never quit and never give up—you can make a difference.

Victor Neufeld
Support crew member, GrandpasCan 2011
Lead pastor, North Kildonan MB Church

All readers will find much to stimulate their thinking in this book. The story of Arvid Loewen's journey is inspirational. Its breadth and scope will provoke both thought and emotion. As he has done throughout his journey, Arvid helps us think more clearly about the things that are truly important and the difference one man can make in the lives of thousands.

Doug Warkentin
President, Warkentin Group, Private Wealth Management

To collect Arvid's dentures out of an Alaskan roadside ditch in '97 was an adventure for me. To break the Guinness World Record across Canada in 2011 is a lifetime achievement for Arvid. The years of training, determination, faith and sacrifice in between are God's calling on a man's life to make a difference to street children in Kenya.

Juergen Loewen
Eight-time support crew member

It was our privilege to give Arvid Loewen coast-to-coast coverage on our daily 100 Huntley Street telecast, as we tracked his courageous trek across Canada. Our Crossroads Relief and Development team are proud to have been connected with Arvid and Mully Children's Family for a number of years. Arvid's huge heart for helping those less fortunate is an inspiration to us all!

Ron Mainse
Spiritual director, Crossroads Family of Ministries
Executive producer of *100 Huntley Street*

Arvid is the fastest cyclist I have ever met. What makes Arvid so wonderful and unique is that he uses his ultra-marathon cycling to honour and glorify the Lord Jesus. He is making a big difference for many at Mully Children's Family in Kenya, Africa.

Albert Martens
Extreme running, Power to Change

Arvid's grit has challenged and inspired me for years as he lives out his mission with a passion and commitment that blows my mind. This book provided poignant "behind the scenes" detail that only increased my respect for his faith, tenacity and willingness to sacrifice. Pedal through the pages of this book along with Arvid if you need a good kick in the pants to discover and live out your own calling. Simply: "Wow."

Carolyn O. Bergen
Marriage and family therapist
Director, Bergen & Associates Counselling

Go, Grandpa, go!

Arvid's eight grandsons

Dedication

My wife, Ruth: you are my best friend, most loyal supporter and accountability partner. Our life has been quite the adventure thus far, and I look forward to how God will continue to lead us.

Our children, Jodi and Bernie, Stephanie and Josh, Paul and Jeanette: you have played a major part in shaping who I am. Being your dad has taught me much. Thank you for blessing me.

Our eight grandsons, Niko, Oliver, Jaden, Emerson, Kieren, Bryce, Lachlan and Jonah: you make life even sweeter. May each of you aspire to make a difference in the world for the glory of God.

Table of Contents

Foreword
November 10, 2013

It was June 1999, and I was sitting in the front seat of an RV making my way through Canada's immense Rocky Mountains. But this was anything but a vacation. Amidst the picturesque offerings of mountain grandeur, what I was actually fixated on, just on the other side of the huge picture window, was a small man on a bicycle. He'd been climbing the excruciating grade of the Coquihalla Highway for the past hour at 8 km an hour and simply hadn't stopped pedalling. As a media coordinator, I had been asked to tell the story of Arvid's first Vancouver to Winnipeg ultra-marathon cycling attempt. I couldn't imagine how what I was watching was possible. Fourteen years and thousands of kilometres later, there is still something unbelievable about the story that follows. Unbelievable, that is, if you aren't prone to acknowledging the strength of a vision and the presence of God.

I actually cycled a few kilometres alongside of Arvid on the bald prairie of Saskatchewan during that first trip. We still share laughs about it to this day, given how difficult I found it to keep up with a man who had been on a bike for 18 hours a day, climbed the Rockies and was bucking stiff prairie winds. I quickly realized that I wasn't going to be part of this story by riding a bike. But those five days from Vancouver to Winnipeg did invite me into a much larger story, a story of faith, compassion and tenacity, a story of setting aside the false belief that the world's problems are too big for any one person to make a difference.

I invite you to read this book with an open heart. If I know Arvid at all, I know he would never want you to read this story as if it was about him and his cycling accomplishments. His singular vision has always been that we would have eyes to see the world through the eyes of Charity, the tiny rescued girl who renewed his sight and filled his heart.

When Quitting Is Not an Option

I count it a privilege to have been invited, on several occasions, to share Arvid's story with the public media. Today, I suggest to you that this story is worth reading because it offers a picture of a life worth living.

David Balzer
Winnipeg, MB
Assistant Professor of Communications and Media,
Canadian Mennonite University
Media coordinator (Spoke '99, GrandpasCan 2011)

Acknowledgements

God: You have led me all my life. And now in these recent years, I have sensed your love and leading in very profound ways.

Ruth: I could not do what I do without you by my side.

Paul Loewen, my son, the author: What a rare privilege this has been. You had this idea long before I did. You have lived much of this story first-hand. The experience of writing this book together is something I will always treasure.

Bernie and Jodi, Josh and Stephanie, Paul and Jeanette, and my eight grandsons: You are my best support crew, whether you are on the road with me or supporting me from at home.

Charles and Esther Mulli: For entrusting me, a virtual stranger at the time, with three of your children as I dreamed and planned Spoke 2005. We are blessed to have been able to work alongside you and value our ongoing partnership and friendship. There is no doubt that God brought us into one another's lives. To God be the glory.

Mulli children Miriam, Jane, Grace, Ndondo, Kaleli, Mueni, Isaac and Dickson: For welcoming and accepting Ruth and me as partners in your ministry.

MCF beneficiaries who have travelled across Canada with me—Lydia, Paul, Mumina, Mary, Charity, Rama, John, Benedict: Your presence on the road with me has been a huge encouragement.

David Balzer, media coordinator for Spoke '99 and GrandpasCan 2011: You have been instrumental in helping me use cycling as a platform to make a difference. Your expertise and creativity in delivering the story to the media has opened many doors.

Paul Boge, media coordinator for Spoke 2005 and GrandpasCan 2012: Your presence on the road with the MCF contingent was invaluable in creating awareness for them to tell their stories.

Media, local and national: You have made it possible to spread the word about MCF all across Canada.

Bikes and Beyond: You have provided premium bikes and service for me. Thank you, Phil Roadley and staff.

Larry Willard, publisher, Castle Quay Books: You were keen about this book project from the first time we communicated. Thank you for believing in it. It has been a pleasure working with you.

Marina Hofman Willard, executive editor, Castle Quay Books: You kept us on track and on schedule. Thank you for your expertise and for making this such a positive experience.

Donors: Thank you for your support of MCF. Together we are making a difference.

Event sponsors: You make it possible for me to do what I do.

Support crews: Thank you for your tireless and selfless service to keep me on my bike.

Prayer warriors—friends, family, the MCF family: With God all things are possible.

1

The End

RAAM 2008

Click.   Click.   Click.
   Click.   Click.   Click.   Click.   Click.   Click. Click.
Click.Click.ClicClicClicCliCliClClClClCCC.

The ticking of my wheels picked up speed as I crested the slight hill and started moving downwards again. Behind me, I could hear the revving of the support crew vehicle taper off as they, too, coasted with a bit more speed. That slight uphill was nothing compared to what I had already experienced in the first five days of the ride.

Five days? I asked myself. *Has it really been that long?*

Is that all it's been?

"Hey, Arvid!" Ruth called out of the side of the van, pulling up beside me. "Up ahead is the McDonald's they were telling us about. Free food for all Race Across America riders and crew."

Biking 20 out of every 24 hours takes a toll on the body, and there's almost no way you can replenish the energy you're expending. With that much output, you're forced to take in as many calories as possible—through whatever means possible. Milkshakes and Big Macs had become some of my favourite. This would be a great place to load up. I needed somewhere between 8,000 to 9,000 calories in 24 hours. If you've ever tried to eat that much, you'll realize it's more or less impossible. Which is why I was losing weight. It was day five, and I'd already dropped a few pounds. By the end of the ride I would be down 5 to 10 lbs from my starting weight. A quick weight-loss program if I've ever heard of one.

When Quitting Is Not an Option

"Sounds good," I said. "We'll stop there, and I'll take a short break. Can't waste time," I added as they drove ahead to the golden arches in the distance. I was alone in my thoughts again, with only the sounds of my bike ticking and the hum of the tires on the road.

Ultra-marathon cycling is a solitary sport, one that puts you against the road. There are other competitors out there, but the battle comes down to you versus you. In the end, if you lose, it's you defeating yourself.

I snapped my head up just in time to turn into the parking lot, taking my foot out of the right pedal and coasting to a stop. Josh was there to grab the bike from me as I lifted my foot over the frame. I shook my head, trying to clear a slight pain that seemed to have settled in at the back of my neck.

"Do you want a Big Mac, Dad?" my daughter, Stephanie, asked. "Vanilla milkshake?"

"And a Coke," I nodded, my throat a little hoarse. I couldn't tell whether the headache was from a lack of sleep or something more serious, but the caffeine couldn't hurt. By this point in the ride I needed every pick-me-up that I could get.

"Rider 132." Someone was coming my way, looking at his clipboard. "Arvid Loewen?"

"That's me," I responded, taking a sip from the bottle and stripping the gloves off my hands. Over time it seemed like they fused to the skin, the sweat bonding them together.

"So you're a solo rider?" He put the clipboard on the ground and lifted a camera to his shoulder, adjusting the lens.

"That's right," I answered. "Solo. All 3,000 miles from coast to coast."

"How are you feeling today?"

"Tired," I responded, laughing out loud. "Not sure what else to expect." I stretched my leg out, feeling the tightness in my hip. People always asked how I could possibly sit on a bike seat for 20 hours a day. I usually told them that by the time you stayed on a bike that long there were far more significant things to worry about. The pain in your butt was only the beginning of your problems.

"You're nearly halfway there," the man said. I wasn't sure whether it was a comment or a question. *Halfway,* I thought, *halfway would be nice. It's all downhill on the other side, isn't it?* It's a little ridiculous to think that biking five days continuously would only get you almost halfway, but traversing the entire continent in less time than many people drive it is no small accomplishment.

"Nearly halfway," I admitted. I didn't like thinking about it, though. I was stuck in the middle of the ride, and there was a lot of ground yet to cover. Those on the outside seemed to think that, somehow, past the halfway point it was bound to get easier. With ultra-marathon cycling, with anything ultra-marathon, the biggest challenge is always yet to come. The ride's not done until you cross the finish line, and not a millimetre sooner. I was a lot more than a millimetre from the finish line.

"How has your ride been going?" he asked. I didn't answer immediately. How can you sum up five days of intense heat (the Mojave Desert), oxygen-thin elevations (the Rocky Mountains), torturous mental exertion (sleeping less than two hours a night), mind-numbing terrain (the flats of the prairies) and more challenges than you've ever experienced in your life? To answer his question would have taken a few hours, but I didn't have the time, because ultra-marathon cycling adds another mental component to the drama: everything, and I mean everything, is on the clock. Every pit stop, every fitful nap, every bathroom break, every second of every day is a part of your time. Already, sitting outside and waiting for my Big Mac was starting to feel like a waste of time, though my legs appreciated the break.

"It's been going well," I said. "As well as I could have hoped."

"What do you think are your chances of finishing?" He moved his eye out from behind the viewfinder, as though he wanted to see, without looking through a lens, what I was about to say. He wanted to catch my reaction.

Stephanie reappeared with my Big Mac, and I took a moment to set it down on the table beside me, then plunked down and got ready to eat. He was still looking at me, waiting for an answer. Finally I decided to give him one.

"Fifty-one percent," I answered.

I wasn't sure if I believed what I had just said. I was in a fog, mentally not even close to 100 percent, and the ride was taking its toll on my mind and my body. Though I am a prairie boy and the bore of the terrain didn't bother me, five days of sitting on my bike was having an effect.

"Are you going to get anything, Josh?" Steph asked. Josh, her husband, was part of our crew.

"We've been in the vehicle for four—no five—days already," he said. "I've had enough of fast food. I think I'll just get a salad." He still regrets not taking advantage of free McDonald's food.

Only a few bites in, I was already almost done the burger. Grease is helpful—once your throat is raw, it coaxes the food down.

When Quitting Is Not an Option

"Ruth, do you think you could pour the milkshake into a water bottle?" I asked her. "I'm going to head to the washroom." I stood up from the table and went towards the restaurant. The air conditioning would be a good respite for just a minute. The large McDonald's sign dominated my view for a moment, and I saw what was written underneath: "Welcome Race Across America riders and crew!"

For 13 years, Race Across America (RAAM) had stood out in my mind as the pinnacle of ultra-marathon cycling. It was the Tour de France of the ultra world, though without all the doping and off-bike rest. No teams, no drafting, no sleep. And here I was, right in the middle of RAAM. For years I had secretly dreamed about it, told no one, and aimed for participating in the world's toughest bike race.

And here I was.

As I stepped into the cold of the restaurant I shivered, not because of the temperature change but because of where I was. Because of what I was doing. A pain shot through my neck, and I clapped my hand to the back of it. There was nothing there. Nothing wrong with it. I took my helmet off—all of a sudden it felt really heavy.

I went to the washroom and questioned what I was feeling. Everything seemed to be normal. I looked at myself in the mirror. Since the beginning of the ride it looked like I had aged five years, if I was being generous. Maybe it was more like ten. My skin was hanging a little looser on my face, the wrinkles pronounced from the heat of the sun constantly beating down on it. My eyes were surrounded by bags, sleep deprivation taking effect.

I blinked my eyes and snapped out of it, then strapped my helmet back on. A little bit of pain wasn't about to slow me down.

I walked back out, adjusting to the bright light of the day. Another rider had arrived in the time I was inside, and I tried to assess who was hurting more. Cyclists have a habit of looking at each other's calves, thighs, butts and midsections. You can size each other up pretty quickly with a quick glance. But the farther you go in the ride, the less those matter and the more the face matters. You can train your body to cycle fast and hard, but eventually it becomes a mental exercise. Judging by his face and what I had just seen in the mirror, he was hurting even more than I was.

Ruth rolled the bike up to me, and I clambered on. "The milkshake is in the bottle," she pointed, giving me a peck on the cheek. "Still 51 percent, eh?" she asked.

"That 1 percent makes all the difference." I forced a smile, forgetting why, exactly, I was doing what I was doing.

Little did I know that percentage was about to drop—dramatically.

The sun was starting to set, disappearing behind the Kansas horizon. Fear climbed into my throat and lodged itself there. The nights are always the worst. It's no wonder that people experience more depression when the days are shorter—the dark surrounds you and saps you of energy. But we didn't get breaks and took them only when absolutely necessary, driven by the wobble of our tires as we struggled to keep our eyes open and our heads up.

My head dropped, but it wasn't sleep that was the problem.

I pulled it back up, feeling some tension in the back of my neck.

Is my head getting heavier? I thought. But that was ridiculous. It couldn't just get heavier. *Then why is it so hard to hold up?* There was only one answer to the question, but I wasn't prepared to accept it.

I heard the surge of the van engine behind me, and it pulled even with me. "You okay?" Ruth leaned out the side window. My son, Paul, was driving, his wife, Jeanette, in the front seat. They had switched with Josh and Stephanie, who were sleeping in a hotel. In the morning Steph and Josh would have to drive to catch up.

"Why?" I asked, my voice hardly a croak.

"It looks like you're falling asleep," she responded. The crew, forced to drive directly behind me at night, had nothing to look at other than my slow, meticulous form in front of them. I should have known it wouldn't be easy to get anything past them.

"It's my neck," I said, diagnosing the problem more accurately than a heavy head.

"Is it sore?" Ruth asked.

"Yes. But that's not the problem. I can deal with pain. But it's getting weak—I can't hold my own head up." The words sounded strange as they came out of my mouth. Holding up our own head isn't something we usually worry about. It's not something we even think about. But here I was, struggling to lift my own head because it weighed too much for my neck muscles.

"Can you hold it up?" Paul asked, leaning towards the window while still watching the road. "You know, rest it for a while?" I propped my elbow into the aero bar pads, then plopped my chin in my hand and let it rest. Awkward, yes. Functional, I suppose so.

"I don't think much can make it better than taking a break," I admitted. "I just can't afford to stop." The clock was ticking. Mercilessly. Relentlessly. I sat up straighter, thinking that if I kept my head in alignment with my spine instead of leaning forward and having to tip my head backwards to look at the road, it might be easier. But it still felt heavy.

"Let us know if it gets worse," Ruth said, and the vehicle dropped back. According to the rules they could only drive beside me for a minute four times an hour. And I could never, ever, touch the vehicle.

Alone with my thoughts again, I fought the heaviness of my head. I tried shifting to different positions, but nothing seemed to work. No matter which way I sat, turned, twisted or stood, my head was simply too heavy for my neck. Though I was completely conscious and awake, it lolled down to my chest like someone asleep. If I hadn't been questioning my finishing the ride, it would have been a comical situation. Unfortunately, when an integral part of your body starts to collapse on you, things don't feel comical.

I propped my head up with my right hand. It worked, but the back of my neck still hurt. It forced me to constantly lean forward, an uncomfortable position for too long of a time. It also forced me to steer, shift and brake with only one hand. This put added strain on my other arm, as well as my wrist. After a few minutes I switched hands, fighting to get comfortable.

This continued for 24 hours. And it only got worse.

My wrists were swollen from the pressure of holding my head. The "rest" I was giving my neck wasn't helping. If something didn't change, my ride was over. Finished. Another Did Not Finish (DNF) in a career riddled with a mixture of successes and failures. I had come to the conclusion that my percentage had dropped from 51 to 10, maybe 5. There was no way I could ride this way for five more days—I had reached the end.

My RAAM was over.

Consuming milkshake before getting back on the road

Through the mountains and into the Prairies

Looking bored as neck problems begin to set in

Determined to Succeed
Paraguay

We made our way through the trees in our bare feet, trying our best to be silent. Small steps and watchful eyes would hopefully keep us a few steps ahead of our quarry. The afternoon was bright and harsh—as always—and beat down on our bare backs. My older brother, Art, was holding the slingshot taut, aimed down at the ground. With only a split-second's notice he could have it up and at the ready. Our prey was small but dangerous. Thankfully we could hear them far in advance.

The buzzing was obvious, and my brother signalled for me to stop with a slight movement of his hand. The signal would have been imperceptible to anyone else.

"Up there." He flicked his head towards the tree straight in front of us. It was, maybe, 50 feet tall. My little eyes followed the trunk until what my ears heard matched what my eyes saw. A bees' nest, some 40 feet up in the tree. It was a good 8 inches in diameter and 15 inches long—we had definitely found the sweet jackpot.

"You have a shot?" I asked. He responded by nodding. We didn't quite speak, didn't quite whisper. The sound was somewhere between the two, and it blended in with the sounds around us. The last thing we wanted was for our attack on the hive to be spoiled, sending us careening through the trees with nothing to show for it.

"I've got a shot," he said, lifting his arms up into the air. Being older and stronger (for a while, anyway), he always took the shot. With his arms held high in the air, the slingshot cocked and ready to fly, he whispered out of the side of his mouth, not moving his head or letting his eyes leave the target.

"Remember," he said, "when it comes down, you get it. If they attack, run—but don't forget the hive."

When Quitting Is Not an Option

Right, I thought. *Why am I always the runner?* "Okay," I whispered, sneaking closer to the tree. We were both about 15 feet from its trunk now, the sound of the hive buzzing in waves, rising and falling. He pulled the slingshot tighter, his aim true, and let the first clay bullet fly.

Thwack, it hit the hive. Instantly the buzzing increased in volume. The number of bees outside of the hive increased exponentially. There was a cloud of them now, attacking the tree angrily. Something had disturbed their home, and it was going to pay.

Without taking his eyes off of the hive, Art put another bullet into the slingshot and pulled it back. I held a two-foot club in my hand, spinning it lightly. It was the perfect size and weight, and its role was still to come.

He let loose the second bullet, and it missed the hive by an inch. Standing right beside him, I could trace its flight. The cloud of bees felt that they'd been grazed, and the intensity and volume of the buzzing increased.

Within a few seconds he had let a third bullet fly, and this one found its mark. Another tear appeared in the side of the hive. Like alarm bells had gone off in their home, the rest of the bees swarmed out to inspect what was going on and destroy the intruder. But they had no idea the intruder was far below them.

One more bullet to the hive should have done it—the bees were out of the hive now. The slingshot was the easy part. Art lowered it and hooked it onto his shorts, letting it hang and holding out his hand. I deposited the club into it like a relay baton. He swung it once, twice, testing its weight. Then, with the skill born out of practice, he cocked it back and let it fly. Now that the bees were out of the hive—supposedly—he would knock the hive off the branch, and it would fall to us. Empty of anything other than honey, it would land at our feet. The bees would be stuck upstairs, confused about why their house had just disappeared.

That was the plan, anyway.

His aim was true and the throw was strong—it knocked the hive off the branch. It careened its way towards us—though we still stayed a few feet back—bouncing off of branches until it hit the ground right in front of our feet. It had gaping holes from the bullets, where his shots had torn through it.

I went forward, diligent in doing my job. But something was wrong.

When I picked up the hive, I knew.

The sound of the bees had travelled to us as the hive came down. There were still bees in the hive.

"Run!" Art yelled, and I listened. But I didn't forget what he'd said earlier—don't forget the hive. I took off running in Art's direction. Fear was written all over his eyes as he saw what was in my hand—and what was coming out of it.

Like Olympic sprinters out of the starting blocks we ran—not towards something but away from something. By now the cloud at the top of the tree had realized where their family and friends were and joined in the pursuit.

We hadn't followed a specific trail, so it was a full-speed tilt through trees and bushes, the branches scraping at us while we dodged the trunks. I bounced off one, then another, clinging tight to the hive—a source of food for a family with little. We came out of the trees and into the open, our bare feet pumping up and down like pistons, our little legs a blur. Behind—and with—us came a horde of bees. Sting after sting after sting after sting. I was trying to swat them, but it didn't work well with the hive in my hands and bees still pouring out of it.

Art was ahead of me, and we both knew where we were going. A large puddle—deep enough to swim in—was there for the cattle to drink from. Without hesitation we jumped headlong into the water, me still clutching the hive for all it was worth, and held our breath underwater. The bees couldn't come down, but with the enveloping water and the still beneath the surface came the catch-up of the nerves—and the realization that my body was stinging like it was on fire. There wasn't a part of me that didn't feel like the bees were still leeching their poison into me.

I held my breath until I couldn't anymore, hearing Art thrashing around beside me. I surfaced, only to spit my air out and grab another breath. At the same time I caught a glimpse of the sky around me—dotted with black and yellow bees like stars in the daytime. I didn't need to be up longer than a second to realize they were still angry. Going back under I held my breath longer, my body fighting against the need to surface.

Several times later—finally—the bees had calmed down enough to leave. I left my head above the surface and waited for Art to come back up. Still stinging from the swarm we'd faced, his face broke into a smile the second he came up.

"You got it?" he asked.

I held up the hive, now soggy but still good, and smiled—13 bee stings were a small price to pay for our sweet loot.

When Quitting Is Not an Option

When my forefathers arrived in Paraguay from Russia, they were given a tent, an ax, a spade, and an ox to share with another family. Given to my grandparents by MCC (Mennonite Central Committee), these tools made life possible, though certainly not simple. It was a meagre beginning, and it set the tone for the years that were to come, including my childhood.

Paraguay was never my family's destination, fleeing from Russia due to religious persecution. Health concerns made Paraguay the only option available. They would take anybody that could breathe. Dad's family had aimed for Canada but missed by a few thousand miles. Nevertheless, we were in a country that didn't care what we worshipped or who we were, and it was now home.

With the tools they were given, my grandparents and their families set to becoming agricultural farmers. This included growing peanuts, cotton, and a small amount of grain. Agricultural farming is very dependent on the weather—particularly rain. The landscape of the Chaco (our territory in Paraguay) is mostly flat, like the prairies, with open fields and meadows. The natural grass (bitter grass that the cattle and horse can't eat) grows three or four feet high, surrounded by bush. There are very few forests but a significant amount of dense bush. The roads were mud, subject to the dustiness of the dry winter season and the sogginess of the rain. Depending on their condition at the time of travel, they could make getting somewhere very difficult.

In winter the temperature dips colder but rarely below zero Celsius, the main difference being the lack of rain. Dust and sand whip up in columns and clouds, getting into every nook and cranny. The houses aren't sealed, but the northerly winds would break any seal anyway, scattering the dust and sand in a layer that cakes just about everything. It provides a strange contrast, because the land is often green and yet suffers from significant drought. It's this drought that has earned the Chaco the nickname "Green Hell," a gritty yet accurate representation of some of the difficulties of the land.

With the dependency on the weather to co-operate, farming was not simple. Over time most farmers switched over to raising cattle. For my family this was on a very small scale with a small margin of success. The difficulty in growing up in this environment laid the groundwork for my understanding of what poverty is. We grew up without treats, with (hopefully) one pair of shoes at a time, and several instances when we were forced near to going hungry. I have a very vivid and clear recollection of the closest we ever came to not having food.

The strong northerly winds whipped into our home, and I coughed because of the dust. I had just come from outside, but it was too cold to remain out there for long. Though our house wasn't insulated, at least it was a partial shelter from the wind. It was quiet in our house, which wasn't uncommon, but something about it felt strange.

I went towards my parents' room and was about to barge in when I fell silent. Thankfully my bare feet were quiet on the ground. I stood just out of sight, listening.

Mom was in the room, Dad, somewhere else. She was quiet, her voice hushed and quiet. When I listened closer, I realized what she was doing.

Praying.

Frozen in time, I wasn't sure whether I should bolt and pretend I never heard or stand and listen. For better or worse, I chose to listen. The words were quiet and quick, and there was emotion laced in with them. Was she crying?

It must be something big, I thought. I couldn't tell the words apart, and I didn't want to be caught. At any moment a sibling could come walking by, and the game would be over—even though it had been accidental.

I heard the telltale sounds of Dad coming home and knew I had to move. Dancing away quietly, I stayed out of sight as he came into the house. He went straight to Mom, and I couldn't help but creep closer.

"Did you get any?" she asked.

"No," Dad responded. From my vantage point I could see him put his hands on her shoulders from behind. He stroked her arms, and she continued to cry softly.

"Nothing?"

"We have no more credit. We haven't produced enough." I knew now what he was talking about. We didn't really deal in money all that much in the settlement. Instead, a running tab of plus or minus would be kept at the store. When we had peanuts or other produce to sell, our number would go up. Then when we bought, it would go down. Apparently it was so far down that they wouldn't give us any more bread, any more food.

We have no food, I realized. Disappearing from their door, I went to the kitchen (a separate building) and decided to check it out for myself. There was some sugar but no flour. Without flour, you can't make bread. It was winter, and we weren't harvesting anything. *We have no food,* I realized. Fear gripped me and hit me harder than any of the north winds ever had.

I heard something and had to look. Hiding beside the door, I saw Dad heading to the barn. His head was hanging low, and his stride was stunted, and—I wasn't sure how to describe it. Somehow he looked small, as if the weight of the world was pressing his shoulders down into the ground.

Mom hadn't left the house, and as soon as Dad made it to the barn I made my move. Scrambling out of the house and running full tilt to the other side of the barn, I moved into position to watch. With his back to me, he headed to where we kept the horse food. It was called kafir, a grain grown specifically for horses. Its grey-white cob wouldn't do for human consumption.

But—what was he doing?

He was pounding the kafir into a powder. His work was laboured, deliberate and methodical. It was an act born out of desperation, an act of submission that a father never wants to have to resort to for his own children. But when there is no other option, the food for horses can become food for humans.

Baked into something resembling bread, the kafir tasted awful. It was a dense consistency and could probably have been used as a hammer. In order to make it even remotely palatable, Mom sprinkled it in water and added a half teaspoon of sugar. It was the only way we would eat it, and for the time it was the only food we had. When it hit my belly, I realized just how desperate we were. No produce. No credit. No flour. Nothing but kafir. I didn't resent the situation we were in, but seeing Dad's concession made me realize that God cares deeply for his children and wants to give them bread to eat.

Our homestead was one of 20 in the village of Friedensfeld, a kilometre-long stretch of road divided into farms 100 metres wide. Each farm was one kilometre deep, though some had land beyond it. It was modeled after the Russian settlements from which the families had all come, and how much space you had for agriculture depended on where the bush started on your land. Over time the bush would be brought down and the farms expanded, trying to push the amount of food we could produce. This village—Friedensfeld—was in the settlement of Fernheim in the Chaco, a small section within the country of Paraguay. It was (and continues to be) a country that knows what it means to be poor.

Determined to Succeed: Paraguay

Before Dad owned the world's first hybrid truck (a Chevy motor with a Ford body can be considered a hybrid, can't it?), our family had only one bike. It was a beautiful black Heidemann single-speed adult-sized bike. As a young kid I would see my older siblings hop onto it and pedal off, and I was desperate to copy them. Not one to take labels (like adult-sized) to heart, I decided that I was going to ride the bike, no matter what came in my way. The problem was I was five years old and much, much too short.

But that wasn't about to stop me.

An adult would climb onto that bike by swinging a leg over the bar, sitting on the seat and pedalling the way it was designed to be done. Not me. Since my head was barely higher than the seat itself, that wasn't an option. But a bike isn't a completely solid object, and the middle of a bike happens to be a large hole. For me, this was my opportunity. Slinging my leg through the triangle formed by the bars of the bike, I could get both my feet on the pedals if the bike was tilted 20 degrees to the side. My back end would be sticking out in the air, my head was under the handlebars in order to be able to see, and my arm had to stretch across to grab the opposite handlebar, but I was biking.

And that was all that mattered to me.

It was 500 m to my grandpa and grandma's house down the dirt road, which had more bumps and potholes than anything I've ever seen in Canada, but I was determined to get there using my bike. With my body positioned like someone doing yoga, I pedalled as fast as my little legs would take me. One of the older men in the village couldn't stop laughing as I rode by, shaking his head.

"That kid has determination like nobody else I've ever seen," he'd say. It was uncommon for a kid to ride a bike—never mind an adult bike that was far too big for him. My determination set the stage for more struggles, challenges and victories to come in life.

The horse's hooves beat the ground beneath us in a rhythm that I had become familiar with. The reins were gripped tightly in my hands, my brother hanging on to the horse without his hands behind me. The kafir fields stretched out before us, and we leaned forward with excitement. We hit the beginning of the kafir and started screaming. Galloping beside the field, we let our lungs take control of the situation. Sometimes the yelling was words, sometimes it was just noise.

When Quitting Is Not an Option

As soon as we began yelling, the horse pounding the ground beneath us, there was a reaction. From amongst the stalks, hidden until now, came the sudden whooshing and beating of the wings of hundreds of pigeons. Afraid for their lives, they took off into the air. They had been sitting on the tops of the stalks, pecking away at the kafir. Since it was the food for our horse and part of our livelihood, it was our job to protect it.

Not to mention that it could also be a lot of fun.

We got to the end of the row and pulled up, turning around. They had settled on this side now, and we went back at it, leaning forward and making our throats hoarse. More pigeons took off. They usually fled at our noise. I pulled the horse up short, reining it in with instinct. We stood still, beside the kafir. My brother didn't have to ask or speak; he knew what I had seen. Up ahead was a flock of parrots, still on the kafir. They didn't flee as quickly, but that was OK. We didn't want them to. Art leveled his slingshot at the bird, taking aim. He was shooting over my head, and with action born of experience I ducked down so the bullet wouldn't hit me.

The shot was true and the bird fell off the stalk with a thud. It was flopping on the ground, and I had to move quickly. If it regained its senses and took off, it would all be for naught. I dropped from the horse and darted between the stalks, picking it up and flinging it on the ground. The slingshot bullet and the impact of the ground was enough to finish it off instantly.

"You got it?" Art's voice rang out.

"Got it!" I called back, celebratory.

"Good," he responded. "Get the beak."

I reached down and grabbed the top of the parrot's beak. Without the beak, we had no evidence that we had killed the parrot. Without the evidence, we couldn't get paid for killing it.

With a quick cut from my pocket knife the beak came off, and I took the top half. I brought it back to my brother, handing it up to him on the horse. The horse whinnied and snorted, stamping its foot. It wanted to move. And we wanted to hunt, so my brother quickly dropped the beak into the shoe-polish container, and I climbed back up onto the horse, swinging up easily and lightly.

The hunt continued, each parrot's beak worth seven cents from the mayor of our village. A single hunting trip could net 10 to 15 parrots, more money than we could earn from any other job we could find.

30

Determined to Succeed: Paraguay

Right from a young age my life included working on the farm. Chores were common and included bringing the cows in at the end of the day, watering the horses, feeding them, collecting eggs from the chickens, cleaning the yard, weeding and raking. Making money was no simple task. In order for my parents to get us gifts for Christmas they had to sell eggs outside of the market, egg by egg, penny by penny. Since our society dealt only in a line of credit (and ours was so bad they couldn't buy gifts), this was the only way for them to buy us a gift. They'd work at it the entire year, earning enough from eggs that we didn't get to eat for a simple gift.

Just like any other kid, I had a wish every year for Christmas. But unlike most kids, my only wish was the same every year: a soccer ball. It's not that I didn't get one—I sometimes did—but I used it so much that I would need a new one by the next Christmas. The balls were simple and plain, and they'd bounce in every direction off the mud clumps that decorated the landscape.

On our property was a large bottle tree, with gigantic needle-like points coming off of plum-sized protrusions. One bounce off the bottle tree and a ball was popped like a balloon.

But the game didn't end there. With no other access to sporting equipment, we'd open the ball up and patch the rubber bladder with bike patches, then close the material up and sew it together. It was probably the only time in my life I'd ever be caught with a sewing needle in my hand. Given to us at Christmas, the soccer ball would become a project throughout the year. Patched up over and over, we could often stretch out its tough existence until the next Christmas, when we'd hopefully have a new one.

My brother is three years older than I am, so by the time I was getting seriously into playing soccer he was already in junior high school, living in a dorm a significantly distant 9 km away. I was the youngest of ten kids (nine made it through infancy), and my brother was the second youngest. Older than him were my sisters, leading to my far-older brother at the top of the food chain, who had gotten married when I was six and was subsequently gone from home.

Some of my soccer playing was done with my two friends, Jacob and Abram, but they were nowhere near as enthusiastic about sports as I was. Given their lack of interest, it wasn't long before my skills distanced me from them. With only 20 homes in our village, there weren't too many other kids to play with.

Our farm was on the edge of the village, and some 500 m away was a native reserve. There were somewhere between 50 and 100 people living in the reserve, and their livelihood came mostly from begging or being employed by the farmers in return for food and (possibly) some money. They were quite frequently dependent on handouts or job opportunities, and the faith-based nature of our village led to us seeing them as poor whom we could help. Given that they were South Americans, soccer was something they were very interested in.

Finally I had someone to play with.

While we would have considered ourselves far from wealthy, I was the only one around with a soccer ball. Over time I had cut some small trees and built soccer goals, and we'd set them up on the cow pasture behind our farm. Right there, in my own backyard, we had our own official soccer field. Saturdays or Sundays were game days, and I'd wake up in the morning with an itch in my legs to get out onto the field, test my skills out against the natives, and have a real game. The size of the scrimmage would vary from day to day, though it usually hung around the 4 to 10 players range. It didn't matter to me, as long as I was playing soccer.

It was the closest I would come to a real game of soccer for a long time.

Once or twice a week wasn't enough. I wasn't a cocky kid, but I had a drive to succeed like no one else I knew. This meant that I needed to practice, even if no one else wanted to. Since my brother was off at school (sometimes home on the weekends) and my friends weren't as interested in the activity as I was, it meant I needed to come up with something on my own, a way to train and get better without relying on anyone else. If I had wanted to play forward or defense it would have been easier, but I always found myself gravitating to the net. You can dribble, deke and shoot without anyone else on the field. But it's hard to make saves if all the ball does is sit on the ground.

Our homestead was four buildings: two barns, the house and the kitchen (separate from the house). The kitchen was the only building with any type of heating at all—it had a simple woodstove. While it didn't often go below zero Celsius in the winter, zero Celsius is very different when all you have to do is run from your car to the house than when you have to cover yourself up under a blanket and go to sleep in a house that isn't remotely insulated. That combined with a dry and strong wind that whips into the house and brings with it sand and dust can make for a very uncomfortable winter.

While the barns were often built with wood planks, the homes and kitchens were built out of mud bricks with straw in between. The mud would be packed into a brick form, let dry and pulled out once it was dry enough to retain its shape. Then it would finish hardening out of the form. Anyone who's stood in a mud field knows well enough that with rain mud turns soft and gooey, completely losing its shape. To combat this we would coat the bricks with a chalk-like paint to seal them. This meant the rain stayed out (mostly) and the houses would stand for longer. This paint was white, and the chickens had it in their minds that this was food. They would peck away at the white chalk until they'd thoroughly weakened the house, so everyone resorted to mixing soot into the bricks along the bottom of the house, preventing the chickens from pecking at it. The roofs were made of tin or aluminum, but it was the walls and not the roofs that I was interested in.

Patterned by design and weathered over the years, the walls were often irregular and unpredictable—perfect for a goalie. To hone my ability I would kick the ball against the walls. The ball bounced back at me to the left, right, up, down—I could never predict it. Over time I got better and better at reacting to the bounces and I could stop it from flying past me. I had to be sharp, ready on my toes to make the catch or block. Depending on how close I stood I'd have to do more than step—I'd have to resort to lunging and diving after the ball, scraping and bruising my legs, sides, hips, shoulders and arms countless times.

But it was all worth it to stop the ball from getting past me.

And it was preparation for a hobby and career of using my physical gifts and strengths to reach others with God's good news.

It was on that mud yard behind the barn, flying through the air, that I developed a saying I've become known for (among my family, at least): If you can touch it, you can catch it. (The catchphrase worked great when my kids were small, but eventually they caught on and realized they could repeat it to me mockingly when I dropped anything thrown at me.)

A soccer goalie only faces a handful of shots in a single game, so controlling the shot is of the utmost importance. If you don't hang on to it, the ball bounces right back out into the 18-yard box. Your defender might get it and clear it away or send it to the sidelines, but it might also end up at the foot of an attacker. With the large size of a net, they've got a lot of options for putting it behind you. I began to develop the ability to turn any contact with a shot into a catch. When you consider the size of a soccer net (or no net, as it was for me when I kicked the ball off the side of the barn) and the relatively small percentage of the net the goalie's body covers, it's quite remarkable how low-scoring a soccer game truly is. But stretch out the goalie's body in the middle of the air and somehow he can reach a little farther if he needs to. The ball touches just the finger, and somehow he can bring the hand around to make the catch.

Without an attacker's face to analyze or eyes to look into, everything that came off the side of the barn was a guessing game. I began to develop the ability to anticipate the ball's angle and react in a split second. Over time it was something that would set me apart from many other goalies.

But that's getting ahead of the story.

School in my village was a one-room experience. For the 20 farms there was one teacher, and he covered everything from grade 1 to grade 6. If you were destined to take over your parents' farm and needed to get to working, grade 6 was often as far as you would go. Since there weren't very many people in the village, the school began and took place on a rotating basis. One year it would be grades 1, 3 and 5. The next year it would be 2, 4 and 6. This meant that the teacher only had to juggle three curricula at a time instead of six. But it also meant that, if you weren't quite old enough (six) when it was a grade 1 year, you had to wait two years to get into grade 1.

That was me.

So I began grade 1 an entire year behind most North Americans. In our grade 1 class (though two birth years because of the delay) there were four of us: my friends Jacob and Abram and a girl named Annaliese. There were usually somewhere between 10 to 15 kids in the entire school, so it was a completely different experience than anything you'd typically see in North America.

The morning was the same as any other, though my feet didn't walk to the school with the same bounce and spring they usually did. When Jacob and Abram came running by, I didn't run with them. The walk seemed to stretch into an hour, the school building looming and seemingly ever-distant.

The first subjects came and went the same as they always did, but my attention wasn't quite there. Along with all the usual subjects, we also had singing. This was fine when the 15 of us in the classroom were singing together. But today was different. Today our teacher was going to be testing us. And testing meant that, one by one, we would have to sing.

As it came around to my turn, my hands began to sweat. Stand me in front of a soccer net with a ball whistling at my head and I was in my element. But this, this was unbearable. I had already chosen my song, one of the only ones I could adequately remember, and started out by singing loud enough that all could hear, "Hanschen Klein ging allein in die weite Welt hinein," translated as "Little Hans went into the wide world alone."

Towards the end of the first verse my volume had already diminished, and I was fading.

"You can stop," the teacher said.

I nearly bit my tongue, I stopped so fast.

Abram was whispering to Jacob, and I couldn't hear what he was saying.

"I know more of the song," I said, though I didn't want to sing. I just didn't want to hear what he would say next.

"That's okay, Arvid," he responded. "You failed."

I could hardly believe it. It was grade 2, and it was the only time I had ever failed a test—and remains that way to this day.

Some of the people in the class laughed. He hadn't even given me a chance. "You should really only sing when you're alone."

To this day I have listened to him. If those around me in church were to all of a sudden stop singing, you wouldn't be able to hear me. I move my lips, but hardly any sounds come out.

If things weren't going well in music class, gym was a different matter. The volleyball court was split down the middle, and the teams were lined up on the sides. Even though I was younger than a lot of the students in the school, I was always picked near the top. The team captain was on the opposite side from his team, standing at the back line of the volleyball court.

The game of dodge ball started, and I moved away from the centre of the court, standing near the sidelines. It was the best vantage point. Only from there could you see the entire team—on my left—and their captain—on my right. Since the team could lob balls to their captain, the attack could come from any side. One came at me from the right, aimed down at my feet. I dodged it deftly, avoiding being hit while moving across the centre of the court so as not to remain a stationary target too long. I pulled up on the other side, glancing left and right. The captain was usually the strongest player, so you had to be wary of him. But there were numerous attackers on the other side of the court, so you had to keep an eye out for them as well.

Because of my speed and skill, it didn't take long for them to start attacking me. A few of the weaker players would already be hit, though they didn't have to leave the court. Getting hit meant your team lost a point. Catching the ball meant you gained a point—and this was where I became the biggest dodge ball star Friedensfeld had ever seen.

Another throw came at me, and I started to move. It was coming too fast, and my hands snapped up to catch it. I wasn't fast enough, and it bounced off my arm. The other team was already celebrating—this was early in the game to have a hit against me. But the ball had lobbed up and away, and I reacted quick. With a dive like a soccer goalie, I flew through the air with my hands outstretched. I caught the ball between my hands and cushioned the landing, rolling back up onto my feet, ready to dodge again or attack the other team.

"Nice one!" Jacob called out. The other team jeered but didn't have much to say.

"Stay alive!" I called back to him, jumping over another throw and spinning to face their captain at the same time. I had seen the ball lobbed to him over my head and knew an attack would be coming. Just as he cocked his arm back to throw, I dropped the ball in my hands and maintained my position. From only 15 feet away I reacted quickly and caught the ball, gaining my team another point. They cheered, and I smiled. Frustrated, their captain threw another ball wildly in my direction as the game came to an end.

We had won, my last-second catch the deciding point.

The training against the barn wall had honed my reflexes, and dodge ball had made my hands a trap for any ball that came near me. Combining these two skills laid the groundwork for the years to come.

Dad never gave up on his dream of coming to Canada. Though the process would span several decades, it was finally coming to a head as I went through elementary school. When the school year finished (in November) after my grade 6 year, we thought the process was almost complete. We would be moving. With time, we would become Canadians. The religious persecution that had forced Dad to flee Russia combined with the health concern that prevented him from going directly to Canada had meant long and hard years in Paraguay.

Canada looked like the Promised Land, and for many of us it was. But just like the Israelites, we were delayed for a while during the time that things sorted themselves out.

Because we were almost accepted, I didn't go to grade 7 nine kilometres away when the school year started again in February. We were going to be going to Canada, and I'd be joining the school year there.

Our long journey to Canada was delayed, again. This time, thankfully, only until the winter (Canadian summer). In August of 1970 we set out for Canada, elation evident in the smiles on our faces as we boarded a plane for the country of promise.

Arvid, standing on the cistern in a family photo.
Note the Heidemann bike Arvid rode as a 5-year-old.

With his parents, sitting on the Ford/Chevy hybrid truck

Arvid in the centre of his family photo wearing a plaid shirt

New Beginnings
Canada, Part 1

I followed Art's feet out of the airplane, not wanting to make my first stride in the new country a stumble. When I crossed the line from the airplane's walkway into the airport, I took a deep breath.

This was Canadian air.

We had arrived, and there was a whirlwind of emotions bubbling up from inside of me—we had left a difficult country, but it had been our home; we were in a new place, full of promise; this land was full of unknowns, including work, housing and a language that I'd never spoken. What if we never earned enough money? What if Canada wasn't all it had been talked up to be? What if we had to return to Paraguay, defeated? After all, selling literally everything we owned had purchased four flights—but there were seven of us. We'd had to borrow the money for the remaining three, so it was with a lot of excitement but a little bit of hesitation that I walked into a new country.

We had to wait for our luggage—a few bags of clothes, all that we had—to arrive on the carousel. The words on the signs were all in English, and Mom was pointing while talking to Dad. Thankfully, there were also pictures, and even I could figure out that the luggage was off to the right.

"Arvid, slow down!" Mom called out. I was running ahead of them, always the scout. At 13 I could dodge not only the dodge balls in gym class but also the people moving through the airport. I stopped before I got out of their field of vision.

"It's down there!" I called. The stairs down to the next level were strange—they were moving. I took a hesitant step onto their surface, joined by my brother and sisters.

Rushing off the escalator, I was the first to arrive at the carousel. Pulling the boarding pass from my pocket I compared the flight number with the numbers on the wall. Our luggage was coming one carousel over, and I waved for my family to join me. We moved, spread out in a line with my parents holding the rear. Even though they weren't moving all that fast, I could tell they were excited. I hadn't seen a smile stay on Dad's face for that long since—well, perhaps never.

"We have the green bag," Mom was telling me. "And don't forget the red suitcase."

"I know, Mom, I know," I spoke back to my mom with a wave of dismissal. She licked her finger and came at my face, but I dodged it deftly. If having your mom clean your face with her spit is embarrassing in Paraguay, I knew it couldn't be any better in Canada.

She made a move to chase me, but there was no competition. I ran away, running around a few other weary travellers. One older gentleman glared at me, and I used my charm to let him know that I wasn't up to anything suspicious. Finally, a smile cracked his face as he followed my gaze back to my family. There were regular travellers in airports, and then there was us, clearly out of our element but clearly loving every second.

"Mom, look!" my brother was saying. I followed his pointing hand and saw a shop, the beginning of a line of storefronts stretching off impossibly far.

"Ice cream," I whispered. A treat that we could only dream of. Mom looked up at Dad, the desire to treat her children evident in her eyes. They tried communicating quietly, but we weren't little kids anymore.

"Can we have some ice cream?" my older sister asked.

"Yes," Dad responded, and we all let out a little cheer. Beside us, the conveyor belt began to move, still empty. He fished his wallet out of his pocket, opening it. I had gotten so used to seeing it empty that something—anything—in it was a surprise. The bills were colourful and strange, completely foreign.

Dad looked at Mom. Mom looked at Dad. They looked at us. We looked at each other.

"You go," Art said to me. I shook my head, more nervous than when standing in front of a penalty shot.

"I think you should," I whispered to him. We went through the entire family until we finally realized that Elfie, the only one with any guts, should do the buying.

"Go buy one," Mom said to Elfie. She pulled one of the bills from Dad's wallet. We didn't know how much it was or what it meant, but she handed it to my sister and spun her in the direction of the shop. Elfie hesitated, but we all cheered her on with our whispers. Behind us, there was a loud clunk as the first piece of luggage hit the conveyor belt. It wasn't ours.

We all watched Elfie without breathing, as if she was going to defuse a bomb. She got to the shop and pointed at the ice cream. She was trying to speak, but it didn't look like any words were falling on understanding ears. But the pointing worked, the money exchanged hands, and she was given the ice cream—and three coins—in return.

Another bill passed, another trip, another three coins.

After four trips and some serious smiles from the ice cream, we figured we had this down.

Finally, all seven of us had a cone. Elfie had gotten every single one. And received 21 silver coins in return. Seven dollars and twenty-one quarters later— we had no idea until later that two bills would have sufficed—we had had our first taste of the country that would become our home.

Canada's immigration department had denied us entry for over 10 dedicated years of our trying to get into the country. Due to health concerns, the number of children, my family's poverty and the lack of family support in Canada, it was tough to meet the immigration point requirements in order to be accepted into the country. Which is why, perhaps, it felt like the Israelites entering the Promised Land as we landed in Toronto at the beginning of August 1970. A thin and athletic 13-year-old with blond hair, freckles and not a word of English to my name, I was nervous yet excited about the opportunities and possibilities ahead.

Everything was big—from the plane we travelled on to the vastness of the land in which we were arriving. After the flat plains of the Chaco, the rise and fall of the Appalachian Mountains was new to my young eyes. But we plunged further inland and flew to Winnipeg, a city with a rising industrial emphasis and a growing population of people just like us—immigrants, refugees, Mennonite folk with only hard work and the fear of religious persecution in our past. We were in a land where we could build our churches, speak our language, work our work, drink our maté (a tea-like drink that's passed around with a communal spoon-like straw), worship our God and continue our traditions. Of course, at my age I wasn't as concerned about our traditions as my parents were. In a country where homes were solid and my town would be thousands of times the population of my village, I was excited about the future.

When Quitting Is Not an Option

Would Canada be the land of prosperity, the land flowing with milk and honey, that we had all dreamed it would be?

It was amazing that we could travel thousands of kilometres away from our home and move into a community with people who understood us. Even those who didn't understand us were willing to accept us.

When we arrived, my dad and older siblings went immediately to work. For the first year the income was pooled until we could buy and pay off our first and only family home. From that point forward my siblings could work for their own income but paid room and board until they moved out.

Mennonites, though not the wealthiest in Paraguay or anywhere, came with a hard work ethic, honesty and loyalty that made them fantastic employees. Dad began working as a labourer and moved to a machine operator, building furniture. The work was different than what we were used to as a family, and the fulfillment it provided was not the same as working on a farm and bringing in your own food, but the work was consistent and the income well appreciated. The Palliser factory was full of others like him, fresh off the boat, as well as immigrants who had been in Canada for several years. There was a camaraderie that pervaded the factory and boded well for keeping employees loyal.

We arrived in Winnipeg in August. Because we had thought we would be immigrating sooner than we did, I hadn't gone to the junior high school class in Paraguay that started in February. This meant that not only was I a year older than some of the others in my grade to begin with, but now I had missed half a year of grade 7. We were forced to make a decision—should I go into grade 7, at nearly 14 years old? Or should we bump me up to grade 8, where there were people a little closer to my age?

Given that junior high school is not the easiest place to be, any teenager with a few strikes against him is likely to get bullied or victimized. With not knowing the language, with my blond hair and freckles, with not knowing a single person going to the junior high school, I already had a few strikes against me. Dropping into a grade 7 class while almost two years older than everyone else would be the tipping point, so I wasn't eager to jump into that atmosphere. Besides, I'd always had an aptitude for math and had never struggled through school.

Though it took some convincing, the school administration finally agreed to let a German-speaking kid from Paraguay into grade 8 with not a single word of English. They did assign a few helpers to move me along, but it was like jumping in front of a soccer net blindfolded.

Having borrowed my neighbour's banana-seat bike, I spent the days ripping up and down the back lane that started at the side of our house. The surface was gravel and full of potholes, but it was like a smooth stretch of asphalt compared to what I was used to. Now 13 and able to ride a bike properly, I practiced my acceleration, turns, skids and pothole-dodging skills.

The crunch of gravel was always the first thing that alerted me to a car coming down the back lane. Pedalling quickly, I would turn to look over my shoulder and verify that I'd heard correctly and they weren't pulling off into a garage or parking pad. Once I knew that they were coming my way, I'd pull over to the side and let them pass. Sometimes the tires would kick up rocks that hit my calves and shins, but I did my best to establish eye contact with everyone who passed so I knew they saw me.

With the sun high in the sky that day, I heard the crunch and turned to look. A car was ambling down the back lane, bouncing through the potholes without avoiding them. I slowed down, my foot skidding along the gravel to help brake. As I pulled off to the right onto the thin line of grass and stopped before a garbage bin, I checked behind me again. The car was getting closer, and I recognized the driver. She was young, and her eyes were wide, popping with every bounce. In the passenger seat sat her dad, perhaps less terrified than the she was.

I turned to look forward again as they were about to pass me. But something was wrong about the sound.

It wasn't going around me—it was coming right at me.

At the last second she had panicked and turned right instead of left—right into me. There was no time for reacting; there was no time for moving. I felt the crunch of the car as it hit my back tire, knocking me over in a tangle of arms and legs. The metal of the bumper passed before my eyes, and then I closed them, horrified of what was happening.

With the dust swirling around my face and the final kick of the car as the brakes stopped it from going any farther, I heard the crunch of the gravel as everything settled. Echoing back off the metal underside of the car came my own breathing, fast and terrified.

When Quitting Is Not an Option

I opened my eyes to look up and—

No, that couldn't be.

It isn't right.

My left leg was between the engine block and the front axle, my bike piled on top of me. My breathing wasn't getting any slower, only faster.

That's not right, I thought.

A leg is supposed to bend, but only at the knee.

It looked like I had a new joint in my leg.

The bone in my shin was sticking out at a 90-degree angle, my leg dangling limply in front of me. For how fast my reaction time usually was, it took a little longer for the pain to hit my brain. But when it did—

If starting school in a week as an immigrant wasn't bad enough, starting school as an immigrant with no friends and a broken leg was like jumping in front of a soccer net blindfolded with my hands and feet tied.

Hospital beds are not all that comfortable, especially when your pastor is walking into the room. Still relatively young, I wasn't accustomed to any type of pastoral visit. Reverend William Neufeld settled himself into the chair beside my bed with a stiff collar and a well-worn (yet somehow still new-looking) Bible clasped between his hands. He cleared his throat, and I waited for him to speak. No way was I going to interrupt my pastor. My parents had left the room, so we were the only ones in it, and I suddenly became very seriously interested in the lines and folds in the sheets on the hospital bed.

"Arvid." His voice was dry, but I didn't think I'd be able to speak enough words to offer him water.

I smiled—more like grimaced—not knowing what to say. "How are you feeling?"

I looked down at my leg—the vehicle that I relied upon to bike, play soccer and move around. It was a horrible thing to lose the use of, but, all things considered, it was a small price to pay for the accident I had experienced.

"Okay," I answered.

"Good, good," he said, the tension seeming to lift as he leaned back in the chair and put the Bible on the counter beside him. But his hand didn't leave its cover, and I waited for what I knew was going to come. My parents had always had a deep-rooted faith, but I'd never been one to follow in anyone's footsteps.

"Does it still hurt?" There was compassion in his voice and his eyes, and I felt the pressure beating in my chest release.

"Some," I said, perhaps acting a little more brave than I felt. "But they're giving me medicine to take the pain away." My mouth felt dry, and I reached over to the other side of the bed to lift the jug of water with the straw that every hospital bed has.

"Good, good," he repeated. I wondered where this was going—no, I knew where it was going. But I wondered when it would get there.

"That was a bad accident," Reverend Neufeld said.

"Yes," I responded. "It was."

"You were very fortunate to end up here—with only a broken leg," he added. "Things could have been much worse." I nodded. This seemed to give him fuel to continue on. "Arvid." He pulled the Bible back between his hands, his fingers finding their home in the leather. "If the accident had been worse—if you had been killed—would you have been ready to meet Jesus?" The words were so heavy I could hardly believe that he was able to look me in the face as he asked them, but his gaze never left my face, while mine wandered around the room.

"I," I began, not knowing how to finish. "I've always gone to church," I argued, like everyone cornered will argue. I was about to continue on and list a resume's worth of good actions from my past, but he cut me short.

"Arvid." He continued to look directly at me—or was it into me?—with a gaze that forced me to look away. "I want you to think about that question. When you're ready, come talk to me. But don't take too long. Before your next bike ride might be a good idea." There was a hint of a joke there, and we both smirked but didn't laugh.

I nodded at him like I understood the question. He began to pray then, his words flowing like water down a hill. I could hardly keep up with what he was saying, but ten seconds in, my mind was already lost. *If the accident had been worse—if you had been killed—would you have been ready to meet Jesus?*

When I got home, I asked Mom the same question. But she turned it back on me.

"Would you have been ready?" I was leaning against my crutches, and I took them out from under my armpits to lean them against the wall. Standing on one foot I hopped into the kitchen as she entered ahead of me. Like with Reverend Neufeld, the silence got entirely heavy and unbearable.

"I guess not," I admitted. "I just—"

"God doesn't want excuses," Mom said. "He wants you." I couldn't argue with that.

"But now?"

"Now's as good a time as any," she countered.

"What do I need to do?" I asked.

The words and prayer that followed lifted a weight off my shoulders, a burden that I alone could not bear.

The bed was warm while I heard the house creaking outside, listening to the wind that used to seep into our home back in Paraguay. Here, though, the windows kept the air out and kept us warm—and, judging by what we had been told, we would need them.

I heard the creak of the floor outside of my bedroom door and shut my eyes tight, pretending I was asleep.

"Arvid!" It was Dad's voice, whispering loudly to see if I was awake. At first I didn't respond, but when he repeated my name and moved on to the next door I knew there was something going on that I didn't want to miss. I rolled over and flung the blanket off my body, swinging my legs to the floor. My right leg did what it was supposed to, but my left stayed resolutely where it had been lying.

I hadn't forgotten that it was in a cast, but sometimes things can slip your mind. I had to lift it with my hands to get it over to the floor, where its loud clunk woke up anyone who hadn't already woken up from Dad's whispers.

"Arvid, come outside!"

"What?" I responded, looking at the window. It was covered in a fog, moisture that had frozen in the cold November. The sky looked white, similar to how it had looked for every day the past week.

"Come!" He waved me towards the front of the house, and I pushed up from the bed, standing without crutches. I could walk short distances without them, so I used the walls for my balance. From my sister's room I could hear her moving about. I hurriedly threw my pyjamas on, wanting to get moving as quickly as possible.

With my hobbling to the door my sister blazed past me, Dad leading the way. There was a smile across his face that sparkled with excitement, and I wondered what it could possibly be.

New Beginnings: Canada, Part 1

Once we'd all arrived at the front door he pulled it open.

A gust of cold air rushed in and made me shiver and pull back into my pyjamas like a turtle into its shell. But it wasn't the wind, the cold or the empty street that Dad wanted us to see.

It was the blanket of white powder that had covered everything—the grass, the sidewalk, the steps, the trees, the small windmill in our front yard.

Snow.

I'd heard about it but never seen it. And certainly never touched it.

I dashed outside, with my cast like a deadweight slowing me down. I made it down the steps and out onto the grass in my bare feet and pyjamas. It was only a few inches of snow—just enough to creep up over my feet and onto the tops of them. My sisters were outside now, too, and one of them was feeling it with her hands. I leaned over to pick it up, feeling it melt on my skin. Dad was still back at the entrance to the house, smiling and laughing. He seemed to be waiting, and I couldn't figure out why—

Until my nerves caught up with what was going on and I realized that my feet were turning bright red from the cold. With a shriek and a scream, I turned to run back into the house. In my rush my feet were slipping, and I could barely get my balance as I pummelled up the stairs, which were also slippery, and hobbled my way back into the safety of a warm home. Dad, who had seen snow plenty of times back in Russia, let out a laugh at my desperate scramble for safety. I shot him a look that only a teenage son can give a dad, then joined in laughing. It was unknown, but it was my life now.

We lived less than a kilometre from the junior high school I was attending, and the next few months had me walking with my crutches through the slippery snow, clutching the bars of the crutches in weather that I could never have imagined. My Paraguayan face, freckles and hair and the injury that prevented me from doing pretty much anything made me a target for taunting and bullying just like anyone else. It doesn't take much to be targeted for bullying in junior high, and my introduction to Canada was no different.

That was all about to change.

First Christmas in Canada, 1970

Junior High yearbook picture, 1971

Between the Posts
Canada, Part 2

By the time I got my cast off in January, I had made enough of a connection with a few guys from my school to know that they were playing soccer. One Sunday evening there was a practice at the high school that backed onto our junior high school (they shared fields), and I decided to go to the practice as a spectator.

The gym was full of boys my age and older. They were quick and strong, and I watched tentatively from the side. I was wearing my runners, just in case. The balls bounced off the floors, the gym walls and occasionally the roof. I was itching to get out there and race around, to feel the ball make contact with my feet, to catch it between my hands and roll out of a dive. I looked down at my leg, thankful that the cast wasn't there anymore.

A few of the players were talking and looking in my direction. After a few drills it looked like they were starting a scrimmage, and I started inching my way closer. The coach looked my way and waved me forward.

"You want to play?" he asked. I nodded, too afraid to say anything. "Okay," he said. "We're making teams." He looked down at my legs. My left leg was significantly smaller than my right, the muscles having atrophied from lack of activity while they had spent the last three months cooped up in a cast, forced to swing like a giant club foot attached to my leg.

"I broke it a few months back," I explained.

"It's good to go, though?" the coach asked. I nodded.

"All right." He clapped his hands on the ball and blew the whistle. The players gathered around, and some laughs were exchanged, though thankfully not at my expense. They were friends and had clearly known each other for a long time. A few balls were bounced, and one of the players tested a few of them out with his feet before deciding on the game ball.

When Quitting Is Not an Option

Players were spreading out as the coach put them on their teams. I went back to the side where I'd been standing, making sure to hide my limp as I walked. I'd been chosen as a goalie because I didn't have great mobility with my weaker leg, but I still wanted to keep my weakness hidden as much as possible. With a blow of the whistle the ball was thrown into play and the game was on.

Adrenaline surged through me. I had played back in our cow pasture with the natives. I had played on my own behind the barn, kicking the ball off its uneven surface for me to catch.

But this—this was a game.

The ball was bouncing lightly on the ground, kicked back and forth by the quick feet of the boys. I watched it with sharp eyes, observing which players I had to make sure to keep an eye on. A burst of speed here, a quick dribble and deke there. Soccer had always been my love, and it was quickly becoming my passion.

The opposing player was coming up the left side with a good lead on my defender. The striker shifted the ball from the left to right foot effortlessly, and my eyes caught a blur of motion out of my peripheral. His body language made it look like he was going to kick, but there was something in me that knew he wasn't.

I jumped into action, springing forward. The ball came off his foot with a sharp curl, two feet off the ground. It was going directly to the opposing striker, but I had guessed correctly. With a quick slide on the ground, right up to the edge of my crease, I had the ball in my hands. I was back on my feet in seconds, scanning the gym and spotting an open midfielder moving up the gym. The ball was at his feet in seconds, and he was off.

Taking a deep breath, I realized I had made my first real save. And it felt good.

The coach was looking in my direction, and I absorbed his gaze without returning it.

Diving, catching, blocking, anticipating. It's all a part of being a goalie. Within five minutes I had made good use of every part of my body. I could see in the coach's eyes that he was impressed. I'd later find out that he'd been commenting on my performance. "Wow! This kid is fearless. He's as quick as a cat," he'd said. "There's potential here."

It doesn't take news—good or bad—very long to travel around a junior high school. By the next morning my school life had changed. I had gone from being an immigrant to earning a level of respect because of my athletic ability. In many ways, soccer was what got me through the rough years as a teenager.

Soccer quickly became a huge part of my life. As soon as the coach saw my ability, quickness and agility, I was involved in a team. I joined the North Kildonan Cobras as a 14-year-old, and within a year I had been elevated to the highest level I could play. While still a juvenile I joined the senior league, including playing a season in the second-highest senior division. Beyond that I moved up to the Premiere division (the highest level of amateur soccer in Winnipeg) and played on the Manitoba all-star team from the second year I lived in Winnipeg until my soccer career ended.

I ended up playing in the Manitoba games and the Canada games, as well as being chosen by a few club teams to represent them when they went to their homeland for a tour against club or national teams. They wanted to keep themselves from getting embarrassed, so their own goalie sat on the bench, a scowl on his face. It allowed me to travel at no cost and play soccer at an elite level, which I thoroughly enjoyed.

The Bermudian sun had disappeared over the hills on the horizon. The game was in full swing, and we were down 2–1. We had travelled to their country to play their national team, but the grass underneath my feet felt the same as it always did—springy and forgiving, until I chose to dive.

The wind whistled through the net behind me, and the net began to move. I turned to look, taking my eyes off the play for a second. It wasn't moving the way it normally would from the wind. There were points of the mesh that were being pulled back, hands hanging onto the net. There was chanting and yelling, the sound just in the background of a game that, though the score was against us, was going in our favour.

There was a yell from up the field, and I turned to look. One of our forwards was moving up the left side of the field, displaying his ball control as he took it inside against one of the defenders. Being in the net, it's easy to see how the play is unfolding. Like the quarterback on a football team, soccer goalies can direct play and correct their players. They have a vantage point that no one else on the field does. But even if I had yelled, he wouldn't have heard me—with almost no bleachers around the field, the fans were allowed within six feet of the boundary line. The lighting on the field was extremely direct and perfectly aimed, its limits dropping off as soon as you crossed the white line. Given that we were in Bermuda, the entire audience of somewhere near two thousand, circling the field and yelling behind me, were not the same skin colour as us and blended into the night perfectly. I shot a glance back at the crowd behind me, catching a glimpse of small glowing white sets of teeth in a sea of black.

Jimmy was streaking up the right side, in perfect position for a cross. Both teams had left their goalies out to dry numerous times, allowing for an open and fast-paced game where the ball spent more time moving up the field than hanging out in the middle. The cross came perfectly to Jimmy, and I saw him put on a burst of speed to pass the last defender, staying perfectly onside. The goalie was scrambling, but I knew how it felt to be in his situation. His momentum would carry him right across. To do anything less wouldn't stop the play.

Jimmy played the ball perfectly, behind and underneath the goalie's jump. It bounced once, curled onto the inside of the post, and was absorbed by the back of the net.

Our team began its cheer, running back to our own side. I pumped my fist in the air, smiling at the fans behind me. They may have been cheering against me, but they were great fans who appreciated sport. I'd already proven my merit against them by stopping some of their top players on fast breaks that should have ended in goals.

There were only a few minutes left, and Jimmy had just tied it up. It was a friendly game, and we determined our own format—neither team wanted to leave it to a tie, so the intensity picked up. Either a team would break the tie or we'd go to a shootout.

Another fast break. A tall forward was moving towards me up the left side. I positioned myself perfectly, anticipating where he would be moving. My defender became a pylon as the man's quick feet brought him around to me. I could play the pass—I had seen the forward making his move—or I could take the shot. I saw his eyes, and my reactions saved me. In one split second I dove left, going for the shot. He'd aimed that way, and the ball went off my elbows and into the ground. I crumpled on top of it, tucking into a ball and not letting go.

The crowd's yells surged out unbearably loud, but I could sense that there was more than disappointment. The Bermudan players were staring their own fans down, and words were being exchanged. It was friendly, but there was an edge. I started to get the feeling that the fans had given up on their team and were mocking them. They'd seen me react point-blank numerous times and knew that that meant one thing—if the Bermuda team didn't win it now, they'd have no chance in a shootout.

Shrill and barely audible above the crowd, the whistle ended regulation. We were going to a shootout. The mocking intensified, the fans not helping their players out but just having a good time. As I came back towards the line in my net, the fans were whipping the back of the net into a frenzy. If the ball did go into the net, it would clobber them. I stepped on the line, flattening the grass and planting my feet.

In soccer a shootout highly favours the shooter. The goalie isn't allowed to leave the line until the player has contacted the ball, so it's purely a gamble. The ball is planted so close and the net so big that to even think that one can react in that much time is ridiculous. The goalie must anticipate, jump and hope. Goalies have to pick a side, and it's not uncommon to see the goalie jumping through the air and the shot dribbling down into the middle of the net. If the player can trick the goalie, the net is his.

The first few shots were give-and-take, the teams even. Then we took the lead. Bermuda was shooting first on the fifth and final shot. We were up by one, which meant that if I made the save, the game was over.

Behind me, the net was an undulating sea of string. I couldn't hear myself think over the sound of the yells, catcalls and screams. The fans were surging ever closer to the lines and net. I felt like they were breathing down my neck, yet I still couldn't see anything other than their smiles and open mouths in the dark.

Their last shooter was one of their best. I'd stolen the ball from him on several occasions in the middle of the game. He met my gaze, then looked away. Some players look where they're shooting. Others avoid where they're shooting. Some try to play mental games; others just shoot. He didn't give any indication—just planted his feet a few steps from the ball. I could feel my pulse in my ears, the crowd washing away to the background fuzz on a radio.

He stepped forward, beginning to run. His cleats dug into the ground, grass clumps flying behind him. I dug my own feet in, moving one step to the right and taking a leap—it was a complete gamble, a guessing game. I launched into the air, my body flat-out four feet off the ground. My hands stretched out. The ball was launching through the air, coming off his foot like a rocket. The crowd's noise rose.

And my hands closed around the ball.

I hit the ground, rolling away with it between my hands. The crowd exploded—all kinds of noises, catcalls, jeers and mocking, aimed mostly at their own players instead of us. I'd earned their respect, and I was thankful we had made friends instead of enemies.

I played hard, tough and aggressive. But my reputation for having no enemies on the field, a seemingly contradictory puzzle, may have saved my skin during a rather tense game.

I was the South-American misfit on a Czechoslovakian-owned team named Tatra with Canadian-born and Scottish imports. During those years the ethnic presence was far greater than it is today. The level of rivalry was intense, especially given that this was Premiere soccer, not national matches. We were playing the Portuguese, a team that stayed very true to its ethnic boundaries. When two players of even skill were available, they would take the one who was Portuguese. Every time. Not only was the rivalry rather intense, but they happened to have very devoted fans. The games could get rough, especially a game as important as this one.

The field at Alexander Park was well-kept, the changing rooms on the far side from me. The bleachers were on both sides, wide banks that sat around two thousand. And today, about 5 percent of those fans were ours. The other 95 percent were for the Portuguese, and they liked to make it obvious.

The game had been close and intense. On the field, I could see everything that was happening. I never had my back to the play, so everything unfolded in front of me. Our forward was streaking up the right side, the ball on his feet like it had been glued there. He stopped on a dime, turning to cut inside. The defensive player got in his way, hacking at the ball. They ran into each other, the ball dribbling away from both of them. The whistle blew—a foul had been called. The Portuguese player, clearly not happy with what had just happened, spat at our player.

Our Scottish contingent, not being shy to express their opinion of things, retaliated. With a head-butt filled with anger our player knocked the Portuguese player onto his backside. Immediately there was an uproar. The crowd surged with anger and—if they had seen the spitting incident they clearly didn't care—began to reach a boiling point. Our players were getting tangled up with theirs, faces red and veins protruding from necks as everyone was yelling. There was clearly a fight beginning on the field, and there was nothing stopping the two thousand Portuguese from storming the field—and storm they did. Like a tidal wave crashing onto shore they hit the grass, anger written all over their faces in plain Portuguese.

The odds for our team had majorly shifted, and my players realized it. With the realization that the game was over, they sprinted for the change rooms. The Portuguese were still yelling, tempers at a rolling boil. The crowd had reached the field now, yelling with their fists in the air. My team made it to the changing room, locking themselves in. They were safe.

I was still on the far side of the field. There was a fence behind me, and bailing over it was an option. I stood in my penalty box, asking myself, *What the heck am I supposed to do?* The crowd was livid, the game definitely over. And I was all alone, a South-American misfit representing a Scottish contingent that had ticked off two thousand Portuguese. Things weren't looking good for me.

The crowd wasn't getting any calmer, so I decided that I'd better make my move sooner rather than later. Besides, I didn't want to sit out on the field for an hour and wait for them to notice that I was there. I left my penalty box— my little island of safety—and walked towards the mob. Still yelling, still angry. When I got within a dozen feet, those nearest me noticed me there. I kept walking—directly at them.

They parted like the Red Sea, and I walked right through. I felt a little like Jesus in Luke 4, a story that suddenly became abundantly real to me. When I walked, they moved to make space for me. People reached out to touch me but not out of anger. I got pats on the back, cheers, high-fives.

"Good game," one said.

"Well played," another added.

"Thanks for being a great player."

"That was a great save!"

"Way to go!"

I walked out the other side, unscathed and completely in one piece. My reputation had preceded me—literally—and I was able to walk through an angry mob of very charged fans.

My team opened the door to the change room when I told them who it was, and I got a chance to see the surprise on their faces before the door slammed shut behind me, the lock clicking into place. Outside, the anger had come to the surface once more, and the Portuguese began banging on the side of the trailer, throwing rocks onto the top and at the sides.

We were hushed in silence, though our atmosphere was anything but silent, for about an hour, until the police finally arrived to escort us from the scene. Making friends instead of enemies had paid off for me—in a big way.

Dad, when he was a teenager, had swum across one of the major rivers in Russia and almost drowned. Though it wouldn't have served any practical type of purpose, he understood, just like many athletes do, the drive to achieve and accomplish. If he had grown up in other circumstances, where he could run for fun instead of to save his life, he would have understood better the intensity with which I approached soccer and sport.

On the other hand, Mom didn't understand my drive one bit. She had always had the idea that a human heart was only given a certain amount of beats to take it from birth to death. If you raised your heart rate, you were shortening your life. In other words, why do something that required energy if you didn't need to? If the life you had (like we had found in Canada) could allow you to sit on the couch when you weren't working, then why would you be running around a grass field chasing a ball?

They had no idea what I had gotten myself into or, especially, at just what level I was playing soccer. After I convinced them to come to one game (and they came to only one), Mom had a few comments. Looking a little concerned, she met me after I came out of the change room.

"Arvid, how come they didn't give you the ball very often? That was not very nice of them.

"And when they gave it to you they would kick it so hard it was difficult for you to even get it!

"Then again, it was nice of them to have that mesh behind you so when you missed the ball you didn't have to run far to get it.

"And by the way…" She was being motherly now, telling me just how to behave. "You should play nicer. Stop taking the ball away from other people."

I was on the cusp of moving up in the soccer world.

"Loewen brilliant in defeat," the headlines read.

We had played a team called Hibernia, a team from the Premiere league in Scotland. The game was in front of 6,000 fans, and we got our egos handed to us on a platter, losing 6–0. But the score didn't adequately reflect just how one-sided the game had been. The attacks were hitting me like rain, coming down one after the other. It was like playing pinball—I would boot it down the field and away, only to have gravity suck it towards me again, another attack inevitable. I played well, taking the ball off some of the forwards with my agility and reflexes. Their team had huge guys, and I made a save when one of their biggest had an open net from the penalty spot. Diving completely sideways, lying flat-out, I took the ball straight in the gut. He left the box shaking his head in disbelief. I had been following these guys and their careers and was elated to be able to hold my own. After the game, the coach of the Hibernia team was quoted as saying, "He's agile with good reflexes and a quick mind."

That same team extended an offer for me to get into the development league for them. It was my chance to go pro, and I was being seriously considered. While the idea of playing soccer professionally was certainly tempting, there were other factors to consider. Injuries are a big part of any sport, and I was no different. Standing in front of a soccer ball travelling at high speeds, as well as players pummelling towards me, meant I got hit or hit the ground quite often. My fearless style of playing had led to a few concussions by this point, and with one concussion the next comes far more easily. Injuries were one factor; size was another. I had never been a big guy. For the majority of my amateur career I could get away with being small—my quick speed and anticipation, for which I was well-known, helped me out in that regard. But the higher you go in any sport, the more all the other players have those attributes as well—and size. Being only 5'8", it was a tough field to crack.

In addition to Hibernia, I went down to the States for an open-trial camp for the newly developed indoor pro league. Because I was an international player, they told me it would be tough—they only had so many international slots available on the roster. Instead, they recommended I go to the New York Cosmos, then the home of Brazilian soccer legend Pele. But I didn't go.

If injuries and size were factors, there was one other significant factor. My faith had been growing over the years, and in the context of amateur leagues it was not a difficult thing to do (though being an elite athlete in a competitive environment at the same time as being a Christian is not an easy thing). But moving up to the professional level would bring with it all kinds of lifestyle temptations that I wasn't willing to bend on. That, and the fact that back at home there was a special girl who was starting to become a bigger and bigger part of my life. If I wanted to spend more and more time with her and invest in our future as a couple (and hopefully a family), being across the ocean would not be beneficial. And so I decided that it was time to make a change and to consider the long-term future.

I would stay in Winnipeg.

If soccer wasn't going to be my career, something else would have to be. After graduating from high school in 1975, I went to the University of Manitoba. I enrolled in the education program. I figured if I liked sports so much, I may as well do them for the rest of my life and get paid for it—so I wanted to be a gym teacher. There was also a good incentive: joining the U of M soccer team. The season started before the fall semester began, and I loved playing. It ran into the autumn, and I could barely think of anything else.

Shortly after classes began, I realized that I loved sports but had no interest in teaching sports. I only wanted to participate. Most of the classes were bearable, but there was one that I just couldn't take. The minute I walked into the class-room I knew I was out of my element. There were mats on the floor, with some soft music playing in the background. I felt more uncomfortable than if I'd shown up on the soccer field naked. The teacher was wearing some extremely tight shorts and shirt, and I had to look away from him. Some of the students filing in were averting their eyes as well. The class was called "Movement Education," and it was about to make me throw up. There was a sign-in atten-dance sheet, and I scribbled my name as if I was being treasonous and wanted to get out as fast as possible.

When the teacher started talking about the fact that we were going to be teaching kids how to move to music, I almost threw up my lunch. The last time I had danced was—never mind, I think I erased that memory from my mind. There was no way I was dancing in front of a group of adults, never mind teach-ing kids to dance. *This isn't gym!* I wanted to scream. And then the teacher dropped the biggest bombshell of them all.

When he moved to the front of the class, leaning over to stretch his body in his bright leotards, I tried to hide behind the other students so he wouldn't even know I was there. It wasn't easy, as everyone kept bouncing around like the floor was on fire.

"Class," he started, "welcome to Movement Education. As we'll be dancing and stretching in this class, it is strongly encouraged that you buy some spandex or Lycra to feel comfortable."

Comfortable? I thought, *Who can possibly feel comfortable in clothes like that?*

While the rest of the class snickered or nodded, I snuck out the back door and didn't come back. There was no chance I was going to be in that class. As I walked away, I distinctly remember thinking, *Like I'm ever going to be seen in spandex!*

"If you can touch it, you can catch it"

When Quitting Is Not an Option

Fearless in pursuit of the ball

Hibs' Tony Higgins takes a tumble after being fouled by Manitoba's Billy Smith.

Loewen brilliant in defeat

Hibernian whitewashes Selects

By Dave Kerr
Tribune Soccer Writer

"He is agile, with good reflexes and a quick mind," was how Hibs' manager Eddie Turnbull described Selects goalkeeper Arvid Loewen. Although the score might not indicate it, Loewen was the man of the match last night as Hibernian of Scotland downed Manitoba Selects 6-0 at University Stadium.

Most of the crowd of 6,000 would agree with Turnbull's assessment. The acrobatic Loewen made a dozen saves that had the Hibs forwards and the crowd shaking their heads in disbelief.

Loewens' individual excellence was equalled but not overshadowed by Hibs Ally MacLeod, who scored four of his team's goals, with George Stewart adding the other two.

The 26-year-old MacLeod said four goals was an exception for him. "We expected to win, we train every day as professionals", He added, "your goalkeeper was quite good, but when your defence is under pressure for 90 minutes something is going to crack."

Indeed the Hibs had the local lads under pressure for most of the match. In the early going, some well-timed tackles by Selects defence, particularly Billy Smith, destroyed many of the Hibs scoring chances.

Selects coach Ralph McKay gave Loewen and the defence much of the credit for keeping the Hibs off the scoreboard for the first 20 minutes.

"This [...]
cont[...]

L[...]
feren[...]
alwa[...]
pate[...]

T[...]
and [...]
save[...]
sure[...]

T[...]
show[...]
plent[...]
and i[...]
of de[...]

A[...]
gins i[...]
free [...]
take.

W[...]
when [...]
Hibs keeper [...] to extend himself with a good save. But the Hibs moved quickly up the park and MacLeod had his second goal, an easy header from a Smith cross. MacLeod's third

goal came from the penalty spot in the 45th minute after Smith had been pulled down.

The second half was much the same with the [...] mith and [...] le often

[...] y with a [...] inutes. [...] th min- [...] ewen at [...] he net.

[...] Manuel [...] closing [...] ing just

[...] Selects [...] goals in [...] ad been

[...]." [...] uld be- [...] ing and [...] team to

[...] as well as could be expected, but as Hibs Smith commented "We're professionals and they're amateurs," and that about says it all.

Newspaper article highlighting Arvid's game against Hibernia

The Fat Years
Post-Soccer, Pre-Cycling

I had decided against pursuing soccer as a career, and spandex and Lycra scared me away from being a gym teacher. I showed up at enough random classes to not get thrown out of university, but I quit after the conference finals of the soccer season. Palliser, the furniture company where my dad and older brother Art worked full-time upon arriving in Canada, was not hiring, but I was convinced I would be able to get a job. It was November, and I didn't want to pass up an opportunity. After all, the Christmas turkey gift from the company to its employees required that the employee be working prior to December 1st.

The smell of sawdust that I'd grown accustomed to when Dad came home from work was strong as I walked into the office of Mr. Reimer, the general manager. He looked up from his desk, knowing who I was but not interested. He asked me a few questions, knowing that he didn't want to hire me and didn't need me. I wasn't even sure he was listening, but I answered them honestly.

"Listen, Arvid." He finally looked up at me, putting the pencil down on the desk with a noise that nearly made me jump. "The truth is that I don't need any employees right now." He rubbed his temples, clearly at a loss about what to do. "But I know your family, and they've got a good reputation around here. They're diligent, and they don't complain." He got silent again, and I decided this was my time to jump in.

"I want this job," I said. "I will do anything you have. I'm prepared to work hard and will work my way up this company." The words felt strange and strong coming out of my mouth, completely masking the mess of nerves that I was underneath.

He looked back at me, recognizing my commitment to what I was saying. "I respect your family," he responded. "And I know what you're saying is true."

With a nod I was hired.

When Quitting Is Not an Option

I left the office with a start date of December 1st—I had a job, and I had a turkey for Christmas. I began just like many begin at a large company, working as a general labourer and doing whatever mundane, repetitive and seemingly mindless task they gave me. It wasn't long before I had moved up the food chain to being a machine operator for various machines, the smell of particleboard now just as strong on my clothes as on Dad's.

From there I moved on to being a computerized-panel-saw operator. It was in this position that I settled in and began to become comfortable. While sports had always been one of my obvious gifts, I'd also developed a knack for math and puzzle-solving. When operating a computerized panel-saw the purpose is to take a large sheet of particleboard and cut it into smaller pieces for use in furniture. This could be any size of rectangle that had to be cut precisely, including taking the grain into account. A bedroom set could easily require up to 60 different pieces. They had advanced (at the time, anyway) computers for figuring out the most efficient way of cutting the particleboard. In other words, how many pieces can you get out of a single sheet? The computer would figure out a pattern, and we would then make the cuts. In many ways it was like trying to play Tetris, like fitting the "T" shaped piece in—should it go sideways, upside down or right side up? It didn't take long before I was disagreeing with what the computer readout was telling us about the way to cut the particleboard. I grabbed a piece of paper and pencil and began to sketch, doing the math and subtracting the lengths and widths from the overall particleboard dimensions. Within a few tries I had come up with a more efficient way of cutting the particleboard that outdid any computer program at the time.

This kind of initiative—and skill—had me promoted to lead hand after a while, and from there it was on to foreman, supervisor and then middle management over a department. Working hard and having a keen eye for increasing production enabled me to do exactly what I had promised the general manager—work my way up the company, eventually becoming the manager myself, though many years later.

I was the plant manager, and my responsibility included the starting of the particleboard plant, sawmill and veneer operation. Eventually I became the vice-president of operations for particleboard, sawmill, veneer and finished goods manufacturing. It was a vertically integrated manufacturing complex with a payroll of about 1,000 employees and a finished goods sales budget of $70 to 80 million. In an industry populated by overseas manufacturing, it was extremely uncommon to go from sawdust to completed furniture in one manufacturing location.

The Fat Years: Post-Soccer, Pre-Cycling

Before becoming the vice-president of operations, I had been general manager in title but VP in responsibility. While I wanted to work my way up in the company, I had hesitations about accepting the title. The amount of stress, responsibility and time that came with the title was not something I wanted on my shoulders. It was, however, being hoisted onto my shoulders regardless of what I wanted.

While this is the picture of my working career, much had changed in my life. By the time 2006 rolled around, I was prepared to be done with the corporate world. Besides, a passion had grown within me that made it easy to leave the company I had dedicated my entire professional career to—but that's getting a little ahead of myself.

Rewinding to the beginning of this chapter, I found my soccer career on the decline just as my working career was gaining traction. Suffering the consequences of many collisions from holding my own in the soccer world, my playing ability just couldn't keep up with the intense pace of the level of soccer I was accustomed to playing. Just being hit with a ball during warm-up would bring on concussion-like symptoms, and I knew this couldn't last.

Attending the church we had grown into as soon as we came to Canada, I had my eye on a young woman a few years younger than me. Her name was Ruth, and though we had never met (and she probably didn't know I existed), I knew that she was the one for me. Whenever possible I would sit behind her in the church balcony. I was always very impressed—she sat beside her mom and dad, unlike so many of the other youth. I figured she was a "good girl," and I got nervous every time I got near her. I don't think I heard a single sermon when she was sitting in front of me (don't tell Reverend Neufeld).

Imagine, then, my horror and shock when one day she decided to sit with her friends. All my dreams had been shattered, and I wondered if I was misled in believing her to be my future wife. Nevertheless, this quiet crush lasted for years.

When she decided that she would go to Bible school in BC the year after high school, I was completely crushed. Having liked her for so long, I was somehow disillusioned that the feeling and attraction was mutual—when she had never even talked to me. Though I had not made a single move or even made my presence known, I gave up on her while she was away. I figured she would meet someone else out there and never return.

When Quitting Is Not an Option

That didn't happen, and she did return. When she came back, however, she was so confident and outgoing that I, a timid and shy adult, knew that I had no chance.

I decided that I had to give it a shot. I knew where she lived and the way she would usually walk to get to church. I decided that I would go to a college and career event (my one and only), and, even though my house was closer to the church than hers, I would somehow be driving by in my bright orange two-seat convertible sports car—a 1975 Spitfire MGB. When I drove down the street she was exactly where I expected her to be. I asked her if she wanted a ride (my first real words to her), and I was completely surprised when she agreed.

Our relationship consisted of a slow start (my fault), though we often went on rides in my convertible and I would invite her to soccer games from time to time. Not exactly a smooth boyfriend, but she was gracious, and the rest was, as they say, history.

In the fall of 1980 we got engaged, and I finally decided to retire from soccer. That next spring a team begged me to come back out of retirement for a tournament in Thunder Bay. The itch to play hadn't stayed away, so I went. At the end of that season, I officially retired.

Those who have played or competed at an elite level know just how difficult it can be to retire. Perhaps it's why we see such high-profile athletes return to their sport (or another). There's just that competitive buzz in their bones that they can't get rid of. They sit on the couch, and their legs shake when they see others competing on TV; they hear a ref blow a whistle and wish they were in the game again. Being a goalie had taken its toll on my body, so I came back for a season as a left-wing for a team called Brazilia. Soccer took a backseat as a priority, especially now that I was newly married, but I was still good enough to play one division lower than Premiere.

The sound I heard was worse than the feeling I felt. I'd had my share of falls and crashes throughout my career, but this was much worse. It was a tearing noise that alerted my ears that something was wrong as I fell to the ground. I couldn't support myself, as my right foot was stuck in a hole. It wasn't even during a game—only a practice—but damaged cartilage and partially torn ligaments are not forgiving.

The Fat Years: Post-Soccer, Pre-Cycling

As I lay on the ground, pain coursing through my body, I realized that something seriously wrong had happened. This could be—would be—the end of my competitive soccer playing. While some of my teammates rushed over to check if I was OK when I didn't stand up, I could feel the blood pounding in my ears as the adrenaline raced through my body. The sounds of the practice going on around me were muted and somehow distant, as if someone had turned the speaker down. All of my body's resources were focused on the pain and repairing what had gone wrong—only it couldn't.

Neither would the doctors. I was put into a cast and forced to walk with a limp. Due to my high pain threshold, they didn't believe it was that serious. If my income wasn't dependent on my knee's health, then they wouldn't do surgery. "Wrap it up and rest it" is what I was told. I am fully convinced that this was the onset of the limp that I still have to this day.

Living with a severely damaged knee for a year and a half could also have been the start of the onset of my osteoarthritis. Forced to climb stairs like a kid—my left leg first, one step at a time—it took that year and a half before I could convince a doctor that I needed surgery in order to live anything resembling a normal life.

When I finally went under the knife, they cut the cartilage and trimmed the ligaments. It wasn't great, but it was good enough to get back to being normal.

For a brief period of time I tried to play indoors with a brace, but I wasn't the same and it wasn't the same. While those on the teams tried to convince me that I could still anticipate just like I used to—and wouldn't therefore need the mobility and speed that I had had—I knew that I wasn't playing up to anything close to my previous potential. A few embarrassing games ate at me as a competitive athlete, and I knew that the former glory (though nothing extravagant) had faded. It was around 1985 when soccer truly ended for me at any competitive level.

The sport I loved and had lived for over a decade was no longer a possibility.

I married Ruth in May 1981, and our first daughter, Jodi, arrived in June 1983. A little less than two years later came Stephanie, and our son, Paul, followed in summer 1986. Our family of five was complete. We moved into a house with a large backyard (for the city) shortly before Paul was born, and I couldn't help but start mentally planning out all the adventures we could have in our own backyard.

When Quitting Is Not an Option

The first part of the yard was normal—a deck, some grass and a play structure, including a large sandbox that Dad and I built. The beam holding the swings was around 11 feet above the ground, and it ran from the top of the slide over to the fence for stability. It didn't take long for my mind to start adding to the structure, and I turned my dreams to reality by building a platform above the swings, 11 feet high, for a zip-line to run down from. Nearly a hundred feet long, the zip-line ends just before our back fence, which borders on a gas station. The design began with a complicated contraption that had to be removed and carried back to the top every time but eventually evolved into a smaller, lighter and faster carriage with a rope coming down that could be pulled back to the top. The kids—our own, their friends and even a few that liked jumping over our back fence—loved it.

Not having had snow (or very cold temperatures) as a kid, I was keen to take advantage of them. As our kids grew we decided to build an ice rink. The first attempt involved a smaller rink—perhaps 30 by 50 feet—and a wooden structure I built at the back of the yard about 8 feet tall that was the beginning for a toboggan slide. We had so much fun with the slide that the next year it grew by about 6 feet. I moved the start to the railing of the zip-line platform.

Starting at 14 feet high, the toboggan slide crossed the yard, ran the length of the yard at fence height, crossed the yard, dropped down to the ground, then circled back underneath itself and came out some 350 feet of distance travelled from the beginning—right at the foot of the ramp to carry the toboggans back up. It was 1992, the year of the Winter Olympics in France, and we set up two Canadian flags at the start and end of our luge. We'd race down the track, its not-quite-Olympic-smooth surface jarring our bones as we forced ourselves into an aerodynamic position. Our top recorded speed was 27 miles per hour. Not bad for a backyard slide!

The toboggan slide was so popular that one evening we heard the sounds of our plastic toboggans careening down in the dark. Going outside to check who might be using the slide (our kids were all inside), I saw a young girl and her even younger brother.

"Hi," I said to them. "Are you using the slide?"

"Yes!" they responded.

"You know, this is actually my backyard."

"Our mom said it was a park."

"It's not. And it's also dark outside. You guys should probably go."

They were pretty young, but I had to admire their persistence in going down the toboggan slide. First they'd had to climb over our fence, then try to convince me that somehow their mom had gotten our yard confused for a park—and let them come in the dark of the evening. But off they went.

In the middle of the toboggan slide was another hockey rink, and the kids quickly showed how much better at skating they were than I was. Though I did enjoy skating and picked it up relatively quickly, kids learn much faster. It wasn't long before they were passing and shooting better than I could—though I showed them how much tougher I was than them by skating in December in shorts. Although I'd been born in a country known for its heat, I must have had some Canadian blood in me before even coming here. Either that or that run in the snow in my bare feet had been enough of an initiation to make me a warm-blooded Canadian.

When the snow and ice had all melted, the grass underneath was a sickly yellow—after all, our motto had always been that we were raising kids, not grass. And so instead of nursing that open space back to a green haven, I turned it into a soccer field, perfect for 3-on-3 with adults or more with kids. While I was still able to keep the ball out of the net when Paul and his friends would play (though he probably claims otherwise), I noticed that I was beginning to live a rather docile life. We would go biking with the kids in a four-seat trailer I built, but the speed and competitiveness I had been used to had disappeared from my life.

I had entered into the years that my son Paul now (lovingly) calls "the fat years." The years where I did little and noticed myself gradually slipping in my ability to stay ahead of my kids. There comes a time in every dad's life when he gets passed or beaten by his kids, but I wasn't prepared for that time, and I was convinced it wasn't going to happen yet—as long as I could do something to prevent it, that is.

The early spring mush was in full swing, the sides of the road littered with a combination of gravel, salt and freezing cold water. I snugged the water bottle into the metal rack on my yellow Canadian Tire mountain bike, then spun the pedal with my left foot.

It had been years since I'd played a competitive soccer game and probably even longer since I'd stretched before any exercise. That fact was apparent as I attempted to get my leg over the frame. Glad that no one was watching, I brought the frame lower than usual. No longer was I the flexible pretzel that climbed through the frame of the black Heidemann bike on the dusty roads of Paraguay. I was wearing a wind-resistant jacket that billowed around me in the cold air, and I brushed any thoughts of caution away. Though I was born in a hot climate, I had adjusted well to the Canadian temperatures, and a little breeze wasn't going to stop me.

"Have a good ride!" Ruth called from the garage as the door closed. The mechanical whir continued for a few seconds before it engaged with the concrete in a sound that was a little too final for me.

This'll be fun, I thought, *and good for me.* The bulge around my waist agreed, so I climbed onto the pedals and took off. For a high-calibre athlete like me, 40 km on a bike should have been a walk in the park (a small park).

For the first while, everything went according to plan. I was able to look around and have fun, take in the scenery. When you spend most of your travelling time in a car you don't realize just how encapsulating a vehicle is. But when you're on a bike you get a chance to actually experience the travel. You've got full range of your vision. You can feel the ground passing beneath you. You connect with the terrain because it's your own power that's got to get you up (okay, so maybe not in Manitoba) and over it.

Around the 20-kilometre mark I started to feel it. My legs, accustomed to sitting in a desk chair, were not quite up to the task. Every pedal turn felt a little bit more like they were turning to jelly. The wind seemed to be getting colder—or was it getting stronger? The sun up in the sky wasn't as hot, and the cars seemed to be coming closer to my body—or was it my imagination?

I was biking a loop, and thankfully I was past the halfway point. But it still meant I had a long way to go. I knew my distances (my bike didn't have an odometer), so I knew I was approaching the 30-kilometre mark. There was a garden store up ahead, and my legs were shaking with exhaustion. That, combined with the cold, made it impossible to see anything farther than the store.

I had to stop.

"Excuse me!" I called out, hoping someone would help me. A man just about to climb into his car noticed me. "Could you spare any change? I, I, I don't think I can make it any further, and I have to call my wife—to pick me up."

He looked me up and down. I probably didn't look like I belonged where I was, but I'd somehow managed to fail to complete a 40-kilometre ride. My athletic ego had shrunk down to the size of a pea as he handed the coins over. When I slotted them into the payphone, the nagging voice enjoyed mocking my failure. I had come to discover something that I didn't even know existed—the proverbial DNF. When Ruth came to pick me up and load the bike into the back of our old Toyota van with fold-down seats, I knew that this wasn't over.

I would be back.

The relationship between me, the bike, the road and the threat of a DNF would continue.

Arvid and Ruth in their dating years, 1980

A wonderful spring day for our wedding, May 2, 1981

With Jodi, Stephanie and Paul the family is complete, Christmas 1986

The backyard winter wonderland, enjoyed by kids of all ages

If At First You Don't Succeed
Cycling, Part 1

For some, discovering how much it sucks to not finish a ride would destroy their motivation to ever ride again. But instead of destroying my resolve, it fuelled it. I had made it 75 percent of the way, even though it was a short ride. In the difficult moments in a bike ride (just as in life), everything seems impossible, and quitting seems like the only option. The minute the switch flips and you decide to call it quits, suddenly in hindsight all the challenges seem somewhat smaller and less significant.

It can't have hurt that bad, you argue. *I wouldn't quit next time.*

Next time.

The next time I tried a long ride it was with the same cheap mountain bike. But this time I would push beyond 40 km and ride all the way from our home to Winkler, a distance of roughly 130 km. When I arrived in one piece I knew that this was what I wanted to do. Inspired and intrigued by a sport I had discovered, I went out and bought my first real road bike, a green Trek Touring bike. It was lighter, and I felt nimble and agile when I stepped on its pedals.

Before the days of the Internet, when things went only at the speed of telephone tag, it took effort to find information. I looked up any type of long-distance rides, figuring that the longer they were, the more of a challenge they presented. I wasn't entirely sure if I was the only one in the world who liked doing what I was doing, but I soon discovered I wasn't.

I discovered randonneuring, a sport of cycling ultra-marathon distances in which you rely on your own ability to provide support. You carry your supplies, food and water with you (though often stopping to refill at farmers' houses—with or without permission). Every year there was a progression of rides throughout the season: 200 km, 300 km, 400 km, 600 km and 1,000 km.

When Quitting Is Not an Option

I seemed to have good timing, because I discovered the sport after the annual 600 km and before the 1,000 km.

Perfect.

There was no way I was waiting for next season to get involved, and, as the 1,000 km was the only ride left in the year, it was the one I gunned for. I knew the starting point, so I got Ruth to drive me and my touring bike out early in the morning.

The sun was coming up over the horizon as we pulled up to the gas station parking lot. The air was crisp and fresh, and I felt a shiver run through my body as I stepped out of the van. Having decided that I would never be caught dead or alive in spandex, I was wearing a hybrid version of cycling shorts that looked like a regular pair of shorts but had a chamois (padding) in them. It didn't matter how hard they peer-pressured me, I wasn't about to give in. It seemed likely they'd try, though, given what they were wearing, making it extremely difficult to know where to look.

They all had slick helmets, cycling gloves with a hole on the back, spandex jerseys with the standard triple pocket on the back and shoes that clacked on the concrete with metal clips to connect to the pedals. Ironically, these are called "clipless" shoes. "Clip" shoes are what I had, with the mesh cage over the shoe to hold it in. Clipless is another stage up in quality, allowing you to apply pressure in both directions and preventing your foot from slipping out when you stand up to apply extra pressure on a climb.

"You're Arvid?" asked a skinny guy who looked like he never went through a stage called the fat years.

"Yeah," I said, looking back at Ruth for confirmation—not about my name but about the fact that I was about to do one of the stupidest things in my life, never mind testing out wearing runners without socks for the first time for a full marathon.

"You done any of the other rides?" he asked, looking me up and down. Wearing normal runners and my half-hearted shorts, and with the cheapest helmet Canadian Tire offered, I knew I didn't look all that convincing.

"No," I admitted. He looked over at one of the other riders, and I nearly lost my breakfast when I realized it was a woman. *Women are supposed to be smarter than this*, I thought. Glad I didn't say it out loud, I waited while the two seemed to be glancing back and forth.

"I'm Susan," she said, showing a little bit of hospitality. She came over to offer her hand and tipped her head in the direction of the skinny guy who had talked first. "That's Brian, my husband."

"Usually you have to do all the previous ones in order to do any of them—especially the 1,000," Brian said, his eyes seeming to be sending a very direct and unmistakable message to Susan.

"It might not be a bad idea for you to wait out the winter and give it a shot next year. Start with us on the 200 and move all the way up to the 1,000," Susan agreed, her voice gentle but also relatively strong. If she was willing to put herself through 50-plus hours of biking, she had to be strong. Or crazy.

I looked over to Ruth, who already knew that I was the latter.

"I can do it," I said, though perhaps it came out a bit stronger than my mind's voice.

"Okay." Brian shrugged his shoulders, and I smiled back at Ruth. Susan was moving to get something from her pack when Brian interrupted her. "We can't stop you from riding with us. But you're not signing any of the documents or waivers. As far as we know and care, you're just some guy that bummed along for a ride. We basically don't even know you exist. Got it?" His words may have sounded harsh, but taking on an incompetent and inexperienced cyclist is a big deal. In any type of cycling, drafting is a calculated risk. Basically, you tuck yourself in behind the cyclist in front of you and ride within six inches of their back tire. It can lower the effort required by up to 30 percent if you do it right. But it also means that a touch of the brakes from the front cyclist can result in a cascading wipeout if the following riders aren't vigilant. On the other hand, a klutzy rider in such close proximity can endanger the entire peloton (the French word for the main group of riders). One wobble of your skinny tires can send everyone down to road rash—or worse.

"I got it," I said, agreeing to their terms. Accepted into the group (somewhat begrudgingly) I was introduced to all of them. Brian and Susan, the married couple and de facto leaders, Robert and Ben. We'd be a group of five meandering our way through Southern Manitoba and into the United States before coming back up (hopefully) some 50-plus hours later.

I walked over to Ruth in the van, who seemed to offer me one last out with her raised eyebrows.

"Here goes nothing," I said, giving her a kiss.

"Be safe," she said.

"I will," I agreed, saying goodbye to the three sleepyheads in the back of the van. They grunted and groaned their goodbyes, watching Dad leave on a strange and unique experience. It was about to become commonplace, however.

"All right," Susan said, the only one welcoming me when I came back with my bike. I needed to adjust my shorts, but there was no way I was doing anything down there in front of any of them. "What's the longest you've ridden?"

"A couple hundred," I said, being a little elusive. Brian gave a snort, his back turned to me. "A couple hundred" could be anywhere from two to five by my reckoning. I had the distinct impression I was about to get my butt kicked by the road.

I shifted sideways, trying to adjust my shorts.

"Listen," Susan said, tightening the lid on one of her water bottles and sliding it into its cage. My bike had two cages, fewer than theirs. I'd probably be stopping a lot more to fill up from hoses. "If you've got a problem with your shorts, fix it. If you've gotta burp, let 'er rip. If you have to fart, blast it. And if you have to puke, just don't hit any of us, and aim for the ditch. If you're going to try to be a polite hero, you're gonna wind up lying in that ditch with a stomach so full of gas you're likely to explode."

Perhaps she caught on to the fact that I was a little taken aback by her abrasiveness. "Welcome to the world of ultra-marathon cycling." She reached out and shook my hand again with a smile. "You'll hate it, just like I do. But something deep inside of you will keep you coming back for more—I can't explain it; it's just the way it is."

I took her words to heart as I stepped on the pedal, pushing off from our starting line.

While many races have guns, crowds and television crews, randonneuring and ultra-marathon cycling races have none of those things. They have the cold, quiet realization that between you and the finish line is nothing but saddle sores (only the beginning of the pain), stomach problems, sleep deprivation, flat tires, sore legs, sore stomach, sore feet and a ton of open road. They have a parking lot at dawn, with the early morning risers going for their coffee wondering just what on earth you're doing up this early in the morning on a bike. It's a quiet sport, an unknown sport, and perhaps because of or in spite of that, a sport that puts people to the test like none other.

Randonneuring and ultra-marathon cycling are not technically the same thing. In order for someone to become a randonneur, he must complete an event of 200 km or more. Riders may travel together or alone, and they are required to be self-sufficient between checkpoints (tens of kilometres apart). Randonneuring events are technically not races, though whether the riders see it that way or not is up for debate. Finishing a randonneuring event enters you into a club for which there is no real prize other than the sense of accomplishment.

Ultra-marathon cycling, on the other hand, does have races. It is governed by the body called the Ultra-Marathon Cycling Association (UMCA) and is more strictly regulated. Though the rules are not always exactly the same across the board, they usually follow something along these lines: From the start line to the finish line the clock is ticking. There are no breaks. Every time I stop to eat, visit the washroom, sleep, adjust my jacket, fix a flat tire, my time counts. Because of this, an ultra-marathon event can become extremely mentally taxing. Every time I step off the bike the mental clock is ticking. I see other riders pass me and wonder when they will stop. I debate between getting back on and riding slowly or resting in the hopes that I can ride faster again.

All the regular rules of the road are required to be followed, and they add their own specific rules. Unlike randonneuring, riding in packs and drafting is not allowed. In other words, you can't follow a rider and hide in his or her slipstream. When a rider is caught up to, passing riders must actually establish themselves two bike-lengths behind and then pass on the left, leaving adequate space so they do not take advantage of the air bubble around the rider. They then have to be at least two bike-lengths in front of the rider before they can go back onto the shoulder.

Some races disallow crewing, some allow it, and others require it. Your crew can be your lifeline in ultra-marathon cycling. They drive behind you to protect you from cars; their lights blast the road at night so you can see better; they get food for you, help you dress and undress, find you a place to sleep, cheer you on and do all kinds of other tasks. There are rules about how frequently the crew can pull up beside you and how long they're allowed to stay there, touching the crew car (a big no-no), checking in at time stations and being sportsmanlike. The rulebook and route sheet for RAAM is several hundred pages long—a daunting task for the crew, whose role it also is to make sure the rider remains mentally competent after hours and days on the bike without sleep.

In order to prevent crazies like me from joining the toughest races without any experience, there are qualifying rides. The small randonneuring rides were qualifiers for a ride like Boston-Montreal-Boston or the Rocky Mountain 1200. Yet rides just like those two actually serve as qualifiers for another ride: RAAM.

When Quitting Is Not an Option

Race Across America is such a difficult event that to have someone who isn't qualified show up and drop out within the first few days is a drain on their resources and time.

In order to qualify for RAAM you need to finish other rides (like the Furnace Creek 508) in a specific (and difficult) amount of time. These qualifying rides are gruelling and push riders to the limit. Yet they are just the beginning. Race Across America, even though its qualifying requirements are strict, still has a drop-out rate of around 50 percent. It's just that tough.

If I wanted to someday get to the start line of any of those rides, I had 1,000 km ahead of me when I turned that first pedal stroke.

Within the first few kilometres I realized just how much the rest of the riders didn't think I could make it. When you're cycling in a pack it's common courtesy to take turns at the front breaking the wind. You'll see a line of riders heading down the road with one at the front. Depending on the size of the pack, that rider will only last up there for a short while before "peeling off" to drop back, slowing down all the way to the end and then latching back on the group. In this way, everyone rotates through a spot at the front.

Everyone except me, it seemed.

Whether out of sympathy, annoyance or mistrust, I never got the spot at the front. The rider dropping back from the front would join the group in front of me, nudging me to the side and back. It meant I stayed in the back the entire time, though I have to admit that I didn't mind all that much.

When we crossed the border into the United States and explained to the border patrol agent what we were doing, he shook his head like we were nuts.

I'm not convinced he was wrong.

For those who have gone for long bike rides, 10 to 12 hours is doable. Maybe 14 to 16. But once you cross 16 hours you realize something: that's as long as the light lasts. When you get into the dark, things get funky.

First off, your entire depth perception disappears. All you see is the beam of light coming off the front of your bike and the twinkling of some faint stars in the sky. Because you have no perception of depth, your concept of speed decreases (you also can't see your bike computer, so it's really a guessing game). It always feels like you get faster in the dark, though when you see your speed you realize that you dropped somewhere between 3 and 4 km/h without meaning to. It's like the air gets thicker at night, even though it's really all in your head.

But that's not the most difficult part. The toughest part is knowing that you're literally in the dark for the next 6–8 hours. The lights are shut off, and it's you and an inky-black sea around you. When the next sunlight is that far away, it feels like forever. Time stretches on into an eternity. It feels like the sun will never come up. Your mood drops like a rock in a fish tank. And all you want to do is give up, go to sleep and wake up with the sunlight.

Somehow, I made it through that night and found myself fighting off sleep as the morning sun crept its beautiful long fingers over the horizon. A smile crossed my face—despite the fatigue, pain, exhaustion, hunger, thirst and utter hopelessness of the night, a brand new day had suddenly dawned, and everything was going to be all right. The day was a clean slate, even though my body felt like it had been dragged over the concrete for the last 24 hours. Away from the city, my family, my home, it felt like nothing else existed at all. It was me and the bike, and the bike was kicking my butt.

With the sun back, I could see the faces of my fellow riders. If their faces were any indication, I must have looked horrible. Staying up all night makes a person tired, but physically exerting oneself moment after moment wears on the body like nothing I had experienced before.

The riding continued with intermittent breaks to fill up on water, go to the washroom or buy snacks along the road. I was dragging. My legs felt like they weighed a ton. The muscles couldn't push anymore, so I found myself lifting up with my feet instead of pushing down, anything to do something different and take the pressure off the bottom of my feet.

Brian kept looking back at me, expecting me to crack any moment. My eyes were closing, and I fought to keep them open, barely able to keep my bike in a straight line. They may have been cheering me on or they may have been ridiculing me—I don't even know. At some point, my body decided it had had enough. I wasn't going to be able to stay awake any longer.

We rolled into a small town, its population less than the number of kilometres I had biked since the last time I felt comfortable. My eyes were alert now, looking for a hotel or motel—anything with four walls and a bed. Even the walls were optional. So was the bed by this point. All I wanted to do was sleep. Brian looked back at me with a smirk on his face, and I knew he knew. I had dragged it out—800 km—but my body had had enough. I needed a break.

"Guys, I've gotta stop," I croaked, my throat sore.

When Quitting Is Not an Option

"Packing it in?" someone said. I shook my head.

"Just some sleep," I argued, convincing myself. I wasn't willing to give up. Not now. Not yet.

"Okay," they said. It was obvious that they were tired too. But as this wasn't their first ride they had come to a greater understanding of just how much of a ride was left. At this point I wasn't willing to turn the pedal once more, and I coasted with my foot off the pedals to the side of the road, onto the driveway to a small motel that I normally would have reconsidered.

"I'm just going to sleep for a few hours," I said. "Then I'll be back on the road."

"You're on your own," Brian said, making sure everything was clear.

"I'm on my own," I responded, nodding and feeling my eyelids take longer than normal to bounce back up.

"Okay," they said, barely pausing as I climbed off my bike. Exhausted, I let it fall against the motel's wall a little harder than was probably good for it. But it didn't matter. For a brief moment I wasn't touching the bike, wasn't sitting on the seat, wasn't feeling the tape around the handlebars. I watched as the four of them disappeared off into the distance, looking like they still had energy to spare compared to me. I booked the motel room, barely wheeled the bike to the door, got it unlocked and hit the bed. I was out.

I didn't give up. When I woke up, I resolutely climbed back onto my bike. Ruth had had to pick me up after 30 km. This was 800 km in, and I wasn't willing to stop. I pedalled the last 200 km alone, no more drafting, no more moral support. Just me and the road, navigating back to Winnipeg.

I arrived home some 60 hours after I left, only a few hours behind the rest of the riders. I took off my shoes and let my feet air out, realizing that I probably needed the real shoes with the real shorts. My feet were sore, and I hated it. I hated every part of it. But Susan was right. I had finished my first long ride, and I wasn't done.

I wanted more.

Paris. It's the city of love, and it's also known for the Tour de France—the most famous cycling event every year. The Tour de France covers some 3,300 km in 23 days. It's what's called a "stage race," which, though it also involves a bike, is very different from what I do. In a stage race, all the riders start together each day. At the end of the day there is a stage winner (whoever crossed that day's finish line first), and the total times of each day's riding are added up. Over the course of 21 days the person with the lowest total time wins the race. It's much faster, because the stages are short (100 to 220 km generally), and the entire group spends a lot of the time together. In the main group (peloton) speeds can stay around 40 to 45 km/h because of the efficiency of drafting. In ultra-marathon cycling, where you bike alone for 800 to 1,200 km at a time, speeds usually stick in the 22–32 km/h range.

I was heading to Paris for a bike ride, but it wasn't the Tour de France. It was Paris-Brest-Paris, a 1,200 km round trip that was a randonneur ride. In other words, there's no official winner (though we all know there's a winner), there's no support allowed on the road and drafting is allowed. Paris-Brest-Paris is the largest ride of its type in the world, with around 3,000 people in the race (most ultra-marathon events have between 5 and 50 riders). In order to qualify you needed to do the 200, 300, 400, 600 and 1,000 km randonneuring rides in the same year. Paris-Brest-Paris only takes place once every four years, and I had a chance to go with Brian (the one who was hesitant to welcome me), Susan (who told me to fart when I needed to fart) and Ben. In a ride of this size, you depart the finish line in waves. Riders are riding so close together that you have to be extremely careful with how much you twitch. Moving a few inches might knock the next guy over and start a domino chain through the peloton.

The time limit for the ride is 90 hours, which can be calculated to 13.3 km/h. That might sound slow, but when you incorporate sleep, eating, washroom breaks, changing clothes and just plain ol' exhaustion, it usually means you need to ride somewhere around 18–20 km/h when you're on the bike and take as few breaks as possible.

Nervous to get going and hit the road, I ate a massive pasta dinner the night before (carb-loading). The pasta had a dressing on it that had a distinct smell. I can still remember it quite sharply, mostly because my stomach immediately let me know that it didn't like the dressing and decided that it wanted to leave the dressing (and the pasta) all over the floor of the restroom.

So I hit the road on my first bike race with nothing in my stomach other than a bunch of jittery nerves.

Apparently jittery nerves are not enough to fuel the human body. I did my best to refuel along the way, but I didn't have a clue what I was doing. I was eating anyway and suffering badly. My system wasn't able to process anything, even though I was able to get it down my throat. I had eaten a lot but metabolized virtually nothing. Inside of my stomach was a bag of food, just waiting for its exit cue. Three hundred km into the ride I was in shutdown mode, only 25 percent done. At the last station I had consumed a bunch of cantaloupe. It, too, sat there. Until finally its cue came—

And it found its new home all over the side of a concrete barrier in a small town.

Now actually feeling quite a bit better, I got back on the bike and kept moving. Though I had no energy, and that situation wasn't about to rectify itself, I was determined not to quit. Some people give up when things get tough, but I hadn't come all the way to France to bike a quarter of the way. Besides, my determined streak decided that I could keep biking on no food.

Even though I felt better, my stomach hadn't gotten any better at keeping anything down. I tried non-alcoholic beer, which came back. Water decided that it didn't like my unfriendly stomach and found its way out of my system. The only thing I could keep down was coffee. I rode all the way to the turn-around point, another 300 km and a total of 600 km, on nothing more than coffee. Once there, there was nothing to do but turn around and come back.

Though I had seemed to go "mind over matter" successfully, there comes a point where the mind can no longer tell the body what is or isn't working. Eventually the body's signals get too loud—either that or the mind's get too quiet, confused and scrambled. I made it back to Cantaloupe Corner, the concrete barrier I'd visited 600 km earlier.

I had nothing left. It was time to quit.

Seeing the cantaloupe stains out of the side of my gaze, I walked away from the barrier a hobbling man. Randonneuring rides have no crew—only checkpoints to keep you from cheating. Thankfully, Cantaloupe Corner was right beside one such checkpoint. I hobbled towards the station, passing a few other cyclists that looked as bad as I felt. When I got to the temporary desk set up in the station, the person looked at me with sympathy in his eyes.

"I'm done," I said, the words barely making it out of my raw and hoarse throat. He grimaced at me and nodded. Better than a cheery smile, I suppose. I handed in my number and felt my balloon deflate as I did so. That was it. I was no longer registered. They would stop looking for me on the road, stop expecting me at checkpoints. And certainly not at the finish line.

If At First You Don't Succeed: Cycling, Part 1

"Do you have a way to get to Paris?" they asked. I shook my head. In all my preparation, I had never anticipated what would happen if I quit. Paris was 300 km away, an insurmountable distance at this point. I couldn't wrap my head around getting there. "Okay," they said, then conversed with each other in a language that was as good as gibberish to me. A few seconds later a voice boomed out over the speakers that were set up.

"I just asked if there is anyone who can help you. We'll see," he said. I nodded, thankful for his effort, and went towards the nearest patch of grass. I sat down, letting my bike fall beside me. Why stand when you could sit? A few seconds later, I lay down. Why sit when you could be horizontal? Giving up was a weight off my shoulders, but with it came the burden of finding my way in a foreign country.

But lying on my back, staring up at the blue sky, all I could think about was that, hopefully, one day I'd get my digestive system back. I started to dream about the foods I would eat but realized that none of that would happen if I didn't get up and make an effort. I sat again and looked around. Cyclists were coming into the station, eating food and continuing on. Some looked like they belonged in this race and still had energy. Others looked like they'd been run over by a truck.

I sat shakily, resting on my knees. Across the street was a young couple, their eyes on me. I felt feeble and surely looked feeble. Having heard the announcement, they seemed to be analyzing me. In most sports when one person or a team loses, another wins. In cycling it's much more personal. When you lose it's because you lost, not because someone else won. There's no one to beat (if you're only in it to finish), so you defeat yourself.

I was about to look away when I heard one of them calling out. Turning to look, I saw concern on their faces. They were waving me over to come to their side, and I was about to step onto the road when another rider whizzed by. Well, whizzed might have been an exaggeration. But compared to my current ability to produce forward motion, he looked like a speeding blur.

Once I realized I was crossing a road, I made it safely over. We gestured back and forth, squabbling in our own languages, hoping that the other would suddenly understand. The woman had a few words in broken English, and it was clear that they were interested in helping me. When they waved me forward, I followed along behind them. All I had with me was my bike and the clothes on my back, which were freshly stained with cantaloupe-coffee vomit.

When Quitting Is Not an Option

We arrived at their condo complex, and they led me inside. I left my bike in the front entrance and followed them to where I would sleep. It was a reasonable room, and the bed looked so comfortable I could hardly believe my eyes. My only sleep so far had been in the makeshift cots at rest stations and the side of the road, my wheel pointed in the direction I needed to head in case I couldn't remember who or where I was when I woke up.

The woman left the room and came back in a few minutes. When I saw what she was holding in her hands I nearly laughed out loud. They were shorts that I could wear, but they were clearly her husband's. He was a tiny Frenchman who could hardly have weighed more than 120 pounds. I shook my head, but she wouldn't take no for an answer. She threw them on the bed and left the room.

I closed the door behind her and moved to the bed. Exhausted and smelly, I took my shoes off and sat down. There was something funny about my feet. And then it hit me. I had come into the race with several warts on them. After 900 km on the bike the warts had decided—like the contents of my stomach— that there was no way they were going to stay there. They wanted absolutely nothing to do with me and left, and they never came back.

I removed my own shorts and looked at the tiny shorts once again. Since she'd been so adamant, I had to slip them on just to prove to her that there was no way they were going to fit.

Apparently cycling 900 km on coffee fumes is good for weight loss, because the shorts fit. As tired as I was, I had to laugh out loud at the situation. When I came out of the room she had a smug smile on her face, the "I-told-you-so" smile that gets anyone annoyed. But I was so tired and so thankful that nothing could annoy me.

She directed me to the table, and I sat down in front of a plate full of tomato and onion salad. *That'll fill up one tenth of my stomach*, I thought, but I figured she'd been right once so I may as well let her make my decisions for the time being. When I put the first bite in my mouth, I realized she was right again.

The salad went down and stayed down. I learned that tomato and onion salad is amazing after a bike race and a great way to kick-start my metabolism again. To this day I often follow a ride up with something along those lines. The smell from that salad was so poignant and the moment so powerful that I can distinctly remember everything about it.

Two nights later, we were getting a little bit better at communicating. They had a friend who had also been in the bike race and was arriving in Paris. They told me they would drive me there.

"I have to pay you for your help," I said. But they waved it off.

"No," they communicated. "We don't want your money."

"Can I give you something? Anything? For helping me?"

The man looked at me, a now skinny and defeated Canadian whose butt had been handed to him by the terrain. They exchanged some words in French that were like the rapid fire of a machine gun. Then he looked back at me.

"You make a promise," she said. I cocked my head to the side, confused.

"I'm sorry?"

"You make a promise that you do not quit riding your bike." The words were strong, and I could tell that she was serious. When a ride turns sour, it's not uncommon to decide in the moment that you've had it with cycling. Everything looks insurmountable, and you never want to see that saddle once more. *I'll never ride again*, you think. But give it a few days (in this case, two), and things can already start to look better. You start realizing what you did wrong and start thinking about what you'll do better next time. And before you know it, you've mentally agreed that there will be a next time.

"Okay," I agreed, nodding to make sure they understood. "I will not quit."

"And," she said, and I waited for an agreement that I owed them something. But it didn't come. "You promise that you will come back in four years and ride this race again."

"I will." I nodded.

I did.

Joined by three Manitobans: Ben, Robert, and Brian,
at the 1,200 km Paris-Brest-Paris, 1995

On the roads of France

DNF
Cycling, Part 2

On a business trip in Italy, I received a generous offer: a brand new, handmade Wing aluminum bike. Just lifting it up I could tell the difference in weight. My passion for cycling was growing, and a new bike seemed to fit in just right. Since it was a gift from a business associate, I had to clear it with my bosses. They gave me the OK, and I felt like I had to break in my new bike with a ride worthy of its light weight and expensive construction.

Not one to shy away from some of the more difficult races, I decided that the Furnace Creek 508 would be my next challenge. If anyone has ever been to Death Valley, California, they'll know that it doesn't get its name by accident. It is a brutal environment where the sun beats down on a mountainous terrain of rocks and sand. It holds several unique distinctions.

First, it is home to the lowest place on earth. Death Valley scoops as low as 282 feet below sea level. Being that low, it should be filled with water. But Death Valley also has the distinction of being the driest area in North America. But elevations (especially low ones) aren't all that important in cycling.

No, Death Valley's second distinction is what makes it a perfectly unique (and tortuous) place for cycling: it is home to the hottest recorded air temperature anywhere ever. In 1913, Death Valley hit 56.7 degrees Celsius. In the summer the lows only dip in the range of 28–30 degrees Celsius, making it the perfect testing ground for just how insane ultra-marathon cyclists are.

The Furnace Creek 508 rides right through the heart of Death Valley in (thankfully) the only slightly insane heat of the beginning of October. Its motto is "Where the West is Won," and it is well-known as the world's toughest "short" bike race. I use the word "short" in quotations because, to most people, 508 miles is not at all short. But RAAM holds the distinction of being the world's toughest bike race (3,000 miles). We'll get to that later. Since I was only a rookie to the world of UMCA, I figured the toughest "short" ride would be the best one to start with.

"You'd like to do what?" my boss, Frank, asked me. I was in a senior management position, and he'd known about my newfound passion for cycling, but this was taking things to a new level.

"Ride in the Furnace Creek 508," I answered. "It's an 800-kilometre ride through the heart of Death Valley."

"I know Death Valley," Frank answered, "and you can't bike through there."

"I guess we'll find out," I responded.

"Do you know how hot it gets?" he asked.

I nodded. "I've been training in heat," I said. "I close the door, start biking on my trainer and run a few space heaters. It's probably not good for the carpet, but—"

"That's insane, Arvid."

"I won't be alone," I responded. "I'll have a crew, and there will be other riders."

"A crew?" He looked at me, his eyebrows raised. He was behind his desk, a large wooden desk that would intimidate many. By now, though, we had become good friends and enjoyed the friendly ribbing that came with the territory.

"You interested?" I joked.

"Maybe, maybe." His eyes seemed to drift off and avoid my gaze. "What does being a crew entail?"

I'd never had a crew for one of my rides before. Ruth and the kids would sometimes come out on the road and meet me for a bit, driving beside me to talk or pulling up and cheering from the side of the road, refilling water bottles and getting me whatever food they had brought along.

"Everything and anything—whatever it takes to keep me biking. That's the crew's one task, to keep the rider on the bike." I didn't want to say too much and scare him off. Forty to fifty hours in a car isn't a fun prospect when you mix in a stinky cyclist and strange cycling food, combined with the heat of a desert and exhaustion from no sleep.

"Food, water, gas?" Frank asked.

"Mine or the car's?" I laughed.

"Preferably the car's." He chuckled, but there was a sparkle in his eye. I could see that the idea intrigued him. "You know," he laughed again, "adventure like this might be just the thing I need. I'll talk to Dave, see if he's interested." Frank was one of three sons of the founder of our company. Art and Frank had taken over the furniture business years back. Dave was down in North Carolina, getting himself into his own kinds of adventures.

"Okay," I said. "That sounds good. Let me know."

I left the office and let the door close behind me. *He has no idea what he's getting himself into*, I thought. Then again, neither did I.

The crew was inexperienced, but so was the rider. This was the biggest physical challenge I had ever set before myself, and I was nervous. There were three in the crew: Frank DeFehr, Dave DeFehr and Graham (from LA). It was probably the wealthiest crew anyone had out there in California. The ride started in Valencia, California (right next to LA). This was my first bike race, and I'd chosen the welcoming Mojave Desert.

Those who have gone on longer bike rides will know that within a few hours the butt can begin to feel sore. It can become downright irritating. Most people, when they find out what I do, ask the same two questions. First: "Did you bike here?" Usually the answer is no, except for the business meetings in Toronto that took me eight days to get to from Winnipeg. Second: "Doesn't your butt hurt?" I usually answer the same way: "By the time I'm into the ride, my butt is usually the least of my concerns."

Aside from general pain, muscle fatigue, mental exhaustion and the sleep deprivation that comes with biking through the night, one of the biggest challenges while riding an ultra-marathon race is food intake. Now, one would think that this is a simple science: eat. Unfortunately, as my Paris-Brest-Paris experience taught me, the process is much more complicated than that.

The human body is a relatively efficient machine. We intake our fuel (food and liquids), store it (as glycogen in our muscles or fat in our, er, fat) and output it as energy (in my case, cycling). The more energy required, the more fuel we need to intake. But we run into a problem when we go beyond one-, two- or three-hour sporting events. The problem there is that we burn up all our glycogen (short-term energy) and go into our fat (long term), but it doesn't convert nearly fast enough to be of much use to us. The body falls behind and begins producing lactic acid (that thing that makes your muscles hurt when you use them), and we lose weight because our body is using all of its resources to keep us moving. In order to continue moving forward in an ultra-marathon event, the body needs to continue to intake more fuel (food).

Most people need from 2,000 to 3,000 calories in a day just to live. When I'm on the bike, I need between 7,000 and 10,000. If you've ever tried to eat 10,000 calories worth of food, it's a lot more work than it seems at first. Frankly speaking, you can get tired of eating. And that's under the best of circumstances. Compounding the difficulty of taking in enough fuel on a bike ride are a few factors:

1. Time—You're always keeping one eye on the clock and one eye on the road. Eating food quickly doesn't make it go down well.
2. Digestion—Digesting on the move is not always comfortable or pleasant.
3. Throat—Breathe into a fan for a few hours and see how dry your throat gets. After hours and hours on the bike, it can get quite painful to even so much as swallow. To add to that, so much food going down the throat can make it feel like sandpaper.
4. Fatigue—Those who have done a lot of physical exercise may understand that being active, though it's burning calories and emptying your stomach, doesn't always make you hungry. In fact, it often does quite the opposite.
5. Heat—This one's a doozy. Heat does strange things to the digestive system. Though your body is crying out for food (because all of its stores are gone), when it's hot and you're exhausted it does exactly what it shouldn't do: gets rid of everything. Through vomiting, diarrhea and sweating. It does everything it can to get it out of your body because it thinks that the system is in shutdown mode. It's often not a pretty sight.

Because of all these things, cyclists rely on a few different methods of getting food into their bodies. They look for food that has a high calorie content, slides down the throat, sits well in the stomach, digests quickly and has long-lasting energy. In addition to that, they rely on powdered meal replacements. At the time of Furnace Creek 508 I was using a powder called Spiz, which made digestion easier (since it was added to a liquid) and wasn't harsh on my throat. It made life entertaining to see the accomplished owner of a national furniture company hunched over the seat, water bottle between his knees, trying desperately to mix the right ratio of powder into the water while avoiding spilling all over his lap. But such is the life of a crew member.

The heat of the desert and the difficulty of intaking calories led to brutal experiences with losing my food on the side of the road. If Frank had known what he was going to see, I doubt he would have agreed to the trip, no matter how much of an adventure it was. In order to cope with my inability to keep my food down, I started popping Tums like they were candy. As the heat of the desert waned and the night took over, things with my stomach were still getting rougher. Around midnight Frank decided to read the instructions on the Tums bottle and realized that they had a max of eight per day. I had already had around one hundred. He cut me off Tums.

The mountains in the Mojave Desert are harsh. At night they are especially daunting because the top is so far away and you have no idea how much longer you have to climb. The gradients are sharp—far steeper than anything I had ever ridden before. It was in the dark of the night that I experienced something called "Black Holes," in which you're pummelling downhill at 75–80 km/h with the lights of the crew vehicle illuminating some 30 feet in front of you. That's just enough (at that speed) to move over an inch or two to avoid bumps or potholes. The problem is that light doesn't bend sharp enough, so when you crest a hill in the pitch black the vehicle lights are pointing at the sky in front of you while you're dropping like a rock. Unless the vehicle is immediately behind you (which is dangerous in and of itself), the light doesn't come down with you for a few seconds. Biking at 75 km/h, you have almost no idea where the road is until the lights land on you like a rainfall and illuminate your path once more.

While it was downright freaky for me, Frank was having a conniption in the vehicle every time I did this and disappeared completely from their sight. Feeling the weight of responsibility every crew member does, he was worried that when the lights found me I'd be splayed against the rock face because I couldn't see the edge of the road. I was new to the sport, and some of the difficulties and challenges and my ignorance could have cost me dearly.

While it was exhilarating to pummel downhill, I didn't understand the challenges. I biked hard and braked only when absolutely necessary. There was a lot of sand drifting across the road, and I took one particular corner too quickly for the conditions. I came into an S-turn and couldn't stay in the lines. I crossed the oncoming lane and was able to hold—just barely—the last foot of pavement before I would hit the dirt at a ridiculous speed. My heart pounding, I knew that I would have to take the downhills slower or they might be my last. Still, I managed to hit 95 km/h on one of the downhills that trip—my fastest speed to this day. At that speed the vehicles have more trouble handling the corners than the bike does.

There were lights in the sky, and I had long since stopped noticing the stars. All around me was a sea of inky black, broken only by the slicing headlights from the van behind me. Though the desert was silent, I could hear the engine rumbling at an idle. It was going so slow that it was hardly moving at all, the driver dancing between the gas and brake pedals. I was beaten down. I hadn't taken in any food in hours. The weather had taken its toll on my skin, my body and my spirit. And now the terrain was having its way with me—a 14 percent gradient that just kept climbing.

I longed to see the sun, anything to give me a slice of hope. But it was evading me, toying with me any time I looked up and caught a glimmer of the headlights bouncing back off a rock. I was weaving back and forth, my granny-gear (the gear-ratio for steep climbs) not enough for me to even climb directly up the road. Cutting a zigzag back and forth made it easier but increased the distance my wheels had to travel—a trade-off I was willing to let go at this time of night in this condition.

Not only that, but the midnight headwind was whipping off the top of the summit, somewhere so far ahead I couldn't even picture it. There comes a point in an 800 km bike race when you break down and start counting progress by less than a kilometre—sometimes even by the cracks in the pavement, the intermittent yellow lines on the road or the individual pedal strokes that it takes to get there. I had hit that point and hit it hard. I couldn't make it any farther, and I pulled over to the side of the road. I didn't even need to apply the brakes to come to a stop within a second.

The squeal of the van's brakes hit me as they pulled up beside me, and I didn't even turn to look at my crew. I couldn't face them. I wasn't done, but my body was trying to tell me it was. "Frank," I said, my voice hoarse. The skin on my face was ragged, dry and full of salt. When you sweat and it instantly gets evaporated into the air, a layer of white salt develops. Furnace Creek was the perfect place for that to happen. "Frank, how much farther is it to the top?"

"I'll go check," he responded. "We'll be back in a second."

"I'll be right here," I admitted, letting the bike fall to the ground and sitting down in the ditch. I couldn't even hold that position and knew that I had to take this moment to rest. I lay down in the middle of the ditch on the side of the desert road in the black of the night and closed my eyes. It didn't really get any darker with them closed, once the van was gone. I listened to it driving away, despairing at how far it seemed to be going. And then I couldn't hear it anymore.

I waited.

And waited.

It was rest, but it was agony.

Finally, a vehicle was coming my way. The headlights were blinding as I tried to sit up and shield myself from them. They did a five-point turn, not wanting to risk touching the soft sand of the ditch and getting stuck. And then they were back beside me.

Frank opened the car door and stepped out. Every sound was amplified, and I waited to hear the verdict.

"Almost there," he said. "Just around the next bend."

He helped me to my feet and picked up the bike. I looked at the bike and hated it, every inch of its aluminum snobbiness staring down at me in victory. But I wouldn't let it win—not yet. My body was shaking as I tried to climb onto the bike. I got onto the frame, but I couldn't get started. Starting on a 14 percent gradient is difficult under the best of circumstances, never mind when your body seems like it's frozen and jelly at the same time. No matter how hard I pushed down on the pedal I couldn't get the wheels to turn.

"I'll walk," I said, croaking it out into the darkness. As I dismounted from the bike I caught a glimpse down the way we had come. The outline of distant mountains was visible, and snaking its way somewhere across the valley was the road we had travelled. I could see headlights piercing the night far below. Someone that I was ahead of—for now.

"Okay," Frank said. Gripping the handlebars and walking with the telltale limp from my soccer injuries, I started to walk up the road. Every step felt like a victory, an accomplishment that most would never hear about. Frank walked beside me, not pushing me but also not letting me stop. He couldn't know how much pain I was in, but I didn't need him to, either. Like a good crew member, he knew when to be silent and when to speak. This night, alone in the dark, was a time to be silent.

When the ground stopped climbing at such an insane rate I decided to get back onto the bike. This time it worked, and I began to crawl up the slope one revolution of the pedals at a time. Frank climbed back into the van, aided by the engine in conquering gravity.

We rounded a bend, and the road still climbed. Then another bend, another bend, and more climbing. I wasn't entirely cognizant enough at the time to realize what was going on, but it began to settle in, five bends and more climbing later. In between the climbs were small dips that, to me, felt like a mere breath of fresh air.

Finally, the road evened out, and looking out at distant mountains, I realized I was at the top.

I pulled to a stop. I needed a rest before going down into the darkness. Frank stepped out of the vehicle, and I pulled him to the side. "Frank." I hardly had enough energy to speak. "Were you talking about that first summit?"

I realized that what I had considered the first mere speed bump on the way to the true summit had been, to him, the top of the climb. There had been three climbs back-to-back, with only minor descents in between. "Around the next bend" had become a significant distance because of the misunderstanding.

"Don't do that again. If it is 3 km to the top, you tell me how far it is."

We looked at each other, our eyes wide, completely overwhelmed with what we had gotten ourselves into.

In California, I ran out of fuel. I had finished about 650 km and had 175 km to go. By this point no food of any kind would go down, and my cycling had diminished to a crawl, even on the flats. I had climbed 25,000 feet (nearly the vertical height of Everest). It was done. My tank was empty. I had to give up.

I had come to learn that the letters DNF haunt a cyclist in those moments. Climbing into the vehicle, seeing the bike strapped to the roof, is a horribly deflating feeling. At the same time, you're just glad to be off the stupid bike.

I had ridden my heart out and failed. We had a celebration dinner, and I even had to quit that early. I left the restaurant, making my way into the parking lot with the hobble of someone twice my age (I was 39). Our motel was across the street, but my mind wasn't in a functional state. I stood there, confused and probably scaring everyone else away. Finally I wandered back into the restaurant and back up to my crew.

"I, I can't find the hotel," I said. The lights reading MOTEL were visible through the restaurant window. They could have laughed, but thankfully they didn't. Frank's wife, Agnes, got up and offered to escort me to the hotel.

I didn't finish, but the experience of failure was worth a dozen successes.

With crew members Dave DeFehr and Frank DeFehr at Furnace Creek 508, 1996

When Quitting Is Not an Option

The end of the road: DNF after 680 km

Oh, The Things You See
Stories from the Road

I'd like to say that after the DNFs in Paris and California everything turned rosy and peachy. Unfortunately, it didn't. Over the next six years I would take part in three to four rides over 500 km a year. Usually this included two to three training rides and one race per year.

I have often said that there is nothing quite like experiencing the countryside from the seat of a bike. When you drive through it in a car, you get to see out your windshield, and you see the terrain, but the engine's doing the work for you, making a trip through the Rockies take only 12 to 15 hours. Taking the same drive with the top down in a convertible is a whole other level of connection. But putting power to the wheels underneath you brings a harmony to you, the road and the terrain in a way unlike anything else. You feel the air, the weather, the subtle elevation changes.

Climbing Rogers Pass in early spring will get you reaching for your jacket and then taking it off again, only to put it back on. Why? Because every time you cross a mountain stream the temperature drops ten degrees, then bounces back up on the other side. You're wearing a T-shirt while 10 to 15 feet of snow caps the mountains you're climbing, filling the ditches beside you. Being in the shadow of a mountain makes you cold, but as soon as you turn the corner you're sweating from the sunlight.

On my own training rides I kept pushing my body to extend its ability. I rode a 500 km personal time trial, a solo training ride from Vancouver to Edmonton, a 1,000 km solo ride in Manitoba and numerous other rides of shorter lengths over varying terrains. Cycling had become a passion, and I found myself pushing my body to its limits and beyond during the races I continued to enter.

Being on the road for 60 hours at a time means you're far more likely to see and experience interesting things. Without being encased in a car, you can see, hear and smell what's going on in every direction. Wildlife that you would have whizzed by suddenly perks up and follows your every move. The slightest change in the outside world has an immediate impact on you, be it terrain, weather, traffic or your own limited supplies and your ability to keep the bike moving forward.

Spending that much time on the road makes for interesting stories, from dentures in the ditch to girls going to a wedding in the middle of nowhere.

Crewing for an ultra-marathon rider is a unique experience on its own. You're in charge of providing food and water, navigating, managing clothing and medication, as well as pretty much everything else. My most loyal and consistent crew member is my wife, Ruth. People have often asked her what it takes to be a crew member. She usually gives a positively worded answer to the question. I, on the other hand, like to tell the story of Alaska.

The year after I dropped out of Furnace Creek I ventured to Alaska with my wife, Ruth, and my nephew Juergen as my support crew. In France I had made it 900 km, so this 600 km time trial (the time limit was 24 hours) should have been no problem. I had read somewhere that, in order for my body to maintain the energy it was putting out, I would need to consume around 400 calories per hour. Determined to not only make it to the finish line but also arrive there in good time, I consumed my prescribed 400 calories each hour.

Even though I had been on a few longer rides I did not have a good understanding of hydration. I was consuming liquids and calories, but I wasn't giving my body enough time to catch up. After 10 hours I hadn't had to go to the bathroom once.

That should have signalled that something was wrong.

Instead, it fuelled my pride and indicated to me that I was doing something right. I figured my body was being so efficient that it was using all the water I was taking in. I suppose that might have been a smidge right, but only because I was taking in such small amounts of water that my body was desperately clinging to it for survival.

I continued to pound back the food, sure that I was doing something right and had figured out some magical formula that would make me into a mountain goat capable of scaling Alaska's passes without much effort.

When you exert yourself to that level, the body has trouble digesting. I shouldn't say *trouble*. What I mean to say is that digestion becomes *impossible*. In order for the body to process what you're taking in you need to either take a break or slow down. I did neither, yet I kept eating.

The math of this equation is pretty simple. By the 16-hour mark my stomach had turned into a watermelon—with its shell. It was hard and completely full. But there was no way this watermelon was staying inside of my stomach.

Everything—and I mean everything—went flying to the side. It splattered (or thudded) on my shoes and my bike and into the ditch. Just when I thought it was over and I could focus on cycling, it would come at me again, reminding me that something was wrong.

Ruth and Juergen had been strictly informed that hand-offs do not occur on a downhill. When you're rolling 40 or 50 km/h with the assistance of gravity, you have no interest in applying the brakes to grab a water bottle or food. Most of the time hand-offs from the side of the road are done at a jog, which means there's a 15 km/h speed differential. Any more than that and it's hard to grab the bottle accurately without careening into the ditch.

When I have a new crew member I like to initiate him or her. Paul (my son) will amp them up, saying that hand-offs have to be done at high speed. He'll get them into a sprinter's stance and count them down. As they sprint off with water bottle in hand I apply the brakes and come to a rest beside Paul. While we laugh, they return with the water bottle. They're not quite as quick to take our advice next time. Needless to say, hand-offs should be done at the top of a hill or on flats, when I'm only going 20 km/h.

Being relatively new to the crewing experience, Ruth and Juergen made the mistake of pulling over on a beautifully wide stretch of gravel—right in the middle of a downhill. As I yelled at them in passing I realized that another round of "what did I eat?" was about to unfold. I threw up everything else—

Including my teeth.

Toothless and gummy, I had to yell to them, "Can you go look for my teeth? They're in the ditch!"

Welcome to a crash course in crewing.

When I tell this story, Ruth seems to have some kind of mental block. She conveniently doesn't remember looking through the vomit to find my dentures.

I had completed 480 km in about 18 hours, but my body had hit its limit. I had taken in a ton of food, not processed it and rejected it. There was hardly anything left. Standing on the side of the road I realized how futile this attempt was. If I wanted to get to any finish line—no matter how long or short—I was going to have to learn a lot about my body and its ability.

I felt the urge to vomit once again and wondered what was going on. There was nothing left to get rid of. Instead, I dry-heaved into the ditch. I felt my teeth coming loose and, not wanting to repeat the previous experience, caught them as they flew out of my mouth. Another crewing experience avoided.

We packed it in, 120 km and six hours short, and drove to Fairbanks. The ride was called "Midnight Sun," and they were right. It was 2 a.m., but we enjoyed a beautiful walk in Fairbanks with the sun still in the sky.

My kids have often joked that their family trips were always tacked on to bike rides. They also indicated that their closets were mostly full with bike ride T-shirts. Neither of those statements is completely untrue. Given that my passion was a relatively solitary venture, I did what I could to involve my kids. This meant family bike rides (sorry, Jodi) and adventures. It also meant that they had opportunities to see first-hand what the rides were like if they wanted to be in my crew.

Race organizers like to arrange their rides to coincide with unique experiences. Iowa was a prime example of that. Not exactly the most interesting state to bike through, they scheduled the Firecracker 500 from July 4th to 5th, a small 500-mile race through the rolling corn hills. I was excited yet obviously nervous. Experience had taught me that nothing was predictable about an ultramarathon ride. You could do well one time, poor the next. You could train, but something unforeseen would happen. You could be stronger, but a muscle you'd never heard of would fail you.

As darkness set over Iowa we began to realize just why it was called the Firecracker 500. Throughout the day we had noticed a ridiculous amount of American flags. One of the houses was covered in dozens and dozens of flags, adorning literally any surface that could hold a flag—and some that couldn't.

A crack rang out in the dark, and I jumped. *Is that a car backfiring?*

Suddenly, the sky lit up in an explosion of colours. A firework stretched across the sky. It took only a few seconds for the next one to ignite, sending red and blue streaks through the night. I guessed correctly—the next one would be white—and realized just what kind of an evening we were in for. In the monotony of the rolling hills and the never-ending dark we were going to be treated to an all-night fireworks show.

House after house was setting off their fireworks. There was no warning where the next one would come from. At times I was convinced we could have turned off the car's headlights and simply biked by the light of the explosions from the sky. Everyone was celebrating—tiny farmhouses and large houses in the towns.

I rolled into the next small town and realized that, midnight though it was, there were people everywhere. It was a town so small that the gas station was closed and the only thing open was the local strip joint. I had to use the washroom and had no qualms about using a bush wherever one presented itself. When you've biked that far you begin to lose some of your traditional decency. The rest of the crew (my daughters, mainly) weren't convinced about the bush. But they weren't about to go into the bar, either. They settled for hiding behind buildings.

Firecrackers began to ignite in the night, popping like mini-guns all around us. I gripped my handlebars as if I had just wandered into a warzone. There was hollering in the night as teenagers sprinted around, lighters in hand and firecrackers following them like live grenades. Horrified yet exhilarated at the same time, I took off on my bike. In the van the rest of the family felt somewhat safer, though the explosions seemed to continue on all sides.

My heart pounding, I made it out of the town. I began to wonder if the teens did this for every rider. Either way, I was glad to be out in the dark once again, the random explosions of light behind me casting shadows on the road in front.

The sun was beginning to set over the ocean as I biked through the beautiful state of Oregon, enjoying the views. Ruth was back in the support vehicle, joined by our daughter Jodi and her friend Stephanie. The air was crisp and cool and everything felt fresh. Rarely did I feel this good this far into a ride, but things had been going extremely well.

I was riding near the front of the race when something completely unexpected and remarkable happened. I scanned the road with my eyes, moving to the side and looking out over the shoulder. *What—?*

There was a man off to the side, only his head visible over the tall weeds. He was screaming, his voice sounding forced and afraid at the same time, yelling, "Help me! Help me! Help me!" over and over. There was no vehicle to be seen. Everything else was eerily silent. It made the image of him even more of a contrast, and I kept looking back and forth for some sort of explanation or reason. As far as I could see, there was nothing. My mind immediately jumped to fear. *If I stop, are we being set up for an ambush?*

But there was no indication that anyone else was anywhere near him. My heart pounding from more than just the exertion of biking, I knew that I couldn't just ignore him and ride on by. I felt like the Good Samaritan must have felt, only not in a story but right smack-dab in the middle of real life.

He was still screaming, clearly in pain. I pulled to the side of the road and put my bike down, getting my walking legs back. The van pulled up behind me, crunching on the gravel. I told the girls to stay in the car, my every moment, word and thought feeling dragged out and in slow motion, the kind of feeling that pervades a nightmare.

The air was thick and my movement sluggish as I began to walk towards him. As I approached, I saw him sitting on his knees. His body was stiff and rigid, nothing but his mouth moving as he continued to beg for help. I tried calling out reassurance, but he was inconsolable.

As I neared him I realized that behind him the ground continued down a large embankment into a very deep ditch. It wasn't a drop-off, but the total elevation change was 15 feet nonetheless. He was mumbling and screaming intermittently, and I finally caught some words. "My wife is down there. My wife. My wife." Down where?

I stepped a bit closer, and my heart jumped into my throat. I could see the top of a vehicle down the embankment. I kept walking and realized that an old, full-size van was resting on its wheels, though its condition clearly indicated it had taken a severe tumble and flip down the ditch, through a barbed-wire fence, and come to a rest right-side up.

We had stumbled on an accident. By the sounds (and looks) of it, a rather violent and recent accident. Horrified of what I might find, I kept going down the embankment. Ruth stayed behind with the man. He was in horrible pain and unable to move, so she encouraged him to remain still while we went to help.

Jodi and Stephanie came with me now, and we clambered down the embankment. My pulse pounding in my ears, I moved around to the passenger side of the van to find the man's wife.

The van must have been full of all of their possessions, because when they had lost control and left the road everything had ended up at the front of the van—pots, pans, clothes, shoes; they were clearly living on the road. In the middle of the mess was a woman, bleeding from her mouth. She was unconscious when we opened the door. Then she came to and started to move, climbing out of the car. I wasn't so sure it was a good idea, but there was no stopping her.

Finally she was down on the ground, looking around. I had my nose in the air, waiting for the smell of gasoline. Something was dripping from the vehicle, but it didn't seem to be gas, and I breathed a sigh of relief.

She looked at me, and I asked, "What happened?"

She was silent, slipping in and out of consciousness. Not wanting her to drift off again, I kept asking her questions. "What happened? Did you hit something?"

"Argument," she was able to squeak out. *How could that...?* I didn't really want to know.

"We need to get them help," Jodi said, eyes wide.

"Stay with her," I told her and Stephanie. "We'll have to get to the nearest farmhouse." We didn't have a phone on us, and even if we did, the likelihood of one working out in the backwoods of Oregon was not very high. I scrambled back up the embankment, asking God for help with every step. My body, tired from the bike ride and not all that agile at the best of times due to the abuse it had received from soccer, felt stiff. Adrenaline took over and I made it up. Ruth was still with the man.

"I need to go to the nearest farmhouse," I told Ruth. "Jodi and Stephanie are with the woman—she's in and out and bleeding from her face."

The man reached out to me and looked me in the eye. Fear gripped my heart as I looked into his eyes. "She grabbed the wheel," he croaked. Like the climax of music in a horror movie, I realized what had been happening. Though he could barely move he mimed someone yanking on a steering wheel, and I cringed.

In the heat of an argument she had decided that everything was over. Though he didn't voice it, I clearly understood it as an attempt to commit suicide.

"Are the keys in the van?" I asked Ruth.

She was about to answer when we heard another sound—a vehicle approaching. *Please be a police car,* I prayed.

It wasn't—but it was someone we knew. George Thomas, the race director, came by. The car pulled to a sudden stop, and he flew out of the door, scrambling around. We were crouched down in the weeds, only our heads visible.

"Arvid!" he yelled, panicking and looking around. I realized what he was seeing—an empty support vehicle and a bicycle lying on the side of the road with no cyclist in sight. He had assumed we were in an accident.

When Quitting Is Not an Option

"Here!" I yelled out, standing up. George ran in our direction, panic on his face.

"Are you all right? What happened?"

"I'm okay, I'm okay," I said. "I had to ditch the bike. There's been a car accident. They were in the middle of an argument and she pulled the wheel—"

"She?" he asked, looking around for the woman and the invisible vehicle.

"Down the embankment," I said. "We need to get them help. There was a farmhouse a few kilometres—miles—back."

"I'm on my way," he said. He took off back towards his vehicle, peeled off and headed down the highway.

Mike—the husband—was clearly upset, in shock and agitated. I don't know how long we tried to console him as he continued to inquire about his wife, make sure that help was on the way and tell us that he was in pain. Throughout the entire time he continued sitting on his knees, clearly in pain but unable to move. I went back down to check on the woman, who was in and out of consciousness and continuing to bleed.

The entire experience had the makings of a scene in a horror movie. I felt like my actions weren't coming from me, because nothing can prepare you to deal with something like that. Yet somehow we were able to make it through it, waiting until the police showed up.

"You were first on the scene?" the sheriff asked.

"Yes," I said. "I was biking and heard him screaming. I scrambled past him to find his wife—down the embankment. I don't know whether he was flung from the van or climbed out. Either way, she yanked the wheel to pull them off the road—"

He raised his eyebrows. "So it was an attempt—"

"I think so," I responded.

"Did it seem like they were having trouble?"

"Definitely. In the middle of a fight."

He nodded like he'd seen this before. "You're in the middle of a race, right?" he asked me.

"Yes," I said, barely realizing it. With all the chaos, noise and confusion I had almost forgotten.

"Well, I'll take your information down so I know how to get in touch with you if I have more questions." He indicated that I could get back on the road.

I climbed back onto the bike, George Thomas continuing to talk to the police officers. I was shaky as I grabbed the handlebars, realizing that the road is a dangerous place to spend your time on—especially out in the open and unprotected—and thankful that we hadn't been in the way when the van careened off the road. Saying a prayer for the couple, their safety and the future of their lives together, I continued down the road.

Because of the delay, I was awarded 50 minutes to my race time. I came in 5th, falling behind my close 2nd-place finish the year before. But I made it to the finish line, thankful for my family and safety.

The air felt different—crisper, somehow. Maybe it was because it was coming over the tops of the distant mountain peaks, racing down their snow-covered slopes and across the open plains to hit me at the airport as I stepped off the plane in Fairbanks, Alaska. After my failed attempt to finish the 24-hour time trial in Alaska, something about that terrain had gotten hold of me. It was less tainted, less travelled.

I walked down the steps with the weight of the world in my pocket. My round-trip ticket from Winnipeg to Fairbanks was as heavy as a brick. I saw them removing the luggage and watched my bike being carried. Sometimes airlines don't handle your luggage all that well, but this time—when I wanted them to accidentally drop it or run it over—they handled it with care, and it made it onto the cart in one piece.

After claiming it from the oversized luggage office, I began to strip it of its shrink-wrapped bubble of protection. I'm not a bike mechanic, but the damage from an impact is pretty obvious. It was fine and made the same clicking that a well-designed bike should.

Taking my bike with me, I smiled at those who gave me strange glances. With my bike clenched in one hand, I carried my small bag of belongings—a few bike repair items and my wallet. I felt like Gideon trying to defeat an army with only a trumpet and a jar. But here I was, nonetheless, 4,400 km from home with nothing but my bike, my legs and my wits to get me home.

That is, assuming I had the guts to go through with my plan. The door to the outside world loomed large in front of me, and I paused before I made it there. Pulling my return ticket from my pocket, I felt that side of my body stiffen. This was it. The moment I had been waiting for. Months and weeks in advance it's quite easy to say just how simple it will be to rip the ticket in half.

When Quitting Is Not an Option

When you're standing there and about to separate yourself from your home, your family and everything safe and predictable, there are a lot more thoughts that run through your mind.

With others buzzing around me and my bike leaning against my thigh, I ceremoniously gave credit to what I was doing, ripping the ticket slowly and methodically. I watched it drop into the garbage one piece at a time, terrified and exhilarated at the same time.

I was biking back to Winnipeg. There was no way around it.

When I hit the highway the next morning, the sun was already high in the sky. I had planned my training ride during the summer solstice, giving me more time to put as much distance on my wheels each day as possible before having to find accommodations—an assumption that would prove challenging at times.

Many would consider 4,400 km the cycling accomplishment of their life, but this ride was a training ride and an experiment for me. I was going to attempt a cross-Canada cycle, something I had always dreamed of, and I needed to know what I was made of. The question for me was very simple: How many hours a day could I ride while still having enough off-bike time to recover and do it again the next day? In other words, what was the maximum time I could ride daily and continue to ride indefinitely? Finding the limit for me was essential in understanding just how my body worked and what I was capable of.

Cycling has a distinct advantage over a sport like running. Running, though it can also be done for ultra-marathon distances, is an impact sport. No matter how slow you run, your joints are continually taking a beating when they hit the pavement. Since cycling is not an impact sport, it is your muscles that fatigue first. Pushing hard will tire your muscles out, but they can recover much quicker than joints. There are very few individuals who can, day after day, put their body through significant running fatigue and recover quickly.

Since I was unsupported (no support crew), I would need to do all of my work for myself. This included finding accommodations, washing my clothes (or not), finding my food, finding water and navigating. This brings down my daily mileage, but it can be an enriching experience on its own.

Wandering down from the northern limits of sanity back into civilization came with some unique circumstances. These included some of the sketchiest accommodations ever, like the wonderful Valleyview Lodge—an old house trailer with extra doors and walls. Two-inch shag carpet covered the floor, and when I walked it and saw little puffs of dust plume up I knew it had never been vacuumed.

At times there was nothing for 100 km, and I'd have to flag down cars or stop tourists to get some water and refill my water bottles. On the highway with only minimal traffic, motorists would often slow down, roll down their windows and tell me that there were bears up ahead. I always took their advice and, alone on my bike, continued on. I figured that, given the fact that at my present pace I was actually getting stronger each day, I could outrace the bears if they got bored of their berries and decided I looked tastier.

Another car was coming from the front and stopped on the side of the road. "There are two grizzly bears around the bend—in the ditch," he explained. I thanked him for letting me know and kept going.

As I turned the corner I saw them—and the words he had said sank in. These weren't black bears but giant and majestic grizzlies. Only a hundred feet off the road, they were on their hind legs in the weeds, picking berries. They paid no attention to the cars (which made a lot more noise than I did), but as soon as I saw them they saw me. Their eyes followed me, moving ever so slowly. I could feel my pulse quicken, and not just because I had suddenly picked up my speed.

I was very thankful that they, being isolated in the Alaskan wilderness, had never heard about Meals on Wheels.

Not long after I passed the bears I came across a Japanese cyclist in his small tent. He was sitting and reading a book, happy and content. The words almost came out of my throat, but then they caught. I never told him about the bears— and I hope he never discovered them (or them, him).

I had made it down to Whitecourt, Alberta, leaving as early as 4 a.m. The sun hadn't even crested the horizon yet when I heard the pitter-patter of a dog running behind me. Being a cyclist and meeting dogs go hand in hand, so I wasn't all that surprised. Yet I hadn't seen a home or civilization in a while and was questioning what a dog was doing out where I was biking.

I turned around to see a dog chasing me and thought, *That stupid dog!*

It kept chasing, and I realized that its snarls sounded a little less friendly than the dogs I was used to. I took another look and realized that it wasn't a dog.

In the dim light I could hardly tell whether it was a wolf or a coyote, but I finally settled on coyote. I tried lifting my pace, but it kept after me. It was gaunt and having trouble running, though its intentions were clear. I started wondering where the next hospital I could go to was (to get a rabies shot), when suddenly I realized that the road in front of me was sloping upwards. I stood up and stepped on it, hardly changing the gears. But I could only sprint uphill for so long, and the coyote seemed to have an abundance of energy, though its muscles were stringy and its ribs visible. Perhaps he thought I would be his last meal ever.

By now he had caught up to me and was nipping at my calves. He was getting bolder and bolder, and the nipping turned to snapping. I could feel him bumping into me as my legs rotated, and I knew there was only one option. I unclipped my foot from the pedal and started to kick.

There's only one problem—when your foot's not on the pedal you don't have the ability to move forward. On an uphill climb, I was suddenly slowing down very rapidly. I was barely moving forward now, and it was circling around me and snarling. Its eyes had the sinister and uncontrolled look of rabies in them, and I knew I was in trouble. With both my feet off the pedals, I was getting desperate as I swung wildly.

I heard the motor of a car churning down the road and breathed a sigh of relief—help was on the way. Scared by the noise, the coyote went to the centre ditch of the divided highway. But like the priest ignoring the beat-up man in the story of the Good Samaritan, the car drove around me and continued on its way.

When the car disappeared, the coyote came back. He came at me from the left and overshot a bit, ending up beside me. With my left foot I landed a kick that connected the tip of my shoe to his temple. I could hear the thud and the crunch and felt the same satisfaction as in my soccer days after a good and solid connection with the ball.

He slowed down, staggering and wobbling. Barely able to make it to the ditch, he collapsed at the edge, and his head hit the ground with a thump.

Just like the car that had passed me by, I decided not to be a Good Samaritan and check to see if he was OK.

I had a board meeting in Toronto, Ontario, that I needed to get to. Most sane people would book a flight, leave the day of the meeting and stay the night after. A few adventurous might hit the open road in their car and spend 20-plus hours on the road and save themselves the cost of flying.

Being who I am, however, I decided I would bike to Toronto.

Sometimes God paints incredible pictures for only the patient, extreme or adventurous to see. This was one of those times. It was around Lake Superior. I would love to go back to the place and see it in the daylight, but I doubt I would recognize it.

Most of my incredible views came from the glorious sunrises or sunsets, from mountain ranges or wide, sweeping valleys with waterfalls ringing their edges. But this was none of those things. Riding unsupported and completely dependent on your own legs, making a calculation for your night's resting place was quite crucial. Around 7 p.m. I decided that I was going to skip the town I was in and make a break for the next place. Unfamiliar with the area, the next place was just a name on a map.

It came and went before I had even realized I had arrived. There was no place to sleep, so I was forced to continue. Being alone on the road can be a wildly disconcerting thing, especially at night. The dark seems to creep in around you and reach out its claws to grab on to you. No matter how fast you ride you can't get away from the black sea that surrounds you. I wasn't mentally prepared to bike through the night, but I didn't have to.

Because it was the most glorious, wondrous night. The dark came, but it somehow didn't land on me. The night was crystal clear, the stars and moon so bright that the trees were not silhouettes but were rich in shades of green. I could see enough by the night lights that I turned my own off, able to see the road, the lines and the bumps and cracks. Usually the night is full of unknowns—animals, road surface, dark—but it was nothing like that. The animals were out in their full chorus, almost seeming to talk to me as I came past. I had adrenaline running through me but not out of fear.

Everything culminated in some of the most incredible hours I've ever spent on a bike. My breath caught in my throat as the beauty around me reminded me of my Creator. I could hardly believe that He had taken the time for me, just one of His created, to take in the majesty and glory of this moment. I pedalled on, revelling in that care and love that He shows each and every one of us.

The dark had come and I had arrived in perfect timing. I had gone 400 out of 1,200 km on a round trip from Boston to Montreal and back. As I pulled my bike into the time station at the community centre I could feel my eyes getting heavy. On the route sheet it indicated that there would be beds at this stop, and

When Quitting Is Not an Option

I was badly in need. I checked in with my rider number, then grabbed some food and headed for a cot.

Focused on finding an empty bed, I didn't notice everything going on around me. There was a whole slew of cots stretched across the centre, only a few feet apart. Many of them were full, riders completely asleep even though the room was decently lit.

When I lay down, I couldn't get comfortable. Every muscle in my body was twitching in anticipation of getting back on the bike. My mind was racing faster than I had been riding, and I couldn't get it to slow down. And when I closed my eyes, shutting out the light, the sounds hit me. Like if living underneath a freeway bridge, they were impossible to ignore.

Snores. Coming from 40 to 50 open-mouthed cyclists, lying on their backs and utterly exhausted. I tried pinning my ear to the cot, covering the exposed ear with the blanket. It was futile. They sawed through my blanket and made it impossible to sleep. I tossed and turned for a few more minutes until I realized it was over.

I had ridden a long day—it was my second time doing this ride, and I intended to improve my time, pushing myself to ride longer days and sleep less. But now my sleep had been stolen from me.

When I got back onto my bike I had some idea of what I was doing, but I didn't fully understand. I pushed through the night, completely missing the sleep but moving forward.

After turning around in Montreal at the halfway point, I came back to around 900 km. Three-quarters done. The dark was crowding in around me, and I was exhausted from riding my heart out without any sleep at all. My body was beginning to revolt against me, threatening to shut down if I didn't give it adequate rest. But I was at a time station, so I knew that I could find somewhere to sleep.

The only problem was, this time station didn't have adequate sleeping accommodations.

Once you're exhausted, any horizontal surface becomes a bed of some sort. I lay down, finding an uncomfortable place to sleep, and dozed in tiny fits. Altogether I slept somewhere near 30 minutes. It had been yesterday—or was it the day before?—since I had last slept. I had pushed through one night with nothing and was going into my second with only 30 minutes of restless, uncomfortable sleep. I had never pushed this far or this hard, but my feet were still going and my mind was still working—or so I thought. I had no idea what it would do to me, but I ventured on.

By this point in the race the group was spread quite far apart, so I was riding alone on the beautiful back-road highways. With 150 km left to Boston and the sun well over the horizon now, sleep decided that after pursuing me for 1,050 km it would finally arrive like a freight train from behind. I was still (thankfully) in control of my bike, but my mind was letting go.

In the distance I saw something unexpected. I blinked my eyes and shook my head from side to side, but it was still there. Three little girls, dressed in spring colours as flower girls, were standing on the right side of the road. I looked past them, then behind me. There was nothing else around—no road, no house, no gathering place. Nothing. Was this a mistake? What were they doing here? *Why would there be a wedding way out here?* I asked myself. But no answer came.

They weren't that far away, and I slowly began to come closer. It was a crystal-clear image. They were holding their flower petals in small baskets with some of the flowers pinned up in their hair, neatly braided. They were smiling, though I wondered when they would notice that their parents had abandoned them out in the middle of nowhere. Surely the wedding party would be arriving soon to take them to the wedding, to make sure they were safe.

I got closer and began to apply the brakes, thinking I would ask them what they were doing. But on touching the brake lever my mind snapped, and I realized that they weren't three girls. They were three mailboxes, standing still, unmoving, all alone.

Pull it together, Arvid, I said. *You can make it.*

A few hours, I told myself. As I passed the mailboxes I had to look back for another glance—yes, they were mailboxes, not flower girls. No, they weren't wearing dresses or carrying flower petals. I shook my head, glad I didn't have to deal with three lost children, then kept biking.

I made it through that bout, but it wasn't over.

You have 110 km to go, I was thinking, *and you have three water bottles.*

How many granola bars? I asked myself. I felt the back of my jersey, searching the pockets. There were only two granola bars. *That'll be enough for me,* I thought.

But what about my bike?

"I need food too," it was saying.

You can have one of the bars.

"And the water," it added.

Good. Three water bottles is enough for me.

When Quitting Is Not an Option

"What about me?" it asked.

What about you? I asked in response, trying to put my bike in its place. After all, I was the cyclist and it was just the bike—I should get precedence.

"I need water and food too. You can't expect me to do all this work without it."

"But, but, but," I sputtered, thoroughly incapable of coming up with an argument.

"You know I need water and food."

"All right, fine!" I conceded. "I'll give you one of the water bottles and one of the granola bars." I immediately started worrying. *Where will I find another water bottle for myself? How will I get to Boston?*

By this point in the argument, I was thoroughly beat. I hadn't been focusing on the biking, and between looking down to talk to the bike and trying to argue with it I had lost a lot of speed.

"This is crazy," I said out loud, to no one in particular. Only the flower girls on the side of the road could hear me, if they existed. "I need to sleep." My bike didn't argue, so I knew that I was doing something right.

I pulled over, not concerned about how it would look to any passing motorist or cyclist, and lay down in the ditch. I kept my helmet on, which actually makes a reasonably nice pillow when you're lying on your back, and looked at my watch. In my dazed state of mind I was able to somehow remember the numbers and recall them, 15 minutes later, when I woke back up.

Not wanting to waste time, I was back on the bike. I finished the ride, besting my time from the previous year and going about 70 hours with somewhere between 30 and 45 minutes of sleep. Glad that my bike had stopped arguing with me, I realized that I had hit my breaking point and resolved to stay away from the red line in the future.

Vomiting my own teeth out of my mouth, running from firecrackers on Independence Day, helping car crash victims, kicking coyotes in the head, riding under a God-created moonlit night, and seeing flower girls turn into mailboxes may sound rather strange, but it's truly only a small glimpse into the everyday experiences of an ultra-marathon cyclist. Pushing your body to the limit is one guaranteed way to encounter a wide range of emotions, moments and memories. Since my beginning years as a cyclist I have matured and pushed myself much harder while maintaining greater control over what is happening around me. This comes with age, experience and trial and error.

Between 1994 and 2001, I DNFed in Paris-Brest-Paris, Furnace Creek 508 (twice) and Alaska. But then I began to finish rides, including my third attempt at Furnace Creek, my second attempt in Paris, the Firecracker 500, Boston-Montreal-Boston, the Race Across Oregon and the Rocky Mountain 1200.

I was maturing as an athlete, but with that came a growth in my faith and a greater understanding that I was accomplishing these feats primarily for myself. With that in mind, I decided to challenge myself beyond anything I had done before—while at the same time making a difference for others.

Midnight Sun (Alaska): Juergen Loewen, Arvid and Ruth

At the Boston-Montreal-Boston finish line after 1,200 km

Jodi and her friend Stephanie were enthusiastic crew members in the Race Across Oregon.

Race Across Oregon finish line: Arvid and Ruth, Jodi Loewen, Stephanie Klassen

Against All Odds
Spoke '99

I woke up with a sick feeling in my stomach. The dark around me was being interrupted by various lights coming in at different angles from all sides, overlapping on the blanket and confusing me. My throat was dry and I reached for a water bottle beneath me—but it wasn't there.

Maybe that's because I wasn't on my bike. I shook my head, clearing the cobwebs that had built themselves up in the last few hours. I'd been sleeping—could it really have been three hours? It felt like I'd barely closed my eyes. I sat up and looked around me. It took a few seconds to orient myself, the parking lot lights not helping one bit.

"Lake Louise," I said. *No, Moose Jaw. That's right, Moose Jaw.* Then it all came crashing together. Things were going well, I was on pace—faster than pace—to get to my destination in time. But even though things were going well, that sick feeling hadn't left my stomach. "Did I eat something nasty?" I asked. But I knew that wasn't the case. Then it hit me.

The sound—coming from outside. I didn't know which way it was coming from, but it was sure louder than when I had gone to bed. And louder means stronger, which could be a very good or very bad thing.

"Ruth," I called out in the dark, patting her on the shoulder beside me. She woke instantly, going from unconscious to alert in a matter of seconds.

"Are you good to go?" she asked, brushing her hair back and sitting up to give me a kiss.

"I just woke up." My voice was scratchy. I caught a glimpse of my reflection in a strip of metal on the motorhome and realized that if someone saw me they would think I was 60—if they were being generous. In the last three days I had aged 20 years.

There was about a foot between the end of the bed and the hallway, barely wider than my shoulders. My watch started beeping in the dark, and I immediately silenced it. I had the uncanny ability to wake up just before my alarm would go off.

We were at a gas station, in the corner of the parking lot. I heard talking—hushed—and realized that Dave and Delbert were in the front seats, trying to catch a little shut-eye while I slept.

"Dave, Delbert," I called out, "which way are we facing?" When I had pulled into the parking lot I had gone to the washroom and climbed under the covers. Since that time the crew had tanked up the motorhome and moved it to the corner of the parking lot. With my eyes closed in the back I had no idea which way was which.

"Home," Delbert called back. Then he sat up straight in his chair and looked at the flags flapping in our direction.

"That's what I thought," I answered, my hopes plummeting into my stomach. In the hours that I had spent sleeping the wind had not only gotten stronger, it had shifted completely—into a raging 50 km/h headwind.

"I was just in the gas station using the washroom," Dave said. "There's a storm coming our way—maybe that'll shift the wind. It's coming from the west."

"We'll probably be moving faster than it," I said, everything collapsing in on itself. More than many sports, ultra-marathon cycling can be adversely affected by weather. While riders are walking or running, the wind can be strong enough that they can feel it. But cycling, because of the increased speed, means that the wind can bring you almost to a standstill, decreasing your speed by 50 to 70 percent. Or it can, of course, increase it substantially if it's in the right direction.

"There's nothing to do but get on the bike," I said. "How far to Winnipeg?" I knew the answer, but I hoped that, somehow, in the three hours that I had been asleep, the two cities had moved closer to each other.

"Six hundred forty-three kilometres," Dave responded, double-checking our route sheet.

"Well, we're not getting anywhere by standing here talking about it," I said.

Sometimes it's easy to see the way things evolve and come together. Other times it's a complicated mishmash of input, thoughts, dreams, circumstances and necessity. This was the latter. I was getting better—a lot better—at this cycling thing. I had gone from an immature and brash cyclist who thought he could go 16 hours on coffee alone to someone who was understanding his body's rhythms and requirements. In Iowa I had entered a 24-hour time trial. One of the racers was an 18-year-old man. About 18 hours in he was on the side of the road at the headquarters, his eyes bloodshot, his face gaunt, shivering uncontrollably, even though he was covered in several blankets. The reality is that ultra-marathon cycling is not usually a young man's game. When it comes to speed, young muscles will easily win a race. When it comes to endurance, maturity and wisdom will see a rider through adversity that makes a young rider crack like an egg.

Not to say that wisdom and maturity come singlehandedly with age. Mostly, they come with experimentation and experience. After several years and a good number of rides under my belt, I had certainly not conquered the UMCA world, but I had learned enough that I was willing and wanting to push the boundaries even further.

With that desire came a realization that, for the most part, endurance sports are rather self-serving. Exercise is a good thing, and it keeps athletes healthy and improves their lives. But going beyond traditional exercise ceases to improve one's body and can be detrimental instead. It's the difference between running 30 minutes a few times a week to stay healthy and running a marathon once a week. Pushing beyond that boundary is painful and, often, degrades the athlete's body.

Ultra-endurance events are not (generally) massive spectator sports. The majority of them are only legitimate races for the top 10 percent that have a shot at winning. The others are there because they want to achieve something—to prove to themselves, those around them and the world that they are capable of pushing themselves to the limits and beyond.

Up to this point I had been very blessed in being able to ask for and receive financial support from my employer, Palliser, to pursue races and training. I realized that in order to do this at an elite level I needed to make a serious commitment. By setting my sights on using my abilities as a fundraising platform I figured there was a greater likelihood that I would continue to get financial support.

At the same time, I realized that as an elite-amateur soccer player I had been relatively shy and quiet about my faith. I lived my faith but didn't make it a mission of mine to use soccer itself as a platform to invite others to faith in Jesus Christ. Bringing fundraising—especially fundraising for a Christian platform—

into the picture meant that I could justify the amount of time and effort it took. But I was treading new ground here. Sports and faith had only recently begun to mix (Athletes in Action, for example), and for many it would still be a controversial decision.

I had an interest in challenging myself, subverting the self-serving mindset that pervaded the sport, justifying the funding I needed and sharing my faith through cycling. Taken together, these factors made it obvious what I needed to do—a longer, harder fundraising ride. At the time I had been reading through the books *Purpose-Driven Life* and *The Prayer of Jabez*, and what I took away from the books was that I wanted God to bless me and expand my territory—not of finances but of influence, making a difference and living a life with purpose. With that in mind, I created the name Spoke '99.

When you look at a bike wheel, every part is important. But it's clear that everything—the tire, wheel and spokes—feed into and depend on the central hub. That made it clear to me: in the metaphor of a bike wheel, the hub is none other than God. If that is the case, the spokes are those who have plugged themselves in and connected themselves to God. What's incredible about spokes is that, though there are many of them, take one out, and your entire wheel wobbles. All need to be present and aligned correctly in order for the wheel to spin "true" (without a wobble). The outside rim, then, is the rest of the world. The part that I, as a spoke, have an influence on. My ride and fundraising effort was merely one spoke in many—but it was integral in the whole.

And thus was born Spoke '99.

A friend of ours, David Balzer, was the department head of English programming for Family Life Network (FLN), an organization that uses creative media and various partnerships to invite audiences around the world to experience what it means to be a follower of Christ. Ruth had volunteered as an envelope-stuffer for them from time to time, and they had the added benefit of having a lot of supporters in western Canada. My goal was to ride from Vancouver to Winnipeg in 5 days and raise $85,000 in the process. Our neighbour and friend Delbert Enns was the executive director. It made logical sense to raise money for FLN and, more specifically, the English programming.

To my knowledge, this ride had never been attempted anywhere near this fast. Though many Canadians have criss-crossed the country, it usually happens at a pace of 100 to 150 km in a day. I was going to attempt to ride more than 450 km per day for five days straight.

Our crew consisted of Ruth, Delbert, Dave and Miroslav. Miroslav was an intern at FLN and a friend of Delbert's from Russia and came along to see the country. Throughout the ride we would be treated to some of his concoctions in the kitchen, as well as his very excited though imperfect English. One time, as I climbed back into the motorhome, Miroslav looked at me excitedly and, in broken English with each word like a swing of an ax, said, "Are you going. To. Stop. Now?" While he meant *take a break*, it sure came across a lot stronger than that. As we were crossing barriers and pushing boundaries by combining faith with cycling, Miroslav was blown away by the fact that faith and sports could come together at all. Numerous conversations about it took place in the motorhome, and he indicated that the connection had not been made in Russia yet.

It was dark still, though I knew the sun would be rising soon. Up above me was the clock on Vancouver's city hall, glowing in the night. I was dressed in a wind-jacket, my cycling gloves on my hands and my helmet on my head. Dave Balzer was filming and Ruth had her hand on my back, offering one last bit of encouragement before we would begin. It was just us—five people unfamiliar with the city, flashing orange lights on the top of our motorhome drawing attention from whomever was up at 4 a.m. on the streets of downtown Vancouver—no fanfare or hoopla.

Delbert offered up a prayer, and I found myself simply nodding, not knowing how to put into words what I felt. The months, weeks and days leading up to an event bring with them a melting pot of emotions. You question every training decision and dietary decision you ever made. You wonder if you even know how to ride a bike (no joke). You just want to get the ride started early so that at least you're doing something to get to the finish line. And then you finally get to the starting line, and your mind doesn't know what it wants—afraid of the pain to come, you want the minutes to drag on. Knowing that the later it starts the longer you have to ride, you want the minutes to rush by so you can just get on the bike and ride. And then before you know it—

"Five, four, three, two, one." I pushed off and felt their hands clapping me on the back, cheers resonating back off the brick city hall building. I knew the first two turns, but there were others that would quickly follow, so I heard them scrambling to get into the motorhome in a hurry, packing up the camera and trying to catch me as I took the sloped driveway and turned right.

It's true that every journey begins with a single step—or pedal rotation—but the ones to follow are necessary if you want to get to the end.

Crossing the Rocky Mountains in a car can be a daunting task, never mind doing it on a bike. Coquihalla Summit, one of the longest (45 km) and most difficult of the passes, ended with a 7 km climb with a 9 percent gradient near the end. Afterwards, Dave shook his head at me in shock. On the radio he would be heard describing me, unable to comprehend how long it was possible to plod upwards at less than 10 km/h—without taking a break. Since I had mostly trained in the prairies, the mountains brought their challenges. But somehow a prairie boy like me found his home in the slopes. They brought with them a serene beauty, mixed together with an unpredictability that made them altogether enjoyable.

The descents could be exhilarating, and hitting the tunnels was a new experience for me. The opening to a tunnel gaped wide, letting me in at full speed. This tunnel was different than all the others—where they were short and had light visible from both ends, this tunnel was longer, twisted, and completely black. I had entered into the tunnel at somewhere near 40 km/h on the descent but then pushed it closer to 60 km/h. The crew didn't respond instantly, and I left them behind for a moment.

When the wash of their beams disappeared and darkness overtook me, it was like riding into an abyss of nothingness. Unable to see the lines on the road, I had to hope and pray that I wasn't drifting too far right or left, about to strike a curb and slam into the concrete wall. My heartbeat jumped into my throat, and I began to count the seconds, waiting for their lights to come back.

Finally, rescue arrived as I heard their engine echoing back to me off the concrete walls and felt the warmth of the headlights cover me like a blanket, spreading in front of me to illuminate the tunnel walls and, more importantly, the boundaries of the road. Thankfully I hadn't strayed far and needed only a minor adjustment.

While the mountains are exhilarating, they can be demoralizing. No matter how much fun it is to descend at 80 km/h and corner like a pro, the climbs take the bulk of the time (though the elevation change should be about the same). I was happy when I crossed the Rockies and saw the city of Calgary on the horizon, beckoning me on to the prairies beyond.

Without explanation, the motorhome pulled ahead of me. I saw Dave give me a knowing glance out the side window and wondered what they were up to. I shook my head, thinking they were off to take a stop at a real washroom or pick up some food for themselves. I realized they had something else in mind when they pulled over only a kilometre ahead, still within sight (this was Saskatchewan, after all).

My head was hanging as I approached the motorhome, so I didn't quite see all their preparation. Before I knew it, I heard the whir of another bike in front of me. Looking all wobbly and like he was on two wheels for the first time, Dave was moving along the road. Though he didn't know how to shift on a road bike, he picked up the pace and matched mine as I approached.

"Your head's been hanging for the last hour," he said. "It looked like you could use some company."

"You sure you can keep up?" I asked, jabbing.

He made a sound that mimicked a gasp of horror, then put on a burst of speed to show me what he was made of. "You do your radio shows on an exercise bike?" I asked.

"I'll be fine," he said, and I knew he was doing the math. *This guy's been on the bike three days. I should be able to kick his butt.*

"Just make sure you keep that thing in a straight line." I laughed. Though I didn't even realize it at the time, the conversation had already picked me up from my funk. With that much time on the bike I can go through emotional highs and lows in a very compressed timeframe. From one minute to the next things can swing radically. There can be external factors—weather, road conditions—or crew factors—navigation errors, positive attitudes—or internal factors—my own fears, hopes and dreams. Wherever they come from, they can shift things in a split second, while the entire ride can have highs and lows that span days.

"I've ridden a bike before!" he laughed, the helmet sliding forward on his head, sized incorrectly.

"Really? Because it doesn't look like it."

If he'd had the ability to punch my shoulder while riding he might have tried. Riding side-by-side can take some skill, and only experienced riders can ride close together. But the highway's shoulder was broad and smooth, so there was enough space for me to remain comfortable.

"Man." He wiggled on the seat, trying to adjust himself. His cargo shorts reminded me of the first randonneuring ride I'd gone on. "How do you get comfortable on these seats? Doesn't your butt get sore?"

"It's similar to acupuncture, Dave," I responded. "When everything else hurts more, you don't notice that pain. That being said," I said with a laugh, "I could use some Advil. Is Advil protein?"

A car zoomed past us on the left and let out a honk. It was short and happy, very different than the blares that you sometimes get from drivers.

"That's the fourth one in the last few minutes," I said. Cars going the other way began to honk as well, a few people sticking their arms out the windows and waving with broad, beaming smiles on their faces. "What's up with this place? Who put the happy juice in their water?"

Dave was laughing, the bike wobbling along with the chuckles.

"What?" I looked at him, thankful that he understood my sarcastic frustration.

"I talked to the radio station back in Swift Current," he explained. "And we made it Honk for Arvid Day."

Another one drove past, slowing down so the passenger could get a glimpse. With several staccato honks they drove off, hand hanging out the window in a wave.

"That makes sense now." I chuckled. "I thought it was a little strange."

"It was—" He paused again to catch his breath. I noticed that his legs were starting to kick out at the top of their rotation—the telltale sign that a cyclist's muscles had had enough. "It was good exposure."

"You sure you're okay, Dave?" I asked.

"I'm fine," he chided.

"Listen," I said, "clearly you can't hack it on the bike all day. What say we..." I looked ahead. Saskatchewan is incredibly flat and incredibly boring. On occasion there is a tree or two to break up the monotony of the terrain. If Columbus had lived in Saskatchewan, no one would ever have had any doubts about the earth being round. "Race to that tree?" There was a solitary tree off in the distance—the only possible end point.

"All right, you're on." Dave smiled, as if he had been pulling my leg all this time. He stepped on it, picking up the pace. The tree was a good kilometre away, though distance on the prairies can be deceptive. It looked a lot closer.

Back at home I had a lot of fun training on Henderson Highway. On occasion I would pull up behind a much younger rider, coasting behind them. They'd look over their shoulder, incredulous that an old man like me could keep pace with them. They'd step on it, and I'd increase my pace—smiling all the way. Sometimes I would let them get away; other times I'd wait for them to exhaust themselves, then bike past them, maintaining a pace fast enough that they couldn't hang on to me. More often than not they would get so frustrated, biking on flat ground at 45 km/h, that I would back off, worried they might blow a gasket.

I played the same game with Dave, watching him struggle and struggle to pull ahead of me, resting just to the side and a few feet back. When he turned to look at me and saw me smiling, I knew I had him. Shifting into the next gear, I stepped up my game and pulled even and then ahead. With him struggling behind I pushed to the finish line, and we coasted to a stop as the motorhome pulled up behind us, ready to accept its crew member back—but there would be no motorhome for me.

Bent over the handlebars, Dave looked completely exhausted. I let out a chuckle, to which he responded, "I think I'm going to throw up." His face was flushed, his shoulders slumped.

"You know, Dave, this is a lot more fun when you're in shape."

He shot me a look that told me to keep it quiet, but it was clear he wasn't going to get any words out of his mouth. He put the extra bike back in the motorhome and (this is my imagination now) slumped onto the couch and didn't get up for the next hour or so. I clipped my feet back into the pedals and hit the road.

It was easy to say that standing around was getting us nowhere, but putting my feet in my shoes and climbing onto the bike was another matter. I stood outside of the motorhome, in the dark, alone in a parking lot in Moose Jaw. Though I sometimes have a crew on my rides, cycling is a solitary sport. The long hours give ample time for thought (and to come up with jokes that my kids tell me lack humour).

A gust of wind slapped me in the face, and I almost staggered backwards off the bike. Footage of the next two days would show the tall grass in the ditches bent nearly horizontal as the wind beat it to the ground. Ruth wrote in her journal that today would be a character-building day.

When Quitting Is Not an Option

I settled into a slow and plodding pace. Different crew members took turns riding beside me to offer me moral support, but they had to return to the motorhome after a few kilometres, exhausted from the relentless winds. Over the next hours I would settle into a rhythm that refused to see beyond the next kilometre, celebrating every time my odometer ticked 100 m further. There was nothing to do but break the rest of the ride up into infinitely small chunks of accomplishment.

That crack.

That driveway.

That tree.

Another ten seconds…

How many hours has it been? I didn't know, but the sun was beating down on my skin like the wind was taking its toll on my face. My cycling gloves have a small circle on them, and a long ride in the sun ends up with a suntanned circle right in the middle of the back of my hand. The top of my head gets "racing stripes" from the air holes in my helmet. My arms and legs develop various levels of farmer's tan (from dark to light) due to the varying length of my shirts and shorts.

The motorhome was parked up ahead with a car behind it. In my exhaustion it took me longer than normal to recognize the vehicle—it was my sister's. There was a man sitting in a lawn chair beside it whom it took a few moments for me to place. I had been alone (mentally) for days, yet instantly my mind reached out for solace to my dad, 84 years old, who had come to the side of the road to see me. Though Mom had never understood any of my athletic desires, there had always been a quiet understanding that emanated from Dad. He was not a man of many words, and he didn't have any to share with me as I pulled up on my bike. But he looked at me, and I knew that he understood what I was dealing with.

Obviously he had never done what I was doing, but I could grasp in that moment that he understood the mental difficulties I was going through. It's not the cycling that draws me back to these challenges time after time but the mental difficulties I face. It's saying, "I can't do it, but I'm going to do it anyway." It's never giving up. It's knowing that you have nothing left, yet refusing to stop.

It all collapsed on my shoulders in that moment. I put the bike up against the motorhome and gave Dad a hug. Emotion washed over me like a waterfall, cascading on my extremely raw nerves. I knew that he knew what made me tick. Though he had never had the opportunity, I know that if he had grown up in a different environment, without all the challenges of the Chaco, that he would have pushed himself to his limits and beyond. He had an appreciation for what something like this could mean to a person, even if he'd never done it himself.

When I broke the hug he gave me a smile that was more of a grimace, and we went into the motorhome together. I sat down on the bench, glad to be off the bike seat for a moment and out of the terrific winds, and ate some sliced cantaloupe. Though the ride was far from over, it felt like a mental load had been taken off my shoulders. Not that others don't, or can't, have a tiny understanding of what I'm going through, but support from Dad was like a tailwind to my struggling body.

Later on, my sister would tell me what he had said to her. Upon seeing my face and the deterioration of my body, he told her, "He will not make it to Winnipeg."

He was wrong, but I was glad that he had the understanding and foresight to know it would have been the wrong thing to say to me.

I celebrated a mental victory when I finally threw Saskatchewan under my back tire and crossed the border into Manitoba. We stayed at Virden that night, but I tossed and turned, unable to sleep. Knowing that the wind was still strong was beginning to get to me mentally. Instead of sleeping, I got back up to get back on the bike. The wind had dropped a little.

It didn't last long. By the time the sun had come up I had a headwind of 60 km/h again.

It would be a long day.

By the time we were nearing Winnipeg I realized that, though it was making a saga out of my journey, the wind had brought the attention of the media. We created a lot of exposure, which is why I didn't quite know what to do when…

I stepped out of the shower in the motorhome, the space cramped. I looked out the window, almost in disbelief at what I was seeing. The skyline of

When Quitting Is Not an Option

Winnipeg was ahead of me, within reach. It might seem strange to take a shower when you're getting close to the finish line, but I wanted to look (and smell) respectable when I arrived at the legislative buildings. If all went as we hoped, there would be plenty of media there. My gaunt face was enough to convince them that I had really done what I had set out to do, so cleaning up the smell would actually allow reporters to get close enough to interview me.

Pulling on clean shorts, I struggled for a moment, my body unable to bend all the way over. But soon enough they were on, and I was stepping back down out of the motorhome, onto the gravel. My bike was resting up against the side of the motorhome, and Dave was keeping an eye on it. Since I'm not the most flexible person in the world, it took some effort getting onto the bike. As I clipped my foot in, Dave asked, "When are you going to arrive at the Leg?"

"I don't know yet." I shook my head, frustrated at the question. When you're 20 percent of the ride away from the finish line, people start asking you to predict your arrival. They're not ill-intentioned, but it's a ridiculously difficult thing to do. Ultra-marathon cyclists have quit rides closer to the finish line than I was now. When your mind is lost and you're simply spinning in circles, sometimes things can snap—and the end can come in a second. But even if I was entirely confident I was going to make it to the finish line, many factors can change the time. Your body doesn't know how close it is to being done the work, so if your stomach wants to throw a party or your system feels like shutting down, there's only so much your brain can do to convince it to get going again.

I started pedalling away, a little annoyed. But soon enough the annoyance faded as I saw the city of Winnipeg scooch ever closer and closer, one tiny bit at a time. The reality of it hit me when I made it to the perimeter, the road that encompasses Winnipeg, and actually entered city limits. There was a silence in my ear that resonated loudly, then—

Sirens. From both sides. Loud and blasting. The wind was still slamming into my face (it had shifted just slightly to the side by this point), and I knew that the way Portage Avenue bent would work a little in my favour. Not enough for a tailwind, but enough for a recess from the headwind.

A cop on a motorcycle pulled up beside me, his lights flashing and freaking me out. I tried searching for his eyes underneath the tinted helmet but couldn't find them. *What did I do wrong?* I was thinking, but didn't exactly voice it. I was about to take my foot out of the pedal and drift to the curb when he said, "I hear you need to get to the Leg in a hurry."

"What are you talking about?" I asked, my voice croaking from the wind that had been ramming itself down my mouth for the last 600 km.

"We'll get you there; just follow me," he said, then pulled in front of me. Before I knew it, more motorcycles swooped in from the side, as well as two police cars. All in all there were eight of them in their escort, and they took their job seriously. Now I knew why my crew had been pestering me time after time about an ETA—the police needed to know when to show up.

Another one pulled up beside me and engaged me in light conversation, though there was no way I had the energy for it. I had just drained my tank to beyond empty over the last 600 km, battling winds that would make most give up.

The one beside me glanced into his mirror, and I could tell that they knew what they were doing. One was directly in front of me, another behind our motorhome. A media crew from FLN slipped in front of me, filming out the back of a minivan. Sirens blaring and horns honking, a few of the motorcycles drove ahead to each intersection, clearing traffic as if the queen was coming through.

I had adrenaline shooting through my body—both because of the police escort and because I was finally within reasonable distance of the finish line—and so I picked up the pace. They took the hint and sped up, pushing the needle to around 40 km/h. I was biking into the wind, completely exhausted from the last five days, and I almost croaked as I struggled to keep up with them. On a few occasions I wanted to tell them to slow down, but I didn't have the voice to do it.

Maybe there was a part of me that wanted to enjoy the speed too, rushing through intersections with red lights, cars stopped and drivers staring to see what was going on. The entire way down Portage Avenue I didn't have to stop once. The cops that had stopped at the intersections would zoom past us to get ahead to the next one.

I could see the cop who was leading me, pacing me, keep looking in his mirror. If he could see my face he would speed up. At any given point it's pretty easy to dig too deep and go beyond the point where your body can't handle it anymore. I was within an inch of that breaking point but thankfully kept up the pace as we turned onto Memorial Boulevard, with the legislative buildings ahead.

A light drizzle had started, and I said goodbye to the police as they swung away, their job done.

"All the best!" they yelled, and just like that they were gone and I was alone. The driveway at the legislative buildings slopes upward (one final climb…) and swings to the left after you turn to the right. I had biked some 2,400 km without serious incident, but the rain just hitting the pavement brought the oil to the surface, and as I turned, my wheel let go and my heart jumped into my throat. A cyclist can feel instantly when the wheel has slipped, and I knew I was going down—in front of a hundred friends and family and media cameras, all waiting for me at the top of the driveway.

I yanked the wheel back to where it should have been and barely averted the disaster. Slowly, now, I climbed the final corner of my journey and coasted to a stop at the makeshift finish line in front of the building.

Tears ran down my face as I realized what I had finished and accomplished. I was humbled by the magnitude of the achievement and what God was able to do through me. I grabbed on to Ruth, my rock, and hugged her while I sobbed, the rain mixing with my tears. My kids were there, and I hugged them each in turn. As the media from CBC, CTV and *Winnipeg Free Press* came to meet me, I looked at my watch. Five days, 11 hours, 31 minutes. To my knowledge, this ride had never been done in so short a time.

It wouldn't be the first time I rode from Vancouver to Winnipeg, but I knew that I didn't want to just stop there.

I was just getting started.

David Balzer, media coordinator of Spoke '99

Arvid's dad (age 84) came to meet his son on the road near Indian Head, SK.
Dad Loewen passed away 9 months later.

A tough morning in Virden, MB, facing strong headwinds

At 12 years old, Paul joined his dad Arvid on the side of the road.
Fifteen years later he is the author of his dad's book!

Winnipeg police escort to the legislative building, Winnipeg, MB

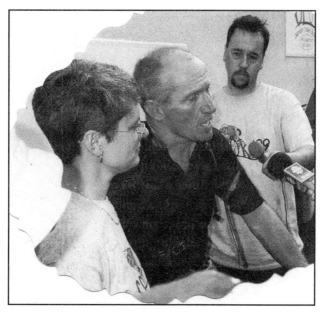

Meeting media who were captivated by our story

The Breaking Point
Spoke 2001

Mountains surrounded me, their glorious majesty making my breath catch in my throat. The road we were on was called a highway, but that's a generous term when it's 700 km of gravel that traipses its way over mountaintops. Instead of diving down into the valleys, like most highways do, the Dempster Highway in the Yukon stays on the ridges. It meant I would sometimes bike through an actual cloud, the mist enveloping me. It also meant that, upon breaking out of the cloud on the other side, some of the most incredible scenery awaited me.

While I had biked the Rocky Mountains in BC numerous times and their impressive height outdid the tallest of any of these mountains, the combination of colours and ridge after ridge made for some of the most incredible views I've ever experienced. That and the fact that it was eerily desolate in the Yukon. In two days of gravel we saw less than ten cars. The solitary civilization on the highway is a small town at the halfway point, whose only service is to repair flat tires—yes, the road is that brutal.

I was riding my Trek Y-Foil road bike and had put studded tires on to gain extra traction. I had never used a mountain bike in my cycling career before, but we had one on the back of the leisure van, just in case. The gravel sent shocks up through my body, endlessly pounding my muscles and joints. By now it had become background noise to my journey, a journey that was turning out to be even more difficult than I had imagined. And this was just the beginning—I had some 7,000 km to go, though thankfully only 700 km would be on gravel.

There was a ferry across the McKenzie River, and we had to make it on time. It only crossed the river twice a day—if we missed it we would be forced to hunker down in our leisure van overnight and wait for the morning ride. That timeline was beating a rhythm like a drum in my mind, and I was pushing myself physically. I knew we weren't far, but we didn't have a lot of time, either.

I pushed harder.

But I was slowing down.

What is wrong with me? Are my legs working? They felt strong, but something wasn't right. And then I realized it—the gravel was wet, sopping wet. I was sinking in, my tires starting to make a significant depression in the surface of the road. I was down to 10 km/h now, even though I was pushing hard.

I stood up, pounding on the pedals, knowing that this would have to end eventually. But it didn't help—my pace slowed to a walk, then a crawl. My wheels were going so slow that the gravel was seeping in over the rims, my tire disappearing entirely under the gravel. And then it happened—

I couldn't produce enough force to move forward another inch.

My bike stopped.

It happened so fast, I didn't have time to prepare. Usually when you pull to a stop you get your foot out of the pedal a while before, so you can remain standing. But I didn't have any advance warning, and I suddenly found myself tipping and—

I hit the ground.

Behind me, the leisure van lurched to a stop. A door slammed open and I heard Ruth calling out, "Are you OK? Arvid!" She was running towards me, the gravel squishing under her feet. Lying on my side, I unclipped my feet and shook my head, still a little shocked about what had happened.

I've hit the ground a few times, most of them at much higher speeds than this. There was the time I touched the wheel of another rider from behind and hit the ground at over 30 km/h, hitting my head, seeing black and splitting my helmet. Then there was the time in Abbotsford when I had my head down and ran into the triangle of concrete where the right lane yields to the right and the left lane stays straight. My wheel hit the solid concrete 10 inches high, and I flipped over, landing on my back with my bike between my legs, narrowly missing the metal post of a traffic light.

This was a different kind of wipeout—a wipeout at a standstill.

My feet were out of the clips now, and I pushed the bike off of me. Ruth grabbed my shoulder and helped me to my feet.

"I think I'm fine," I said, checking my body. My legs were fine, my shoulder was fine, and my head hadn't hit the ground. I picked the bike up; the wheel still dug into the ground. Jeff, the bike mechanic along on the ride, followed Ruth by a few paces. He took the bike from my hand and immediately did an inspection. Because of the wear and tear the gravel can bring, every time I got off Jeff would clean the chain and inspect the bike. Without keeping an eye on it, on this kind of surface it could cease to function within the span of a couple hours. He gave it his OK, not worried about me as much. That was Ruth's job.

"This gravel is ridiculous," I said. I shook my head, frustrated at the situation. I had set a goal of 400 km every 24 hours to make it to my finish line. This road was proving to be a lot more work than I thought it would be. The elevation, the gravel—it was all taking its toll on my body, and this was day one. "This road should only be travelled by helicopter," I muttered.

We had driven it on the way up, a body-shattering vibration so loud that we couldn't speak to each other. When we had arrived at the final 10 km before Inuvik (our starting point), the 10 km that went from the town to the airport and was paved with asphalt, we could hardly believe how smooth the road was. It felt like driving on the clouds or lying on a soft pillow after sleeping on needles. That 10 km stretch was the most well-paved road I've ever driven—either that or our perspective was a little skewed from the previous 700 km.

"You want to take a break?" Ruth asked.

"I can't," I said. "The ferry—we have to make it to the ferry or we automatically lose 12 hours." I swung my leg over the bike and put my foot in the pedal. Jeff steadied me as I pushed forward. I didn't clip my left foot in, knowing that I might need it. Two rotations later I was at a standstill again.

"Looks like I'm walking," I admitted. I got off the bike, held on to the handlebars, and trudged through the mucky gravel. At this rate, a single kilometre would take 15 minutes. But I was moving forward, and that was progress in itself.

Up at the northwest corner of the Northwest Territories is a small town called Inuvik. It is just south of the Beaufort Sea, part of the delta of the Mackenzie River, where the river flows into the Arctic Ocean. For several months of the year the town sees nothing but sun—being far beyond the Arctic Circle. Conversely, during the winter it sees nothing but dark. In and of itself it is an unremarkable town. What drew my attention to Inuvik was the fact that it is the northernmost point in Canada connected by a road. Going from one limit to another is enough to get someone like me excited. And so I drew a line from the top to the bottom of Canada. It started in Inuvik, crossed the border west into the Yukon, swooped down into BC, then cut southeast across Alberta,

When Quitting Is Not an Option

Saskatchewan, Manitoba and into Ontario. There it wound its way down to Point Pelee, a park in Leamington that is the southernmost point in Canada. The ride would cover a total of 7,200 km, connecting Canada's northernmost and southernmost points by road. I had set myself a goal of 18 days, needing to cover 400 km every 24 hours.

This ride would serve as another fundraiser, this time for Mennonite Central Committee (MCC). There was a personal connection for me—MCC was the organization that had supplied my parents with the tools essential for survival upon arriving in Paraguay. Globally respected, MCC helps people from all countries through many of life's challenges.

When we pulled into Inuvik with our leisure van and minivan, it was obvious that we stood out. All the signage on our vehicles screamed outsiders, and it didn't take long after checking in at the small hotel for people to be stopping on the street to ask us what we were up to. When we told them, they wanted to see what we meant. Well, ultra-marathon cycling is a sport that is exciting over the long haul, not second-by-second. Thankfully, our bike mechanic, Jeff, was capable of doing tricks on his bike I couldn't even dream of. Before we knew it we had our entire team out on the schoolyard with dozens of kids surrounding us, as Jeff told them to lie side-by-side on the grass while he jumped over six of them on his bike. I cringed every time, but he never missed.

After that performance, everywhere we went for the next 24 hours we had kids surrounding us, even when we went for a brilliantly bright walk at 2 a.m., the midnight sun making it difficult to sleep even in hotel rooms with curtains drawn.

Starting early in the morning, we left town with a little less fanfare than we had seen during the day. My first 10 km were fast—even though you try to pace yourself, your body has adrenaline pumping through it. That and the fact that it was the only asphalt before I hit the 700 km of gravel. My pace dropped and I settled into my seat, preparing myself for a long two and a half weeks.

"Why don't we stop at the Arctic Circle and have a picnic?" I asked, itching to rest my legs. Three hundred kilometres in, and it was nearing night, though you couldn't tell from the amount of sunlight splashing off the mountains back at me. The land was frozen in a perpetual sunset, the sun ten degrees off the horizon. Normally it would continue its plunge, but in the land of the midnight sun it actually moves along the horizon from west, through north, and all the way back to east, where it rises again in the morning.

We were nearing the Arctic Circle, that line on the globe that you learn about in elementary school but doubt you'll ever see. There's not much above the Circle, considering the ground up there is permanently frozen. At the Circle is a large sign describing it, as well as a picnic area. That's where I was headed.

"That sounds like a good idea," Ruth agreed, "and it'll be good for pictures."

"There was a watermelon in the van, wasn't there?" I asked. Ruth looked behind her, not answering my question. She said something to someone else, and I tried to look back into the windows but was shut out by the reflections. "Why don't we have that watermelon?"

"We'll see," Ruth said, before the van dropped its speed to idle along behind me. I was climbing up a slight hill, standing up on my pedals. The Circle was close now, and I could see the sign, recognizing it from our drive up.

I heard a slight buzzing and turned to look. Since I'm from Manitoba, the sound of mosquitoes is not unfamiliar, but that had been loud. I shook my head and continued on, anticipating the chance to stretch my legs and get off the bike.

I made it to the top and pulled to the side. The van's tires crunched to a stop behind me, and I climbed off the bike—and was hit by a wall. Not the wall athletes talk about but a black cloud of mosquitoes that swarmed me the moment I stopped. I started swatting them.

And didn't stop.

They were everywhere, landing on every visible stretch of skin. At one point I counted 13 mosquitoes on my skin inside the small hole of my cycling glove. Those were easy to swat, but the ones that clamped onto my leg were more difficult.

There were so many that I couldn't swat fast enough. My hand just wasn't big enough. Resorting to something I had never done before, I cupped my hands and wrapped my leg with them. I just rubbed my hands up and down on my calves, getting the mosquitoes to flee. As soon as my hands were gone they would be back.

The door from the motorhome opened up and Ruth came out, carrying a piece of watermelon on a plate. She put it down on the picnic table and started dancing to ward off the mosquitoes. The watermelon was in a circular slice, just the way I usually eat it. But there was duct tape on the side.

"Duct tape?" I asked, swatting another pack of mosquitoes.

When Quitting Is Not an Option

"Bettie," Ruth said, referring to one of the crew members. She and her husband, Henry, were the "Grandma" and "Grandpa" on the trip, taking care of all of us.

Jeff jumped out of the leisure van and came to grab the bike, giving the chain a cleaning. He started muttering about the mosquitoes and didn't stop the entire time. I didn't blame him—I had hoped that this stop would be restful and scenic (and the scenery was beautiful), but we weren't getting a chance to appreciate anything at all.

"The watermelon took a tumble off the counter because of the road and split right in half. Bettie knew how much you like it cut in slices like that, so she resolved to duct tape it together for you."

Up at the Arctic Circle, completely in over my head and surrounded by bloodsucking insects worse than I had ever seen before, I shared a laugh with Ruth.

"Tell Bettie I'll eat it later, but I've got to go. I can't stand these bugs."

"You and me both," Jeff muttered, handing the bike back to me while simultaneously trying to swat every part of his body. "I'm getting back in the van." He ran quicker than I'd seen him move all trip, and Ruth followed suit, taking the watermelon back with her.

Our two-second picnic over, I got back on the bike. The good news was that I could bike fast enough to get away from mosquitoes; the bad news was that the Arctic had a black fly that was faster than me—and just as vicious as mosquitoes.

The bugs had seen how enticing I could be when I stopped at the Circle. They decided to start chasing me. Usually you can outrun bugs on a bike, but these ones were different. They were organized, flying like geese in Vs to maintain good aerodynamics. They would draft behind me, then swing around in packs to attack me from the front.

Back in the leisure van my son, Paul, spent the next hour and a half hunting mosquitoes that had snuck in when the doors were open for a few seconds. Blood stains were all over the interior of the van. The crew could hardly believe the speed of the flies, as the same flies kept attacking the van's front windows. Convinced they could outrun them, they increased the van's speed up to 70 km/h, at which point the flies were still capable of drafting off the van and speeding forward to attack the front windows. All the repellent we'd brought along on the trip wasn't enough to stem the attacks, and we were thankful to finally say goodbye to the bugs a while later when we left their territory.

"How much farther?" I asked the crew. They were rumbling along behind me, the incessant gravel still loud. I wondered what it would be like to bike alone, wheels whistling through nothing but air, only the distant trundle of the van's engine to be heard.

"We don't know," Paul responded. "Do you want us to check?"

"Well," I began, then looked ahead. I had to keep my eyes on the road; otherwise I might hit a particularly large stone that would send me careening to the ground. This wasn't packed gravel by anyone's standards. It was gravel that had been piled high (to avoid the effects of permafrost) and simply driven on. I'd never seen a gravel road in this kind of shape in Manitoba (and that's saying something).

"Wait a second," I said. Were my eyes deceiving me? The road up ahead looked darker. Often, the trees in the distance produce a mirage that covers over the road, but this mirage wasn't green but—

"I think we got our answer!" Paul yelled, smacking the side of the van. Renewed energy hit my legs, and I stood up on the pedals to get a better view. There was no mistaking it now; that was definitely not gravel. Up in the distance a car whizzed by from right to left, heading the same direction I wanted to go. I had been praying for 700 km to finally see the T-intersection. Finally it was here.

A minute later I rolled onto solid road, a few stones still scattered here and there. But then it got silent, and I almost felt like crying. There was a stop sign, and I rested my foot on pavement. Compared to the road I was about to turn onto, where I'd just come from looked like a side road. To think I had biked 700 km on that road to the nearest civilization!

The van pulled up beside me, and I heard the cheering from the crew inside.

"Just over two days!" Ruth yelled. That's how long it had taken me to bike the Dempster Highway, and I was convinced I would never do it again.

When I had been researching for the ride I had scoured the Internet for any information on whether this was even possible—could the highway even be biked? I had found a website with capital letters, boldly proclaiming "I BIKED THE DEMPSTER HIGHWAY IN 2 DAYS." Now, at the stop sign at the end of the highway I had to laugh—and laugh I did. The biker had posted a photo of his bike. It was quite a nice bike, only it didn't look like mine.

When Quitting Is Not an Option

It was a motorcycle.

My body didn't feel great at that moment, but my mind was doing fantastic.

We had turned onto the Klondike Highway, and I knew I had a lot of work ahead of me. I had been anticipating that the winds would turn in our favour, but they didn't. When I calculated my 400 km/day I hadn't accounted properly for just how brutal the Dempster Highway would be. I attacked the highway, even into headwinds, to make up for the lost time. In my mind I intended to catch back up to my required pace or quit trying.

A cough let loose from my lungs, and I felt how congested they were. My breathing was laboured, and I knew I wasn't getting as much air into them as usual. Something was wrong, but I wasn't willing to admit it yet. My legs were still turning—mind over matter, right? I could always force them to turn one more time, just one more. If I did that enough times I would get up the hill. I didn't want to call it a mountain, because then it seemed too tall.

The van was ahead of me—checking in at the hotel where we would spend the night. After numerous days of camping on roadside pullouts and building fires in the ditch, sleeping at whatever angle the ground afforded me, showering in a cramped stall (or outside), I was finally going to slip into the comfort of a hotel bed. How many days had it been now? Five? I couldn't count. Maybe only four.

My legs were like lead and I could barely push. I realized I hadn't taken a breath in a few seconds and pulled in sharply. It was tough work, this breathing thing. I put my head down, not wanting to see just how far it was to the hotel. Off in the distance I had seen the sign, but it was taking far too long to get there. I was alone on the road, completely alone.

"Arvid!" someone called out, and I jerked back to reality. Had it taken me ten minutes to climb that hill? I looked behind me—it was a paltry hill, and it should have been a breeze. If only breathing was a breeze. I had almost missed the hotel's driveway, and I turned in slowly, coasting to a stop a few steps from the van.

"I need a break," I said to Ruth, who was approaching me with a hotel key in hand.

"It's time for a shower and a nap," she said.

"No," I responded, "I need a real break. Ten—no, twelve hours."

Ruth is my crew chief and my constant. She understands me more than anyone, sometimes more than I do. Having been there on almost all my rides, she knew what to expect. This was different. I was huffing and puffing, barely able to walk. I gripped her arm as I headed to the hotel, feeling like an 80-year-old.

The rooms had doors on the outside, and we were on the ground level (essential for cycling), so I could walk right into the room. Paul was already inside, and he turned to look at me. A knowing glance passed between him and Ruth, but I ignored it.

I stripped off my clothes and climbed into the shower, letting the hot water massage me. Usually that revives me, makes me feel fresh. But it did nothing this time. My breathing didn't improve. The pain didn't improve, and I slipped under the covers with only one thing on my mind—sleep.

The crew had energy after the break, and we hit the road one more time. My legs felt better, and my lungs, though still clearly full of fluid, were responding better. I wondered if it was the altitude, but we weren't that high. Was I sick? Had I pushed it too far?

Out of the town there was a slight downhill, and I felt rejuvenated by the wind in my face. One day at a time. One kilometre at a time.

And then the downhill ended.

And the uphill started.

And everything came crashing back down around me. My lungs closed in, making it almost impossible to breathe. I could feel my muscles tightening, my body reacting as if it was on its deathbed. *This isn't right.* I had never felt this way before.

I fought through the climb and coasted down another hill. And another climb.

But I didn't make it to the top of this one. I pulled over. Ruth came out of the van, her face serious yet calm.

"I don't know if I can," I began. She looked at my face.

"Paul was right," she said. I cocked my head, unsure what she meant. "Your lips are blue."

"They're not blue," I said, feeling them, as if I could rub it off. But then I started coughing and couldn't stop. I was used to vomiting on bike rides—but this? This was different.

"How far can you push it?" Ruth asked.

"I can always push it one hill farther," I said, though I wasn't sure if it was true. "It's so early in the ride. I don't want to give up."

"Of course not," Ruth said, "but is getting back on the bike an option?"

"My lungs," I said, "there's something wrong with them."

When I started ultra-marathon cycling, I had made Ruth a promise. If I was dealing with anything that seemed like it would have lasting health issues, I would stop. I needed to always remain in control, and this was the first time that my promise was coming into play.

"Do you think it could be long-term damage?" she asked. We both knew exactly what she was asking, *Is this ride over?*

"I, I don't know," I responded. But what I did know was that there was no way I was getting anywhere with the kind of air intake I was currently capable of.

"When is enough enough?" Ruth asked.

"People always ask me if I know when to stop." I chuckled, which turned into a hacking cough. "I guess we're finding out now."

"Then maybe this is it," Ruth said.

"Maybe it is," I agreed, the words carrying the weight of an anvil. I didn't want to give up—not so close to the starting line, not so far from home, not with all the media attention we had gotten on the start of our ride. But I couldn't risk it, and I also knew I couldn't make it.

The ride was over.

I lifted my foot over the bike and shuffled to the van, barely able to breathe. I had let myself down. I had let the ministry down. I had let my family down.

I had failed, and it crushed me.

If the walk back to the van was tough, the drive home was much worse. It didn't matter that Paul and Ruth said they had never seen me look worse (and they'd seen some unique situations); it didn't matter that my breathing was still laboured the next day. All that mattered was that I had quit the ride and I wouldn't be continuing.

As soon as you say you're done and you put the shoes and bike away, everything looks rosier. You start arguing with yourself that it can't have been as bad as you thought it was or that it surely would have gotten better (it wouldn't have). I had 3,800 km of open road ahead of me to think through my decision. It would be a long ride home.

Our crew stopped in Edmonton and went to the waterpark. I had to field phone calls from media who wanted answers to questions I didn't know if I could even talk about. It was my own fault—I had attempted to create a spectacle and had succeeded; the attention was my own creation. But it didn't make it any easier.

I felt, correctly, like I had failed. I had failed in what I set out to do.

We arrived back in Winnipeg at our house. Unbeknownst to Ruth and me, our kids and friends had arranged a "celebration" for our return. What I wanted to do was arrive home in quiet, get into bed and shut my brain off. Instead I grimaced my way through conversations and stories about what had transpired on the Dempster and Klondike Highways, frustrated that my ailment had seemed to repair itself in the three days of driving home. If I had had to quit, at least my body could have let me look miserable when I saw everyone. It made me question, again and again, the decision I had made on the side of the road in northern Canada.

The sun had long since set, and the mosquitoes were out in full force. I hardly noticed them, my legs one giant mosquito bite from my earlier experience. Our kids, all teenagers now, were helping with the cleanup after the party.

"Go inside," Ruth said. "We'll clean it up." I knew that she knew there was more bubbling beneath the surface, but I wasn't ready to deal with it yet. They had a large garbage can out and were shovelling paper plates and plastic cups into it. I turned to head into the house and realized that, for the first time since getting off my bike, I had my thoughts to myself. The house was quiet, and I walked through the sunroom into the kitchen.

A flashing red light caught my attention, and I turned to see the answering machine. I pressed the button absentmindedly and was puttering around the room. I stopped almost immediately when a friend of ours started speaking. His voice was laboured and slow, clearly emotional.

"Arvid," he began, "I just wanted to welcome you home." He paused between sentences, weighing his words. "I'm sorry to hear how things went out there. I am sure it was a tough decision to come home. But I wanted you to know that how you handled the disappointment has meant a lot more to me than if you finished. It meant a lot to me."

End of message.

Usually after we listen to a message we write down the relevant material and delete the message. My finger hovered over the button, and I knew I couldn't delete it. I would have to play it again for myself and for Ruth.

I began to feel emotion overtaking me, and I headed down the hallway to our room. Lying down in bed, I closed my eyes—not to sleep but to think. I saw what had happened not even as a failure but as a defeat. Up till that point, I had thought that anything was possible. Now I realized it wasn't.

This might not be for me, I thought, referring to ultra-marathon cycling. I had about a 50:50 ratio of success to failure at this point, and the DNFs were piling up. *I might not have what it takes.* The words came out of my mind and felt like weight on my chest. I sank further into the bed, wishing it would swallow me whole.

It would be a year before I went for a joyful bike ride again.

I shelved my feelings and my fears, my failures and my disappointments. When people talked to me about it, I diverted the conversation. As a cyclist I had hit rock bottom. I gave up on cycling; I gave up on my ability to think outside the box and stretch my imagination. By focusing on the failure, I gave up on succeeding.

But I found that from rock bottom you can try to climb up again. Though this time things would be different. Fear of failure is often what prevents us from doing what we are capable of doing. Because we always want to be perceived as successful, we limit our attempts to those that we know with certainty will stick. What ends up happening is that our dreams and our goals get diminished until they're small enough to be easily surmountable, and by that point they're hardly dreams at all.

The message on my answering machine reminded me of all this and prompted me to think about what we are called to do—do we dream big and fail or hardly dream at all in order to succeed? If you can even call it succeeding, that is. And at what point along this whole process are we allowing God to take over? You know, it might not be the way we want it to work out, but it's what God has called us to do anyway.

After I hit rock bottom, I became less obsessed with achieving my cycling goal than even many people in the support crew and friends and family. To some of them, the challenges I faced were simply obstacles that "Arvid can and will always overcome." It's simply not true. I could ride the same ride ten times, succeed the first nine and fail the tenth. There is nothing predictable when you push beyond the boundaries of what you thought was ordinarily possible and stretch all your preconceived notions. And that relates to both the positive and the negative—when you push beyond, you're giving God room to operate, and sometimes He takes those ridiculous attempts and turns them into something golden.

And so I continue to dream big—really big, but I also understand that my accomplishments are only a goal and they take second place to what God can do through any one of these initiatives. While it took me years to come to that realization, letting go of myself and allowing God to take control gave me the confidence to dream big once more and simply go into an event with the understanding that God is in control and the outcome is not up to me.

When it comes down to it, fear of failure is all about me. *I'm afraid to look stupid*, people might think. We struggle with the expectations of others, with what failure says about our character. But failure is what cripples us and ties us to the ground, preventing us from living up to our full potential. Fear is what takes many in society hostage and makes us live a life that's much less than it could actually be. When we as Christians act within the will of God, we should be far more confident in our approach to go forward.

Over time I've become okay with failing—from the perspective of that standard definition of success and failure. God can (and does) take failures and turn them into something far greater. It's why I dream big and don't worry about the success. On the other hand, every dream I contrive has to be completely backed by my effort. I need to put 100 percent into preparation, training and planning. That is the minimum we need to bring to an event in order for God to bless it. If we're doing anything less, we shouldn't be asking God to bless it—like in James, where the author calls someone out for seeing a homeless person and saying, "Be warm and well-fed," then going on his way. If we're not willing to back our words up with our actions and our efforts, how can we expect God to pull through for us?

When we step into God's arena and pull His confidence over us, we realize that we are not alone in this thing. Failure ceases to be a four-letter word, because it's not about us anymore. Instead of shying away from failure, we embrace the possibility that we might fail, because it's only when our dreams are big enough to collapse that we are capable of accomplishing anything extraordinary.

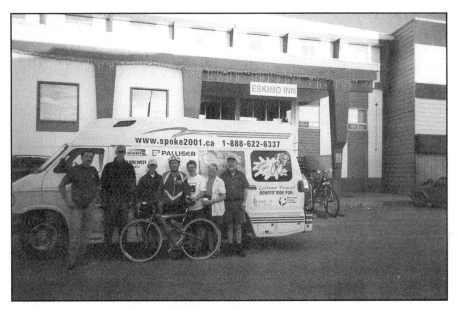

Support crew in Inuvik, NWT: Harv Sawatzky, Jeff Derksen, Paul Loewen, Arvid and Ruth Loewen, Bettie and Henry Bergen

Henry Bergen, support crew veteran retired from crewing in 2011 at age 80

Desolate Dempster Highway

Coming back after finishing 300 km north of the Arctic Circle

When Quitting Is Not an Option

Decision time

Welcome home with family and friends

Closed and Open Doors
Preparing for Spoke 2005

The phone was ringing on the other end, and I was a bundle of nerves. I could hear Herb Buller's breathing from his phone as we waited for the conference call to connect. Finally, someone picked up, and there was a "Hello."

"This is Herb Buller calling." Herb sounded calm. I was glad he was willing to do the talking. If this worked, this could be the biggest moment of my cycling—no, sports—career. Early on in cycling I had already realized that the platform I could create from cycling was far bigger than anything I could have created with soccer. Exuberant to make up for where I was silent about my faith during soccer, I was pouring my energy into this project.

"Ah yes, Herb and Arvid!" The voice on the other end was friendly and warm, and I swallowed back my nerves, as if I could keep them in my stomach. I recognized the voice from our last phone call, when we'd made the pitch. And now we were going to discuss it in further detail.

"Thanks for talking with us," I found myself saying, the words coming from who knows where.

"Thanks for thinking of us," he responded.

I had always wanted to work with and for kids, and this project felt like the culmination of that desire. The humanitarian organization had expressed interest, and so here we were—me with a hare-brained idea and Herb with the strings to pull to get me in touch with the people who mattered. It felt like God had been opening door after door in front of me, a blessing that kept on going.

"Explain to me the motivation," he said.

"It's quite simple," I began. "As a Christian and an athlete I see this as the perfect and complete way to demonstrate Christian service—literally making it a physical act."

"And you think it's possible?"

"Anything is possible," I respond, "but it will be the most difficult thing I've ever done. Pulling another person across the country on the back of a tandem bike isn't an easy feat."

"What if you fail? How do we cope with not finishing, after pouring energy, money and time into the project?"

"That's a good question," I said, the fear of failure still fresh in my mind from two years before. "I can't honestly say. Failure is always a possibility. Rides of this length and magnitude are far from predictable. Never mind when you tack on the extra difficulties. But the platform is worth the difficulties." I continued, "We're going to be taking impoverished children and putting them on the back of a bike, and I'll be pulling them 7,000 km across Canada. How could the media not love that story?"

"The board loves the idea," he responded, the first directly positive words I had heard. I felt a shiver pass through my body. Did this mean that all my dreaming and scheming was coming to fruition? Was I going to have to get back onto the bike and into good enough shape to pull another human being 240 km a day for an entire month? What would that be like in the mountains? I didn't want to think about it, not now.

"We're excited about it," I said. "I'm excited about it."

"And you're sure this is doable?" he asked.

"Yes," I responded. "Yes, I am," sounding far more confident than I actually was.

"Okay," he said, "we'll be in touch. Thanks for your time."

And just like that, the phone call was over. I said goodbye to Herb and put the phone down.

Ruth was in the room, listening to my side of the conversation. "How'd it go?" she asked.

"Good, I think," I responded. "He said they liked the idea and were excited."

"Good!" she responded, a smile on her face.

Days and weeks passed. I nagged Herb to update me on what was happening. I kept riding my bike, maintaining shape. And then, finally.

"Herb, how's the project going?" I asked.

"I don't know."

"Can we call them?"

And we tried.

"Hello, this is Herb Buller calling." I waited.

"Yes." The voice was distant. Not cold, not mean, but distant. When we tried to reach our contact, we couldn't get through. We were routed from one through to the next to the next.

"I'm sorry," someone official finally said, "but they've expressed concern about liability issues with having kids on the road. They've, they've decided against going ahead with it."

Decided against going ahead with it? Those were legitimate concerns, but these were my dreams and hopes. And now my dream had crash-landed, like a plane just off the runway. Down in the wreckage, I felt despair hit me.

Open door.

Open door.

SLAM!

It had closed on me in an instant, and everything came tumbling down. *This is it*, I realized. Maybe I wasn't cut out for this biking thing. The failure of Spoke 2001 had crippled me, and I had spent an entire year away from my bike, struggling with self-doubt and questions. And now those questions seemed to have an answer. *Maybe cycling isn't for me.* If all the doors had closed, should I just give up and go home? Go back to the couch, put the bike up in the garage, and pretend it never happened?

But why...?

Why did I itch to get back on the bike?

Why did I find that God was stirring in me a desire to use this platform for others, particularly kids?

Why had God given me the ridiculous idea that I was capable of pulling someone across the country?

What was it all for, if the bike was only going to end up on the hooks in the garage?

"It's over," I told Ruth. "The door closed."

Clueless and lost, I held on to a shred of hope that there was more to the story.

I settled into the chair, the cushion beneath me releasing a breath of air and the metal frame squeaking a little. I nodded and said hello to others around me as we greeted each other. Someone in front of me leaned over to talk to a friend, a hand on their shoulder. A few seconds passed and then a friend of ours sat down beside me.

"How's it going, Arvid?" Hans Boge Sr. asked me.

"Good, you?" I returned.

"Good, good." He traced the spine of his Bible with his finger. "My son Paul is headed off to Kenya—not sure if you knew that. He'll be going to an orphanage for three months, teaching chemistry and karate." I wasn't sure if I wanted to see those two disciplines mix but didn't say anything. Like a 2x4 swung at my head, Hans' words struck me and dazed me.

If God had been yelling with a bullhorn in my ear it wouldn't have been any clearer. "Here's why the door closed!" He was saying. A door that I'd never heard of had opened.

"What's it called?" I asked.

"Mully Children's Family," Hans responded, hushing his voice as adult Sunday school was about to start. "Run by a guy named Charles Mulli." I thanked him for the information with a nod of my head and settled into my seat to daydream for the next hour.

I'd never met Charles Mulli and I couldn't recall ever hearing of him. This was, to my recollection, the first time I had heard of the organization. When I got home that afternoon I sprinted to the computer—not usually my first place to go—and wrote Charles Mulli a one-page proof of concept for my idea. I addressed it to Mr. Mulli and placed it in an envelope. Before the end of the day I had called Paul Boge and asked him to hand the letter to Mr. Mulli. I don't think he knew what he was carrying, but it was an envelope that contained my hopes and dreams.

Originally my plan had been to be the donkey for the organization. I had no illusions about my ability to be a promoter. I simply wanted to get on my bike and ride, allowing whatever organization I was raising money for to do the promotion. This would be different—Mully Children's Fund (MCF) was in Kenya, Africa, and didn't have an extension in Canada. We would be in charge of the marketing and promotion. I waited with anticipation until, only a few weeks later, I received an email back from Charles Mulli.

My letter had been brief but pretty exact. I had made requests:

1. I would like to borrow three young people from your orphanage and bring them to Canada.
2. They will ride on the back of my modified tandem bike, and I will pull them across the country.
3. They need to be able to communicate clearly and effectively in English.
4. I would prefer that at least one of them be a girl.
5. They need to be comfortable communicating their story.
6. A chaperone from the organization should accompany them.

And last but certainly not least…

7. They need to weigh 100 lbs or less.

I wondered how many requests Charles got every day, week and month. It would help that Paul Boge was vouching for us, but the ridiculousness of my request wasn't changed by anything. What I was attempting to do was preposterous. Why should this man trust me?

Which is why we were completely floored when we opened the email and saw Charles' response:

My wife, Esther, and our eight biological kids have spent a significant time in prayer about this, and we feel undoubtedly that this is from God. We do believe that this is the start of something and that God will bless this. We feel comfortable trusting our kids into your care.

If it was mind-boggling for us, it was just as out of character for them as well. It doesn't take more than a minute with Charles to notice that he cares deeply and lovingly for each of his thousands of kids and would go to great lengths to protect them. To entrust them into my care, on the back of a bike on the side of a highway, was beyond ridiculous.

Yet sometimes God does amazing things with ridiculous.

What amazed me throughout the process was the thoughtfulness that he put into this and every decision. No decision is made in isolation or without consulting God. When he moves forward with something, he takes his first step in full confidence that God is walking beside him. It's a remarkably inspiring way to live life.

With the email came the realization for me that the organization had been found. Now it was up to me to get the kids across the country. I started to look more seriously into the feasibility of the project and knew that I had a lot of work ahead of me. Logistically it would be a challenge; physically it would push me further than I had gone before. Could I even climb a mountain with another person acting as dead weight behind me?

Nevertheless, I was excited. If I've ever had a humanitarian heart it's always been towards kids. Now would come the time for me to put my determination and resolve to the test. The road ahead was a long one.

The clock was ticking. and I could hear it relentlessly as my legs churned another rotation. I pushed my chin down into my collar a little farther, the four layers doing little to protect my skin from the wind. Rarely did I have to dress this warm for biking—if it was this cold, I stayed inside. Especially if I was training. But in this case, with only four weeks to go until I would dip my tire into the Pacific Ocean and fill half a water bottle with its salty water, I couldn't throw away another day, even if it was below zero, sleeting and snowy.

I reached down to grab my water bottle, and when I felt the plastic, I knew what I was about to discover. It took some effort to slide the bottle out of the stiff cage and put it to my mouth.

Frozen. Frozen solid. *Seriously?* I whacked it against my handle bars, nearly losing control and shaking my head to regain my wits. But this wasn't just a piece of ice that needed to be dislodged. All the water had turned to solid ice. I wouldn't be getting any water on this ride. And I had a long way to go before I got home—most of the way around Winnipeg's 90 km perimeter highway. Three times 90 km is 270 km—a day's work for my training. But what was ahead of me wasn't the challenge; it was what was behind me.

I slipped the water bottle back into its cage and stood up on the pedals, putting my weight into my forward motion. But the bike didn't surge like normal, and I had to remember that I was driving the biking equivalent of a limousine—a tandem bike.

Two seats, in line with each other. The back rider merely pedals and has no control over steering, braking or shifting. The back position of a tandem is usually called the "stoker," taken from the job on a train of stoking the engine with coal. In other words, the back person is all brawn and no brain. The front person is the one that knows how to handle a bike. The stoker can often be the stronger of the riders. They get a great view—the spandexed butt of the front rider, though they do have the option of riding without hands, looking around and, if the front rider doesn't immediately notice, taking their feet off the pedals (though it's pretty obvious). The pedals are synced together by a long chain, so you have to communicate if you're going to suddenly stop pedalling with your feet still attached.

You're probably wondering who was crazy enough to join me for three sub-zero blizzard laps around the outside of Winnipeg. The answer is quite simple: No one.

Whereas most tandem riders have a strong stoker to rely on, I was riding empty. Not only that, but I had had a custom-made doll created to adorn the back seat. She was aptly named Sandy—her innards were 50 lbs of sand taken from our backyard sandbox. Not only did I not have a stoker but I had weighed myself down with dead weight. It felt odd biking with it behind me.

A tandem is strange enough to handle with a passenger, never mind a weight that doesn't lean appropriately or put a foot down when you come to a stop at a red light. As such, the usual zest with which I could accelerate was greatly diminished. The bike was significantly heavier than my usual, and I had an extra 50 lbs on the back. Together we weighed roughly 300 lbs, unlike my usual 200 lbs (myself and bike). I had cut the cranks on the pedals down to stubs and fashioned a comfortable seat with a backrest and a safety railing around the entire seat. I'd already taken my son and his friends for short rides, and they approved of the comfort level. Not that Sandy cared.

A car whizzed by on my left, and I shook my head—driving too fast. The road was a sheet of ice, and if they weren't careful they would end up in the ditch. I had to navigate carefully, choose my moments to shift my bike appropriately and plan well in advance. *What am I doing out here?* I asked. So far, we'd had no success getting the Kenyans to Canada. With four weeks left, the departure date was looming. While Charles was working in Kenya, we were doing everything we could here. But it's a hard balance—training for the most daunting physical challenge of your life while simultaneously trying to deal with logistics that would take enough time to cover a full-time job.

My back wheel slipped on the next pedal stroke, and I knew something was wrong. The front had lost traction, and I didn't have time to think. The weight in the back of the bike had all the wrong momentum now, and I hit the ground on my left side, smashing into the ice with my hip and sliding a few feet. The bike slipped out from my legs, and Sandy hit the ground. I was stunned, though thankful that my head hadn't hit. I came to a rest on the ice, my hip sore but all right.

No! I yelled in my head, biting my lip. I had tried moving, and my hip was worse than I thought. I rolled over onto my back, sitting up and taking stock of the situation. Nothing was broken, but it didn't feel good either. Even through my layers and layers of tights I could tell that it would be swelling soon. I struggled to get to my feet, biting my lip. I wasn't sure if my wet face was from tears or the harsh snow and biting sleet. I adjusted my helmet and walked over to the bike. I picked it up, resolving to pay more attention to the surface I was riding on.

Training couldn't wait for another day—I got back on and kept moving, shaking off the wipeout and the chill that had set in in my bones.

The weather didn't really get any nicer, but I kept training. A day or two later I had pulled over to pee into the ditch and left the bike lying on the shoulder. Before I knew it, I heard the sound of a police siren cutting through the freezing cold air, and I turned to see a police officer climbing out of his vehicle. It didn't look like he wanted to be getting out of the heat, and he walked toward me hesitantly. By now I had finished my business and returned to the bike. His eyes were on the bike, showing a lot of concern.

I looked down and pictured the situation from his perspective. With clothing, shoes and braided hair, Sandy looked reasonably like a real kid from a distance—which is clearly what he was thinking.

"Oh!" he said, a lot of relief in his voice, as he neared the bike. Still, there was confusion.

"Good morning, officer," I said, trying my best to sound sane—what kind of a person drags a doll full of sand around in the middle of a May blizzard?

"I thought, I thought it was a kid," he said.

"It's a bag of sand," I said. "Sorry to scare you."

"I'm just glad—didn't think anyone would be stupid enough to take a kid out in this weather." Then he looked at me, taking me in for the first time. Though it would have been extremely stupid to be out in this weather with a kid, it was still really stupid to be out there on my own. "What are you doing out here?"

"Training," I said. "I'll be biking across Canada in three and a half weeks, carrying an orphan from a Kenyan orphanage on the back of my bike."

"Right," he said, as if that suddenly made sense.

"Well, if the weather's anything like this, I'd have something to say if I saw a kid on the back of the bike. I can't stop you from doing this, though. Take care of yourself." He shook his head, burrowing deeper into his jacket. He returned to the cruiser, clearly thankful to be in the warm vehicle. I envied him, but I had chosen my path and hadn't had anything forced on me.

When his vehicle finally disappeared in the fog of the falling snow, I climbed back onto my bike. The bruise on my hip from the wipeout had developed into a hematoma, but I wasn't about to stop. *It better be healed by the time I start!*

Three and a half weeks. And no kids. Every lap of the perimeter I doubted what I was doing. I was injured, training with an injury, and we didn't have any kids. Twenty-five days to the start line, we knew something was wrong. It was a feeling in our stomach when we tried to communicate with those responsible for granting visas. It was the brick walls we ran into when we asked how the process was going. And it was the emails from the Kenyan side, making it sound like this wall was as insurmountable as it seemed on our side.

But there was one thing I was learning from our Kenyan friends, and it was that we have a God who loves dealing with the impossible. Because once things seem impossible, it's finally obvious when God steps in and does something. When we stop being able to accomplish whatever we set out to do, God's hand in the situation becomes that much clearer.

A few of our family and crew members arranged a 24-hour fast, asking God to step in and change things for the better. People cycle across Canada all the time; it wasn't the distance that was the drawing point for our ride. Instead, it was the fact that I planned on pulling a person—a non-participating person—across the country.

While this was the media hook, it also seemed to be the stalling point. Immigration was having a hard time believing that what we were attempting was possible, both logistically and physically. No matter how hard we tried to convince them of what we were doing, they kept repeating, "No one transports someone across the country."

They were convinced that we were up to no good, getting the orphans into the country, smuggling them in only to make them disappear and have them defect. By this point we were getting desperate and had others working on it. Art DeFehr, president of Palliser Furniture, jumped into the fray and got more political parties involved. Joy Smith, MP for Kildonan-St. Paul, spent time in Ottawa lobbying for our group, working tirelessly to convince them that what we were doing was all above board—and possible.

It came down to the point that Art had to promise to personally deliver the kids to the airport and see them onto the plane back to Kenya. We were despairing, and rightly so—without the kids my ride had no one–two punch. I began seriously contemplating starting the ride with Sandy as my passenger, hoping to sub the kids in when they came.

By this time we couldn't shift the dates—Paul Boge's book *Father to the Fatherless* (the life story of MCF founder Charles Mulli) had gone to press, and events were scheduled to coincide with my trip all across the country. The wheels had been set in motion, but we were missing a key ingredient—the passengers.

Knowing that the process was no guarantee, Charles had been training and preparing numerous kids for the task in Canada. They'd sent in applications for more than three kids, knowing that it was unlikely for them to all get approved. After a week fraught with incessant prayers, we heard good news from Joy Smith—15 days prior to the event, their visas had been approved! God had answered our prayer!

I was ecstatic—things were finally on the move. They had been approved, but they still needed to receive their visas (and they were slow in coming). Three kids, all fulfilling my initial prerequisites, were finally chosen and ten days before the ride received their visas. The flights were booked, and they were on the plane the same day, arriving in Canada nine days before we were going to kick off the ride. Ruth and I flew to Toronto to meet with them and spend some time doing media interviews.

I stood anxiously at the airport gate, waiting for kids I'd never met but felt like I knew. The big question running through my mind, though, was *How big are they?*

Finally, amidst a sea of white faces I saw four dark ones—Ndondo, Charles' biological daughter and the chaperone for the ride, Mumina, Lydia and Paul.

Both Mumina and Lydia were just a bit under 100 lbs, but I smiled when I saw Paul. I dubbed him, no more than 65 lbs, my mountain climber, destined to sit on the bike and sway side-to-side during the relentless slow climbs.

It was a whirlwind of activities before we got to the starting line. The Kenyans came to Winnipeg, and we had a backyard BBQ. By now the weather had warmed up, though they used winter parkas and toques (a lot more than any of us did). At one point we stopped to have them introduce themselves and give a brief program. They sang, told their testimony, and in a moment that was entirely emotional and poignant, they recited a poem, "A Street Child I Was."

A street child I was
I had no place to call my home
I had no mother to call my own
No one to care if I lived or died
A street child I was
You say I am unclean and unkempt
Not fit to be seen
You say I am wicked and wild
With a look so mean
But I have to fight just to stay alive
I have got to be tough if I want to survive
I soak to the skin in the monsoon rain
I sleep when I can on roads and deserted dark streets
I ate throwaways from the roadside hotels
Or am forced to dig in the garbage bins
Harsh words, hard blows and careless kicks
On bus stops, stations, markets, streets
You see me everywhere
But you really see me only when you begin to care
Yes, I had no place to call my home
I had no mother to call my own
No one to care if I lived or died
A street child I was

I had tears in my eyes as I realized the weight of the moment. This was the beginning. Everything had built up to this point. I was incredibly nervous—the bad weather had meant a lot less training than I would have liked, and the crash had resulted in a grapefruit-sized lump that still pained me. I was also concerned because my average speed while hauling the sand behind me during training was lower than I had anticipated.

But now, I would have to overcome all my fears and put my concerns aside if this was going to be possible at all. My nerves on fire, I enjoyed the BBQ and the poem, but I had my mind set on the starting line.

A cold early spring training ride with 50 lb Sandy

*MCF kids reciting A Street Child I Was during the Spoke 2005
kickoff at our home*

The entire crew of Spoke 2005

Praying Without Disclaimers
Spoke 2005, Part 1

Walking on my clip shoes can be kind of awkward, and my nerves were on fire this morning. It was early, and the pinkish hue from the sun was setting the world ablaze around me. The approach to the water was concrete, so my shoes were clacking on the ground. Every sound seemed to echo as I approached the water's edge. In my hand was a little water bottle, clutched tightly. It was just a water bottle, but to me it symbolized everything I was doing.

I dipped the bottle into the salty ocean water, letting the power of the Pacific lap into it to fill it up. Behind me the camera crew from CTV was filming, and I was hyperaware that every move was being recorded and would be broadcast on national television. I had set the bar high and the media had responded. The nagging voice in the back of my mind tried to remind me of 2001, that I had bitten off more than I could chew. But I pushed it aside—the only voice I needed to listen to was God's.

Pulling the water bottle out once it was half full, I looked at it again. Some of the sand settled and let me see what was in the bottle clearly: a bookmark with an image of a little girl.

"Arvid," the reporter asked, "what does the bottle represent?"

I swallowed back tears and nerves as I prepared to give an answer. I'd been working on the words for the last few weeks, probably mumbling them in my sleep.

"For me," I began, "this bottle of water represents what I am doing. The waters from the Pacific are us, those that live in the privileged world, and the waters I will add from the Atlantic when I arrive are those that we are trying to help. In the bottle is a picture of a little girl named Charity. She was born to a teenage mom in Kenya. Shortly after, her mom tried to strangle her. But someone intervened. Another time her mom tried to leave her beside the river to die,

165

but again someone intervened. She's now in the care of Mully Children's Family and has a family and hope. No one should be forced to have such a difficult start to life. When the two waters mix, when those who have reach out to those that have not, then we will begin to see lives changed."

"What do you think are the odds of you making it across the country like this?" The reporter, his face stuck behind the camera, indicated the bike I was now standing beside. I was still holding the water bottle, the bookmark jostling around in the salt water.

"I don't know," I said. "Around 50 percent. Well, 51." I laughed. "But I know that I have a 100 percent chance of making a difference."

There were only a few minutes left, and I went to speak to Ruth. There are no words that can be said in the moments leading up to a ride that will even begin to speak into what is about to happen. As soon as I make that first move, things are unpredictable. Within hours the nerves can turn into cramps, and things can unravel faster than you can say *What just happened?* I gave her a kiss and called the crew to gather around me.

Mumina was on the back of the bike, comfortable in the soft chair. A roll bar was around him, acting a little bit like a seatbelt. The pedals had been sawed off, and solid footrests were there. All in all, it was a lot cosier a seat than the one I was about to climb into. As the crew came together, I nodded at each one: Ndondo—Charles Mulli's biological daughter, Paul—my mountain climber, Lydia—the third to ride on the bike (and the lead singer), Stephanie—my daughter, Josh—her boyfriend and the bike mechanic, Paul Boge—author of Charles' biography and media contact, David and Hermine—drivers of the motorhome. God had assembled a good team.

With the clock ticking down, the crew began to pray for me, for this ride and for their friends back in Kenya. It was an emotional experience. The kids, young though they were, had absolute faith in God's goodness. They prayed with an eloquence and passion that I only wished I had, switching from English to Swahili and then back again. I let their words wash over me, knowing just why Jesus told the little children to come to Him. It was so inspiring, so moving, that we all had tears in our eyes as we broke from the prayer circle. I climbed onto the bike, clipped my foot into the pedal and waited for the official countdown. There were calls, cheers and hollers as I pulled away. An entire country lay between me and my destination, and it all started with a simple pedal stroke.

When reality hits, it hits hard. This was a lesson in realizing that ultra-marathon cycling is unpredictable. You'd expect the problems to start halfway into the ride, but my expectations were shattered within the first few hours.

It was hot, very hot. BC had been hit by a heat wave (though it's usually rainy and cool), and it was wreaking havoc on my system. Heat makes it incredibly difficult to maintain food intake. In the Death Valley race it had been heat that had twice been my downfall. I had only started, and I refused to let the heat beat me up.

I could feel the sweat dripping down my back. I reached for the water bottle in the rack below me and pulled it out, spraying it into my mouth. It tasted nasty, hotter than lukewarm. No matter how much ice we put in the bottles it only took a few minutes for it to take on the temperature of its surroundings. Temperatures were over 35 degrees Celsius, and my stomach had already shut down. Welcome to day 1 of 30.

The incessant Coquihalla climb was wearing me down, the weight of Mumina behind me making it more difficult than I had even realized it could be. With a gut-wrenching spasm of my stomach I knew that I needed to pull over. I had barely gotten my foot out of the clips when the food made its return. Hands on the handlebars, straddling my bike and doing my best to prevent it from tipping, I puked my guts out over the handlebar.

Another heave came and caught me off guard. I wiped my mouth, then felt the gentlest of taps on my shoulder. Not used to riding with someone behind me, I turned to see Mumina with a look of horror on his face. Behind me, the support vehicle had stopped, but I waved them away. Mumina's look of horror quickly morphed into a look of concern, and his words, simple though they were, cut me to the core.

"Meesta Avid, I'm praying for you."

Though I'd just lost a bunch of liquid out the front, I still had enough to feel the tears welling up in my eyes. I tried to picture this scenario from the kids' perspective: growing up in slums, fighting for life and hooked on drugs, rescued by a miracle man who gave them a home, food and love, transported 15,000 km to a country they'd probably never even heard of before, seeing luxury and wealth, then plunking down behind this middle-aged white man and being dragged across the country on a bike, only to see him puke out his guts 5 hours into a 30-day journey. Instead of a mental breakdown, Mumina's response was simple and a godsend—"I'm praying for you."

God bless these kids, with faith that can move mountains.

I left the food and all my expectations on the side of the road.

Averaging 240 km/day in about 14 to 15 hours of riding, I traversed the mountains and came into the prairies. They had taken their toll on my body, but I wasn't letting it show. There was too much country left for me to be showing any signs of weakness. Getting to our home—Winnipeg—was only one-third of the way.

The tunnels of the mountain had foreshadowed the ride. A tunnel that curves so the middle is in the dark has three parts: the beginning, middle and end. At the beginning, you're excited to enter the darkness. The light behind you is still shining, guiding you. At the end, you can see the light from the outside once more and you feel rejuvenation in your legs.

But the middle, oh, the middle.

I call it the "middle third syndrome." The excitement of the beginning has disappeared. The adrenaline of seeing the end hasn't hit yet. The middle is that place where you question everything you're doing. You're stuck with no hope, nothing to go on. That middle third changes in length in relation to the length of the ride. It's the part where I feel most strongly the urge to quit. Everyone feels it—the crew, the rider, even the flower girls on the side of the road.

If the first third was this bad, what would the middle look like?

"How much farther to Brandon?" I called out, needing to yell so the support crew inside the Golf could hear me. The wind was whipping me, making my rain jacket flap like a sail gone crazy. It was raining, pouring rain. The rain jacket was just another layer of warmth now; the water had soaked through to my skin and permeated every crack and crevice.

"Fifty, maybe sixty kilometres," Ruth responded. I nodded resolutely. The numbers matched my mental math. When you're on the bike as long as I am, you have lots of time to think. Some of the time I pray, some of the time I dream about what I would do if I wasn't riding, some of the time I come up with awesome one-line jokes for the crew (don't believe them when they say they're corny). Some of the time I crunch the numbers of speed, average, distance, calories and pretty much anything that can be multiplied or divided. By the time the crew has run the numbers through the calculator I have a pretty good idea of the answer myself. But it's good to keep them sharp.

I looked down at the speedometer on my bike. It was hovering down around 12 km/h. It reminded me of 1999, when I'd suffered massive headwinds through the prairies. Was history repeating itself?

"I won't make it there on time," I said, hanging my head. "Not at this speed. Not unless something changes." Ruth, always optimistic blended with realistic, nodded. There was a presentation in Brandon where the kids would be singing. We had done our best to estimate what I was capable of, but the weather had its own mind.

Behind me, Lydia was hunkered down in a parka so that only a small strip of her face was visible. Up ahead, the motorhome was pulled over on the side of the road. Ruth and the follow vehicle pulled ahead to go speak to those in the motorhome. The rest of the Kenyans were out on the roadside, fully covered in their parkas. I pulled in beside them, resting my foot on the ground.

Ndondo approached the bike, and the rest of the kids came with her. "They want to pray for the wind," she said. All around me, the kids put their hands on my wet arms, on the bike, on the seat, on each other and began to pray. They prayed with strength, conviction and devotion. Living in desperate situations and through major crises, they had come to rely on God in a way I had never had to. When the only hope left for rain through a drought, food through a famine or healing through disease is God, you pray with a fervency that I'd never experienced. And they never prayed with disclaimers, as if to soften the blow when something doesn't happen. They prayed for the wind to change direction—no excuses, no exceptions. Nothing but a miracle.

I got back on the bike, a smile on my wet face. My sunglasses kept the rain out of my eyes, and I hung my head to shield it with the front of the helmet. I was moving again, and before I knew it things began to change. I can't say for sure that the wind changed, but the road shifted from northeast to east, and we managed to get a slight cross-tailwind. I thanked God nonetheless, resolving that I needed to come to God the way the kids did: If there's an issue, you simply pray. God is neither too big nor too busy to be involved in the little things.

When Quitting Is Not an Option

Brandon came and went. Portage came and went. Winnipeg was finally in sight (mentally). The weather wasn't as brutal and, as the first third was coming to an end, I was excited about pulling up to the legislative building and seeing family and friends. Until this ride, all my rides had ended in Winnipeg. This time would be different, as I'd be continuing on to triple the distance I'd just accomplished. There had been discussion about whether it would mentally be easier to stop at the legislative building or to skip Winnipeg altogether and take the perimeter. As hard as it might be to get back on the bike and leave the city, I didn't want to pass the opportunity to see loved ones and hold a press conference.

Already things were buzzing; Global TV, CBC and CTV were covering our arrival into Winnipeg, sending crews either out onto the highway or to the legislative buildings. Everyone wanted to know what time I would arrive, but it's not easy to predict. We had scheduled a day off in Winnipeg for some rest and recuperation, as well as in hopes that the media would be interested in talking to us. That day off came at the perfect time, because between Portage La Prairie and Elie—

A sharp pain shot through my right thigh. I nearly screamed out loud, controlling it and only letting a gasp out, so the kid behind me wouldn't notice. I stopped pedalling, looking down at my leg. It felt like my flesh had torn off my bone, the pain searing into my brain and taking over everything. I pushed the pedal around again, but the pain bit in worse than the first time.

What is happening?

I kept looking down, expecting to see loose bits of muscle and skin hanging off my leg, torn and on fire. But there was nothing. My thigh looked normal. I pedalled again. The pain coursed through my body and made me bite my lip. I couldn't fight back the tears. Thankful that the Kenyan kid was sitting behind me, I let the tears flow.

I contemplated pulling over but couldn't bring myself to do it. Even when I wasn't pushing, the pain was shooting through my leg. It wouldn't leave, and I didn't know what to do about it. If this pain continued, there was no way I was getting anywhere, unless…

Resolved to fight on, I decided that I could make it work. With my clipped shoes, I could still provide power on the upstroke, pulling instead of pushing. With no other option, my left leg took over and did 90 percent of the work, my right leg simply hanging loosely on the side and coming along for the ride. It was a testament to the level of my training that, with only one leg doing the work, I was able to make a 300-plus lb. package move at all. The conditions were good, and I wanted to get to Winnipeg. Winnipeg meant seeing my family, and it also meant a day off the bike.

I pulled up to the legislative building with a forced smile on my face. The pain had not subsided at all. If anything, it had intensified. Loved ones swarmed me with congratulations and well wishes, and I let them wash over me. We were going through a crew change, though because of the day off it wouldn't be rushed. Stephanie and Josh were done, as were Dave and Hermine. Bob and Donna would replace them in the motorhome, while my son, Paul, and my nephew Kevin would take over in the follow car.

I had told Ruth, but that was it. The pain would remain a secret, for now. I had wiped the tears from my face before I entered the city and kept them at bay while a few friends drove past us, parking on the side of the road and waving us on.

The news cameras were in my face, and I did what I could to answer their questions. A TV reporter wanted to test out the comfort level of the backseat, so I took her for a spin around the legislative building while others laughed and took pictures. The kids sang, danced and told their stories on camera. A few local politicians were present, and I was thankful for the buzz we had created. But through the back of my mind the questions were churning. *Have I done it again? Have I overtaxed my body, created a media maelstrom that will be my downfall if the ride collapses? Will this be 2001 all over again?*

Off the bike, the pain gradually subsided. In the back of my mind the next time I climbed onto the bike was a giant hanging question mark. It plagued me the next day, a day that should have been filled with fun and joy. It started at 6 a.m., with an appearance with Paul and Mumina on *Canada AM* (CTV), then continued with five other media interviews. The evening was capped with the official book launch for *Father to the Fatherless*, where Joy Smith had a presentation for the children and hundreds gathered to be introduced to MCF in a significant way.

When Quitting Is Not an Option

The light was just arriving on the horizon ahead of me, though its presence was marred by the clouds and rain pouring down on me once again. We saw many beautiful sunrises on our journey, but that was not one of them. Cars driving by cheered us on, honking to show their support. Leaving Winnipeg behind, my mind was full of doubts. *When is the pain going to come back?* I thought, *How long will this last?*

Half an hour, apparently.

The pain arrived with vengeance after a day off. Again, it felt like flesh was searing off of my bone, though nothing on the outside appeared strange. *Is my leg on fire?* I bit my lip to prevent myself from screaming. Behind me, in the warm cabin of the support crew vehicle, they were aware of my difficulties. I'd told the crew that morning, and we'd been praying that the pain would stay away.

But it didn't, and I knew it was over. Tears arrived, both of pain and of futility. I couldn't fight the pain, and I knew I couldn't bike 4,500 km on one leg, no matter how strong that leg was.

The car pulled up beside me, and as soon as they saw my face they knew. "We've got an impromptu performance," Paul said. "A tree nursery said they'll have their workers out at the side of the road."

I nodded, not saying anything. It wasn't much longer before I saw the motorhome on the side of the road and people already gathered. Workers from the tree nursery were out in the cold and the rain, clapping along to the kids' singing and listening as they shared the pain and triumph of their lives.

I appreciated the support but couldn't get my mind off of my leg. Ruth and I had a hushed conversation in front of the motorhome, where I shared the desperation I was in. Unless something changed, it was over. I needed a miracle, and I needed it now.

Fighting the pain, I struggled all the way to Kenora. When we arrived there, I crawled into bed, pulled the blankets close around me and went to sleep, thinking that I had reached the end. At the time, however, the Kenyans had something else in mind. They formed a prayer group for healing, and I slept on. While it's one thing to say that we believe in the power of prayer, it's another thing entirely to rely on it. That's how they lived out their faith.

I woke up the next morning not even sure if I'd be able to stand up. If there's one thing I've learned about ultra-marathon cycling, it's always to leave the decision until the morning, because things look different then. Never make the decision to quit in the middle of mental and emotional pain. It's always essential to get back on the bike one more time and give it one more try. See what happens, and then decide.

With the weight of 830 Kenyans and hundreds of Canadians on my shoulders, I clipped my shoes into the pedals again. I started riding, wondering when the pain would come back. I winced every time my leg went around, expecting my flesh to ignite once more.

But it never came back.

The ride would continue. The miracle had happened. The pain stayed away and has never come back.

I had crossed half the country by this point, though I wasn't expecting anything to get any easier. A ride of this length, with different people from different countries and cultures, can be quite entertaining. The kids had the opportunity to swim in the Great Lakes when we stayed overnight on their shores, and it was at that same place that Mumina learned to ride a bike for the first time in his life. Nothing could quite compare to hearing the laughter (and shrieks) of a teenager wobbling on two wheels.

We'd been on the news after our visit to Sault Ste. Marie, so Sudbury was expecting us. Though entering Winnipeg has often been a grand and enjoyable experience, we were thoroughly impressed by the hospitality of Sudbury. Since they had heard about us, cars were stopping to let us go, honking and waving, being more generous than any other drivers I've met. Even when we more or less missed our turn towards the hotel we'd be staying in, five lanes of traffic opened up and let us through. It was at that hotel that Lydia was given a chance to speak to the media for an extended period of time, sharing her life story.

With their warm winter parkas, the kids looked oddly out of place on the back of my bike. Even as the temperatures climbed (and the rain stopped), they refused to take the parkas off. I issued a challenge: wear shorts, and you get ice cream. It took more than a few days and a high of over 30 degrees for Paul Gachoka to finally put shorts on and take off the winter parka. I'm not quite sure how ice cream made sense as a prize, but it worked.

The hills around the Great Lakes provided good room to let the brakes go and fly downhill. In the mountains, I'd been worried about curves and crazy winds, but the slopes in Ontario are straight and steep. Every time we went down a major hill the kids would ask me what speed we'd hit. When they got off the bike there'd be good-natured joking and taunting each other, comparing speeds. Mumina set the record early on and it held: 72 km/h.

When the Kenyan crew stopped at a restaurant for breakfast one day they had the surprise of seeing themselves on the morning newscast. The people in the restaurant hushed as the TV was turned up, everyone looking back and forth between the screen and them. With the encouragement of the patrons, they gave an impromptu performance, earning themselves applause and support.

One evening, after a cancelled event because we'd gotten some wires crossed, things got a little loopy in the hotel. The kids had always been ready to entertain us, whether it be with dancing, singing or cracking jokes. With a lot of energy (did we feed them sugar?) they launched into a sarcastic recap of the Spoke 2005 promo video that they saw every night. They had the words memorized by now and were dramatizing what was on the screen. But the laughter didn't end there—they were soon mocking my own attempts at getting on the bike. Being inflexible meant it usually took my leg a lot of momentum to get over the bar, and Mumina could mimic it perfectly. They told Charles Mulli's story, imitating his accent and voice with precision: "Born way back..." They went through each member of the crew, imitating our personalities and quirks.

With laughter rolling, the crew got closer and closer as the miles ticked by.

Vancouver to Winnipeg crew beside the motorhome

Custom seat for the Kenyan passengers

Crowd welcomes Arvid at legislative buildings in Winnipeg

Dream Big
Spoke 2005, Part 2

Sometimes it's better not to tell the rider the truth…

We were nearing the southern Ontario basin, and I had scheduled a bike tune-up. Since I was putting on 1,000 km every four days, it was getting a reasonable amount of wear and tear. Kevin and Paul put the tandem on the rack (it stuck out almost a foot either side of the VW Golf) and drove to Kitchener-Waterloo for the tune-up and to get the chain replaced (chains stretch over time). When they came back, they mentioned something about "the bike should be OK," and I thought I heard the words "fell off," but I figured if the bike shop deemed it safe to ride I'd be fine.

Only later did Paul tell me the entire story. The bike rack sticks out off the hitch and has four places for mounting the bike, held by a metal plate and secured by three wingnuts (between each of the four mounts). Thinking it was the safest place to put it, they had the tandem held in the first spot, closest to the vehicle. While they were travelling somewhere around 100 to 120 km/h on one of Ontario's highways it popped loose, the metal bending from the wingnut and up. In retrospect it would have been safer to put the bike in the second slot, since a wingnut could secure it from both sides.

But it didn't hold, and the bike decided it didn't want to stay on the rack anymore. Paul was driving, and he (like me) has the continual habit of checking the rear-view mirror to make sure the bike is still solidly attached. He noticed it leaning askew and hit the brakes to pull to the side of the road. That was enough to jar it loose from its holdings, and it came forward, hitting the back of the Golf (leaving a mark that's there to this day), then landing on the hitch extension that held the rack. He estimates its two wheels hit the ground somewhere around 70 to 80 km/h, bouncing once or twice before skidding sideways while they stopped in the gravel on the side of the road.

When Quitting Is Not an Option

They looked at each other like they'd been caught breaking a window with a baseball, though it was much, much more serious. They popped it back up, put it in the safest slot, and continued driving—heading to the repair shop. When they got there, they mentioned to the mechanics that they should inspect the tires and wheels and check if they were true. When all came back mechanic-approved, they breathed a sigh of relief.

And decided not to tell me until after the ride was done.

Though it added a thousand kilometres to a cross-Canada journey, a large contingent of MCF's biggest supporters were in southern Ontario. We weren't interested in setting any records across the country (never mind that, as far as we knew, we were the first to do what we were doing), so the extra thousand was a small sacrifice to give the kids a chance to see Niagara Falls and Toronto and meet many more supporters.

My brother Art lives in St. Catharines and met us on his bike to escort me to Niagara Falls, where the kids got to see the wonder, take pictures and spend part of an afternoon. I wondered what it looked like from their perspective. At MCF there is a small river that winds its way across their property. Throughout the course of a year it changes dramatically—from a source of life and place to swim to a trickle in an empty riverbed during the dry seasons. When they experience drought it dries up, making the bridges across look foolish. Yet here we were, a giant waterfall continuously pouring water over its edge, the mist billowing up hundreds and thousands of feet in every direction.

We stayed that night in my brother's home, and the crew had their second transition. Kevin and our drivers, Bob and Donna, would leave, while Jodi (my oldest daughter) and George and Erika, along with their daughter Laura, would join us to head to the finish (still 10 days away). The addition of Laura was particularly helpful for the Kenyans, as she was only a few years older than Lydia.

Another red light.

I stopped and put my foot down, resting it on the curb. Behind me was the support crew. Over time I had gotten used to hearing the quiet purr of the engine constantly behind me, the crunching of the tires in the gravel on the side of the road. But here, in the heart of Toronto, there was noise everywhere. Engines, horns, people talking.

A few pedestrians walked by on the sidewalk, looking at our tandem with curiosity. I smiled and waved, prompting Paul Gachoka to do the same. He was behind me, and the rest of the MCF crew had gone to a church in Oakville for a performance. Up on our left was the Gardiner Expressway, snaking its way above the city.

"So, what do you think?" I asked Paul, clipping my foot into the pedal as the light across from me turned yellow. Getting started on a tandem can be extremely awkward, but this was about my thousandth repetition by now. I threw my body forward, getting some momentum behind the bike, and then started pedalling, clipping my left foot in.

"It's big," Paul said.

"For the next day," I explained, "we'll be driving more or less in city the whole time."

His eyes went big, comprehending but not digesting. There were some glass condos on the right, their rippled glass distorting our image as we passed them by. I caught a glimpse of Paul in the backseat. We had bought a Gameboy for the kids to play on the back of the bike. It had become such an obsession for them at all times that we had made a rule—you could only play it while on the bike. Before the rule they'd gotten onto the bike with less-than-ideal enthusiasm. After the rule, Paul and Mumina would fight over who could go on. They mostly played Super Mario Brothers. I smiled as I saw Paul behind me because, though the Gameboy was still in his hands, his eyes weren't looking at the screen. They were taking everything in, swallowing it whole and comparing it to what he had known.

Though we, in our concrete and glass world, certainly have culture shock when we go to a developing country, I can't imagine what his culture shock was like. You see, we have seen commercials, movies and shows that take place in other locations. We've seen pictures of slums (if only for a second, because we pass over them), and we know that poverty and desperation exists. But someone like Paul has grown up in a world much different than ours. Sure, the African children may hear about the luxury in North America, but their access to images is severely limited. Their lives are about survival, about finding the next place to sleep, the next piece of garbage to eat or the next hit to take away the pain.

There were some tall buildings in front of us, perhaps 30 or 40 storeys tall. For the moment it looked like one of them had a peak coming out of it, though

When Quitting Is Not an Option

I knew better. Hidden by perspective behind those high rises was the CN Tower, the tallest (at the time) freestanding building in the world.

"Just you wait," I said. "There's a building coming up you're going to like."

"Mr. Arvid," he said, tapping me on the back. "Why do all the cars only have one person in them?"

I didn't know how to answer him. In Kenya, it's not uncommon to see a *matatu* (bus-taxi) with people crammed into it, hanging onto the sides or even climbing on the roof. Given the level of extreme poverty, the ratio of cars to people is quite low. If you need to go somewhere, you walk.

"Because a lot of people have cars," I answered.

He was silent, and I became silent too. The night before we had driven to a performance on the freeway. We had used the carpool lane, because there were four of us in the car. It was remarkable how few cars could jump into the lane where only cars with two or more passengers were allowed.

Driving in city traffic is always more stressful than on the highway. You have to keep your eyes out for cars, and your rhythm gets broken up by traffic lights. Start. Cruise. Stop. Start. Slow down. Speed up. Cruise. Stop. You can't, even for a second, put your head down and focus on your biking. Though I had chosen the route intentionally (and the best was yet to come), I was getting frustrated. I looked forward to being out of the concrete jungle and back on the road.

We snaked forward with traffic, Lakeshore Boulevard leading us directly under the Gardiner. Our view of the tower was obstructed, and I worried that we would have to pass it by without seeing it. But my fears were alleviated.

Suddenly, there it was, rising up from the concrete like it had simply grown out of the ground. I heard Paul give a sharp intake of air and appreciated seeing something I had grown somewhat accustomed to from a new perspective.

"It's called the CN Tower," I said, "and it's the tallest building in the world."

"We learned about it in school," he said. But he didn't say more, and I knew he was taking it in.

I wondered then, as I do now, what it would be like to see the world from a fresh perspective. If we had come from poverty and pain, ruin and desperation, would we be so quick to judge, criticize and condemn our country? Would we take for granted the things we have around us? *How long will it take someone like Paul,* I wondered, *to lose the appreciation and awe that he just experienced?*

Though the riding had been difficult after Winnipeg and Kenora, I had continued to get stronger day after day. By the time I had finished two-thirds of the ride and arrived in St. Catharines I was in good shape. Usually a ride tears me down, but because of the length of this one I had planned recovery time. Though I biked 14 to 16 hours a day, that was less than on many other rides. As such, I was getting around 5 hours of sleep, enough time for my muscles and body to recover and rebuild. We'd designed a schedule with performances and timing for media in mind, but after St. Catharines and Toronto, I distinctly remember thinking, *How can we move the schedule forward?*

I would arrive at the hotel at the end of the day with plenty of time for supper and a good break. My legs were itching, not out of tiredness but out of a desire to ride more. Not to say it was easy—every day still had its moment—but from a riding perspective I mostly enjoyed it. *What difference does it make how many days it takes?* I asked myself, wondering if anyone would notice if it was a day or two shorter.

But changing the schedule would be a nightmare, so I stuck with it. The weather had turned gorgeous, and we hardly had a drop of rain moving forward. Though the course was still hilly, it remained close to the St. Lawrence and didn't climb too much. Plus, I'd been working out for the last 20-plus days and was strong by now.

I pulled to a stop at the motorhome, and my son, Paul, jumped out of the follow vehicle to grab the bike. With the kid on the back I couldn't simply lean it down to get off of it, so dismounting was more awkward. We were roughly two hours out of Ottawa, and Paul Boge was constantly on the phone, trying to arrange media interviews.

Ruth came walking towards me, and I could tell that something was wrong.

"What's wrong?" I asked, moving out of earshot of the others.

"Paul's been on the phone for half an hour," she said, "and he's not getting through to them."

"Who's 'them'?"

When Quitting Is Not an Option

"*Ottawa Citizen*," she answered. They are Ottawa's biggest paper. Getting them to write an article could mean a huge amount of exposure. We had had an incredible amount of success so far—many cities had articles in their paper, and large TV outlets had joined us in select spots. Regional television had covered us in a few locations as well. I wasn't entirely sure, but the count for articles and interviews was nearing 50.

"You mean he can't get them on the line?" I asked.

"No," Ruth said. I could tell she didn't want to say any more, but she knew I would get it out of her. "They think you're a fraud."

Whatever food was in my stomach plummeted right to the bottom. It's one of the curses of doing something extreme—if you do something ordinary, no one cares. If you do something extreme, some might think you're faking it or, even worse, cheating. "They told Paul they think you're sitting in the motorhome and putting a kid on the back of the bike when you get to the limits of cities."

"That's ridiculous," I said.

"That's what Paul said."

"But they don't believe him?"

"No, they don't," she agreed.

If they thought I was cheating and they decided to publish something to that effect, well—this entire thing could come crashing down around me. Frustration rose inside me and I said, "Do cheaters feel like quitting 10 times a day? Do they lose 20 pounds in 20 days?"

"Arvid, it's not me that's accusing you," Ruth said.

"I know, I know," I admitted.

"Good news." Paul Boge's voice drifted from around the motorhome. He came to talk to us. "They agreed to look at footage from CTV and Global—if those places covered it, then they're willing to at least take a look."

"Good," I said. "They had their cameras out on the road and got some footage. It's no joke."

"We'll deal with it," Ruth said. "Just get back on the bike."

I nodded, the frustration cutting deep. It felt like something was being torn away from me, something that I knew couldn't be taken from me. Yet somehow it felt like they were trying all they could.

It wasn't long after, as we entered the streets of Ottawa, that I heard back from the crew. Paul Boge gave me some great news.

"They're going to come out to cover you at the parliament buildings," he said. "They're in."

And they were. We arrived at the parliament buildings with no fanfare (unlike in Winnipeg), but *Ottawa Citizen* was there, and we enjoyed an amazing picnic on the front lawn. The kids dug into some hotdogs from a vendor and were spun in circles by my son, Paul, on the grass, and the entire crew stood around the eternal flame and prayed for our nation, following it up with singing "O Canada." Considering that we were crossing the entire country in 30 days it was a rather unique and moving experience for me. We finished up (I was always itching to be back on the move) and took a ferry across the river.

We had beautiful weather up the St. Lawrence, and the mornings were incredibly calm and almost—dare I say it—enjoyable. I made Ndondo get up at 4 a.m. and join the crew one morning, just to see what it was like. The Kenyans were getting soft waking up at 6 a.m., and I wanted them to experience ultramarathon cycling first-hand. The follow crew (at this time Paul, Jodi and Ruth) were asleep even less than me. In order to maximize my rest they would be working after I went to sleep and waking up before me, packing the vehicles and getting me up only when the bike was ready and I could literally walk out the door and climb on.

The wind was more in my favour for this stretch than not, and the end was (somewhat) in sight. At Riviere-du-Loup you turn from heading northeast to southeast, avoiding the tip of Maine and then, after a stint going east, dropping south into New Brunswick. But on the run-up to Riviere-du-Loup, things started to sour.

I had started hearing a strange noise coming from the bike. I'm quite familiar with the different sounds that a bike can make when it is in distress, but this was somewhat different. It started just as a soft crunching, like sand had gotten in somewhere. It progressed and progressed, until it was the gut-wrenching sound of metal grinding on metal.

Worse than that, I could feel it. Every turn of the crank was getting harder. Whatever was happening, it was destroying my efficiency. Each pedal stroke required more energy than the last, and before I knew it the circumstances had completely destroyed my mood.

It was only four or so days to the finish, and we decided we would try to make it. After all, we had no alternative bike (the only option, in case of extreme emergency, was using my single road bike with a bag of sand strapped to the back). Since bike shops are only open during the day, stopping to get it looked at would mean losing time. We opted to push on, past Riviere-du-Loup.

Finally, I had had enough. Every pedal crank was loud, and I knew this wouldn't last until Halifax. It had to be fixed or I'd be dead on the road. Jodi and Paul drove the bike back to Edmundston, the nearest reasonably large town. It offered one bike shop, and they went in looking disheartened. As Paul described the problems to them, their faces fell.

"The back crank is grinding," he said. "We can only assume the bearings are shot." Tandems have two cranks—the one I turn and then, connected by a long chain, the one the second rider is supposed to turn. The chain doesn't go through any derailleurs, so the pedals actually spin in sync. On my bike, however, the pedals had obviously been cut off. That back crank is unique—it has a ring on both sides. The one on the left receives the chain from my pedals, the other turns the triple-ring that powers the back wheel. It was that back crank that was causing the problems; its bearings had presumably ground down to dust.

The mechanic took one look at the bike and said, "We can't do anything for it; we don't have an axle long enough."

"What do you mean?" Paul asked.

"Since it's a tandem the axle has to be longer. It's got to pass through two rings and out to the pedals. Our longest would probably be 10 mm too short. It would throw everything off, especially the shifting. That is, if I can even get it in there."

Paul had already explained what the bike was being used for and just how desperate we were. "We have to try," he said. "And we need it tonight."

The mechanic must have seen the look of desperation in his eyes because he finally gave in. "I'll see what I can do."

They got the bike back, short axle and all, and drove back to the hotel we were staying in. We'd had to end the day early because we needed to make it to the bike shop before it closed, so I'd had a relaxing day. There were 750 km and four days left, which gave me plenty of time. Paul explained the bike situation to me, and I tested it out on the parking lot.

"It'll work," I agreed.

It was early in the morning, the brilliant sun lighting up the road in front of me. I had never gotten used to the sunrises—each day they were more amazing than the last. Part of me realized that with each sunrise, too, I was another day closer to my goal.

Because of the tiring schedule of the trip, we had placed Sandy, our extra-weight doll (filled with sand), on the back of the bike and allowed the kids to sleep in. They would catch up to us two to three hours later, and we'd swap her back out for a real, live body.

Standing up on my pedals for a moment, I was cruising at good speed when I shifted into the big ring and—

Shoot! The chain had fallen off. Twenty-seven days into the ride and for the first time the chain had come off.

I pulled to the side of the road, flagging Paul from the vehicle behind me. He'd already seen the problem and was out of the follow vehicle before it had come to a stop, prancing barefoot on the loose gravel.

"Ouch!" he exclaimed, getting to my side.

"I can't reach back to put it on," I said. On my own bike I could reach down and fix the problem, but on the tandem the chain was three feet behind me.

"No problem," he said, pulling the derailleur forward and slipping the chain back on. "It was on the big ring?" he asked.

"Yep," I responded, my foot already starting to move.

"That's odd," he said. "Normally it falls off to the inside."

I was gone and he ran back to the car, nursing his sore feet. I didn't have much sympathy for him (I usually don't for the crew), and I kept biking. I wondered if the chain falling off had anything to do with the repairs the bike had undergone but shrugged it off. It was a freak occurrence, I figured, and it wouldn't happen again. The entire exchange had taken 20, maybe 30 seconds.

Twenty minutes later, with Paul fast asleep (again) in the follow vehicle, I was making my way up a slow and gradual climb that curved off to the left. The shoulder was wide—some of the New Brunswick shoulders are so wide you could fit a car on them lengthwise—and I was enjoying the space.

Up ahead, a half-ton truck came from around the curve in my direction. Nothing abnormal. Until I realized that he was going unreasonably fast and—he wasn't maintaining the curve!

My heart began to beat faster as he entered the oncoming lane. I waited for him to get back into the correct lane, but he wasn't budging. *Move!* I thought.

When Quitting Is Not an Option

But then his tire did what I was hoping and praying it wouldn't—touch the white line on our side of the road. And I realized, he was asleep!

I was freaking out, my breathing getting quicker. Going up a climb my speed was down to 9 or 10 km/h, meaning I was a lot less nimble than if I was moving fast. I couldn't just jump out of the way, which is what I wanted to do. He was bearing down on me, now completely on my extra-wide shoulder.

He hadn't slowed one bit before his vehicle smashed into the guardrail that protected him from a steep drop. The sound of the metal smashing on the rail was terrifying, and I wanted to close my eyes. I had nowhere to go, yet he was coming right at me. He bounced off, back into the lane of traffic, but the curve meant that he came back to the guardrail. He hit it again. Bounced again. Hit again. Came off just slightly. Then finally smashed into the rail one last time and screeched as the metal did everything it could to stop his vehicle.

My heart still in my throat, I waited as he came to a stop in a massive cloud of dust that hid his truck, less than a hundred feet in front of us. I was terrified and could hardly speak. My tongue caught in my throat, and I turned back to look at Ruth and Paul. Their eyes were wide, in shock and horror.

One hundred feet.

Less than one hundred feet.

That's what separated me from becoming the newest hood ornament on a smashed truck. Given that my crew was only 20 or 30 feet behind me, they would likely have joined the wreckage. I was horrified at the possibility but amazed and astounded that we were OK.

As I pulled up beside, I looked into the vehicle. The man was already moving, climbing out. Ruth and Paul pulled over to stop, helping him out. Surprisingly, he escaped with practically no injuries. Within minutes a tow truck and a friend was on the way for him. Ruth and Paul gave him some water and food and continued on to catch up to me.

At the time we didn't make a big deal of the crash. Way before the ride had started we had talked significantly about safety. I had made it clear to Charles Mulli that we were on highways, technically unprotected. Though the kids always wore a helmet (as do I), risk was inherent in what we were doing. Charles was reassuring and reminded me that he was aware of that but he prayerfully considered the risk/benefit and knew that the impact the ride would make was far greater than the risk. Thankfully, that morning we didn't have a kid on the back of the bike.

Nonetheless, I still had the thought, *Wow, that could have been really serious.*

When I talked with Paul and Ruth later, Paul commented, "Remember—the chain came off?"

And he was right: 20 to 30 seconds.

One hundred feet.

Had the chain not come off, we would have been directly in the truck's path. All of us. It would have ended everything. A carelessly tired driver could have derailed (pun fully intended) our ride and the future of our ministry. But he didn't—all because of a fluky mechanical problem.

Or so we thought.

Back in Winnipeg we had arranged a prayer team that would rotate through every seven days, spending a significant amount of time in prayer for myself and the team for an entire day. One of the prayer team members was our friend Weldon. He woke up at 3 a.m., restless and unable to sleep. He started to pray, feeling specifically the need to pray for my safety. He told his wife, Arlene, that he couldn't sleep, left the bed and went downstairs to pray.

Taking into account the time zones, Weldon was praying for me that morning as my chain derailed and as a truck careened around a corner and came head-on. Clearly, his prayers were answered effectively. God could have completely removed the danger, but He did something even more unique—He knocked off a chain, delayed our travel and saved me by a hundred feet or less. All to show us how powerful He is and that He cared about what I was doing.

It's a lesson I'll never forget.

I woke up feeling groggy, which wasn't all that unusual. After all, each day I was pushing myself farther than I'd ever biked before, sleeping less than normal and battling the fatigue, exhaustion and indifference that came with the territory. Every other day on a ride I seemed to be in a funk. Heck, every other hour I passed through a funk and came out the other side (hopefully).

I always have issues.

This day, the feeling was stronger than usual. I couldn't get out of bed. The crew had gotten up, Paul was already outside with the bike's lights flashing and the vehicle all packed, and I was comfy in the warmth of the hotel bed. I could feel my legs under the sheet and didn't want to remove them. I could see my cycling shorts on the floor and shivered when I thought about how cold they would be on my bare skin. My shoes would be tight, cramped almost, and my helmet so uncomfortable. The monotony of the road ahead was like a massive speed bump that you had to hit at 100 km/h to get over.

I'm not getting out of the bed, and no one is going to make me.

I had hit the point that I hit many times on every ride: the point where I no longer want to continue, no matter how close I am to the finish line. I no longer see the value in what I'm doing.

"You're still in bed?" Ruth asked, looking in the mirror and seeing only my head peeking out from the blanket. She was in the bathroom, brushing her teeth and getting ready to climb into the follow vehicle. The hotel room was empty of our belongings. If a crew is good, they'll leave almost nothing for the rider to do other than ride the bike and put on his clothes (and even sometimes the latter is the responsibility of the crew—no joke).

"I'm not getting out," I said. The day could wait. The finish line could wait—if I crossed it at all.

"Yes, you are," Ruth said, coming out of the bathroom. She brushed her hair back with her hand and pulled at the corner of the blanket. "You and I both know you are."

"There's no point," I said. I prepared for a debate, for her to see reason with me—after all, I was the big dreamer in the moment, and if I, having dreamed the dream, wanted to give up, then the crew should support me. That was their purpose, wasn't it?

"Arvid, you're the one that made the decision to do this," she said, and I waited for the consolation and empathy that was sure to come.

"No one held a gun to your head. You decided to do this of your own free will."

When is the support coming? Or is this quickly turning into a three-point sermon I don't want to hear?

"So shut up, get on your bike and ride."

And I did.

That was 3 days from the finish. Even though I had come through 27 days of intense effort and only had 3 left, I didn't have hope to get to the end. I had lost the ability to even comprehend what the end might be like.

Dream Big: Spoke 2005, Part 2

No matter where or when you give up hope along the road, it's essential to always have someone there to keep you grounded. My family, and specifically Ruth, has always been that grounding. When times have been tough, they've known how to get tough to get me back on the ride. No matter how strong a rider is, they will always come to the point where they don't want anything more than to *never* see their bike again. And that's when you need someone who can tell you to shut up, stop complaining and get back on the bike and ride.

The fog cleared and I kept moving ever closer to Halifax. The distance I needed to cover each day was less than before, since I had booked in some extra time—just in case.

Arriving in Moncton, we faced a brutal detour that was a tunnel between trees, hilly and windy and hot. It seemed to go on forever and ever, and I was ready to yell at whoever chose to make certain stretches of highway illegal for bikes. Nevertheless, we found our way into Halifax on the 13th day and, having given the media an approximate time that turned out to be too generous, sat on a parking lot to delay my arrival at Black Rock Beach in Point Pleasant Park (the irony hit us that we had started at White Rock a month before).

My daughter Stephanie, having crewed from Vancouver to Winnipeg, flew out to join us for the last day so the whole family could be there. From the same crew, Dave and Hermine flew out to join us as well. On the ride into Halifax, Lydia was on the back of my bike, drumming away on the *djembe* we had bought them, while my family blared "Dream Big," a cheesy but inspirational song that exemplified many of the traits my goals had come to embody.

And then we came into the park, and I couldn't stop the tears from pouring down my face.

I could see the water and almost taste the salt in my mouth—or was that from my tears? The ground was getting sandy, and I knew I was getting close. The road ended at a parking lot, and I curved through it, headed for the concrete path. I had to dodge a rock and hop a curb, but by this point I wasn't concerned about popping a tire.

Behind me the crew had parked the car, and I could see my family scrambling to get out of the vehicles and get down to the beach in time. I slowed down so they could catch up to me, cameras in hand snapping and recording.

When Quitting Is Not an Option

Hitting the sand, I tried to pedal as far as I could, aware that I was being filmed by two massive cameras, representing CBC and CTV. When the sand got deep enough that I couldn't move anymore, I popped my foot out and rested it on the sand. I would walk the final 20 feet.

Lydia climbed out of the back, handing the *djembe* off. She seemed to understand that I wanted her there with me, and together we walked in the sand. She kept one hand on the bike, my feeble steps making me appear a lot older than I was.

We hit the water and it lapped onto my shoes, soaking into my socks and caressing my feet. It was a glorious feeling, and I let the tears come. "We did it," I said to her, putting my arm around her in triumph. She hugged me back, and when we released I reached for the bottle with the picture of Charity in it. It was still half full, water from the Pacific sloshing around inside.

It had been 30 days since I had dipped it into the other ocean, an entire continent away. In those 30 days I had thought about giving up a thousand times. I had felt pain and become friends with it, knowing that it would push me on. I had climbed over mountains, cycled through rain and cold, and felt more emotion than I knew it was possible to feel.

And here I stood.

The grandeur of the moment swept into me as I realized just how amazing our God is. I felt small, tiny and insignificant, on the crest of a wave much bigger than me. I undid the lid of my bottle, the bottle that had been half full from the Pacific. The moment was heavy as I lowered it until the bottle touched the surface of the ocean and water splashed into it, the two waters mingling and mixing, swirling the picture of Charity around.

It was full, and I closed the cap.

I turned to face my family, my friends and the cameras, raising my arms in triumph.

Paul and Mumina came to join me in the water for a picture, and then my family followed. I felt Ruth's arm behind my back and could feel the emotional wall crumbling.

"It's over," I said. "Thank God it's over."

"No more biking." She smiled.

"No," I said, realizing why my shoulders suddenly felt so light. "I no longer have to worry about carrying a life behind me. I'm not responsible for them anymore." The words rolled off my tongue and took to the air, taking the crushing weight of that responsibility with them. I hadn't realized just how heavy it had been, but now I knew. More than just the physical burden they had been on my cycling, their presence had taken an emotional toll on me.

"Well," she said, "you'll sleep easy tonight."

We emerged from the water a victorious family, and I realized at that moment just how important that was to me. I'd never needed them so badly or depended on them so much. It was fitting that we be there together, to take in the victory as a unit.

Before they would let the media talk to me, Paul spoke up.

"Dad," he said, emotion choking his voice. There wasn't a dry eye around. "We want you to know how incredibly proud of you we are. This may not be the Tour de France, but we thought you deserved this anyways." From behind his back he pulled out something and unfolded it. It was a yellow jersey—the yellow jersey, advertisers and all, that the winner of the Tour de France gets to wear on his back.

I felt a sob coming and didn't stop it. I gave them all a hug, pulling them in as tight as my tired body would allow.

The next hour was a blur—media interviews, including an incredible opportunity for Lydia to share her testimony on national television, a group song and prayer in the shallow waters of the Atlantic, ice cream on the park railing and some more laughter, tears and hugs.

It was over. We had made it.

Lydia sharing her story with the media

Winnipeg to Ottawa crew at Niagara Falls

The Kenyans thought it was cold no matter the weather

Celebrating the Canadian Safari in Ottawa

A welcome sight after 27 days on the bike

The Kenyans liked to entertain the follow vehicle when they got bored.

National media at the ocean in White Rock, Halifax

Arvid with his family at the ocean

When Quitting Is Not an Option

The reason for the journey

Changing Lives
Mully Children's Family

After having seen the kids back onto the plane, something stirred in my heart that I could not quiet. We had gotten to know them better than we had expected, and saying goodbye was an emotional experience. *They have 800 siblings in Kenya*, I thought. And we knew immediately what we wanted to do: it was time to go to Kenya.

We had conceived of the ride as a one-off. It had achieved a high level of success and awareness, and we were thankful that God had blessed the venture.

Am I done? I had to ask myself.

Was that it? As Ruth and I thought about it, we knew it wasn't. But moving forward, pushing more and more into what God had called us to do, would take a level of commitment that stretched beyond anything I had imagined.

Palliser had been incredibly supportive of what I was doing. There were not many companies I knew of that would give a management employee more than a month off to gallivant (it didn't feel like gallivanting at the time) across the country, raising money for an orphanage. Nevertheless, I realized that God had awoken a passion within me that I couldn't deny. No matter how hard I tried to tell myself that that ride was it, that we had done our duty, God wouldn't get the idea of a longer-term relationship with MCF out of my mind.

Ruth and I spent many evenings talking about our future. We were not old, and retirement wasn't an option. But yet I knew that I couldn't put this idea down.

The winter after Spoke 2005 I talked to Art DeFehr, knowing that things were changing at Palliser. The company was being realigned, and I knew that this timing was working itself out for me.

197

"Art," I said, suddenly nervous. I'd been in his office many times before, but this was different. I wasn't asking for a job; I was talking about leaving one. "I need to talk to you."

"Arvid." He smiled, leaning back in his chair.

I struggled to know what to do—sit down? Stand?

"Have a seat," he said, with a spark in his eye that made me realize he might understand. Though I thought I had been keeping a lot of the turmoil inside, it was possible that some of it had leaked.

"With all this going on," I said, waving my hand around me, "I've been doing a lot of thinking and praying. I think it's best—for the company and for me—if Palliser doesn't consider me as a part of the long-term plans."

He looked surprised, but then again, maybe not all that much. Surprised to finally hear the words, unsurprised at what he knew had been brewing.

"Your future..." he let the words out, knowing that it wasn't something I had taken lightly.

"I don't know yet," I said. "The decision's not final. But don't feel like you need to make a space for me."

"Okay," he said.

"I feel like this is a calling. It's something I want to pursue."

He shook my hand, and I was sad to think about leaving. It had been 31 years, and, though the decision wasn't final, I was far more nervous than I had been when I'd stepped into a similar office and requested a job.

Through the months of January and February, Ruth and I came to the conclusion that this was what God wanted. It made no logical sense in the eyes of the world. While all those around us were stacking their RRSPs and hedging their salaries for the future, we were turning away a good income and a stable career. We didn't know what the future held, but we knew that we wanted God to be an even bigger part of it than He had been. On Spoke 2005, we had seen the power of reliance on prayer, and we were about to learn a lot more about relying on God.

I suppose it would have been possible to keep racing and working, but I have always been the kind of person who likes to focus on only a few things and do them well. I didn't know what I would be doing, but I knew that the *why* was simple—I had a burning passion, burden and love for the kids. God had started growing it during the ride, and it was only getting larger. At the time, I didn't tell everyone what my hopes and dreams were—and I still don't. Because I focus on what I truly believe I can accomplish I have a tendency to exceed my publicized expectations.

But that's getting ahead of myself.

My career with Palliser ended in May of 2006. They were incredibly generous and blessed me with a one-year severance to get me started on the path I had chosen.

My salary for the last few years had been more than enough, but I knew that we needed to change our lifestyle. We decided that we would take that one-year severance and stretch it out as long as we could. Though job offers came, we knew that wasn't the point. God had called us to something different, and we were sticking with it 100 percent.

Many people worry and wonder what they would do if their income suddenly stopped. Many also wonder what it would be like to cut loose, give everything to God and make serious sacrifices. We, at our highest income ever, had a chance to experience both. Fear cut deep, but we made the tough decisions that we had to make. Our three kids all happened to meet their spouses around the same time, so in the span of 16 months we got them all married off. Now they were no longer our financial responsibility!

Two years back we had made one of Ruth's dreams come true: owning a VW Beetle. We had never really owned a fun car before. For the first 19 years of our marriage we managed with one car. Once we had five drivers, we bought a second car. So the Beetle (brand new) was a big thing for us. I had decided that if we were going to take the plunge for a new car then we were going to go all the way and get a convertible.

Finally, Ruth had her car. We went on a trip to BC, driving through the mountains with the top down. We loved the car, which made it incredibly difficult when we decided that it was not practical for the lifestyle we were about to enter. I felt horrible for Ruth—she had it for 24 months before we sold it, going back down to one car. While many our age were planning their trips to the south, we cut trips down to size. It was radical and countercultural, and it was extremely difficult.

When God called us to live this life, He didn't promise it would be comfortable.

By chopping the big expenses of an extra vehicle and trips and adding a tenant to our basement suite, we were able to do what many would have considered impossible: we stretched one year of salary out to 29 months.

When Quitting Is Not an Option

The warm air swirled up and filled my lungs. It felt a little bit like being back in my childhood home, back in Paraguay. It had been a long time since I had been close to poverty the way we were now. Still, we had landed in Kenya and been shuttled from the airport directly to MCF's property. We had arrived at the start of their wintertime, meaning that it was still 30 degrees Celsius in the daytime and dipped down to roughly 15 at night. The ground was dirt that turned into mud when it rained. Because of that, most of the little kids we saw running around were wearing flip-flops. They would be much easier to clean than runners. Flip-flops or bare feet, that is.

Our white skin made us stand out, but we didn't feel like strangers. We're not ones to dress fancy, but their clothes were modest—whatever came in donations, mostly. It was our first time in Africa, and Ruth and I were nervous. Until now we'd met Charles Mulli once and then only briefly. Many had asked why we would possibly do so much for those we had no significant connection to. When we had decided to call it quits at Palliser, the next step was logical—if we were going to ask others to give their money to MCF, we needed to have a better understanding of the place. We needed to make sure it was what we thought it was.

"They don't have much," I whispered to Ruth.

"But look." Ruth smiled, and I did. "They're all smiling."

It was true. Though their surroundings were simple—no orphanage is ornate and elaborate, after all—they had smiles on their faces. Different shades of brown and black, different heights and different backgrounds—yet one home.

"We'll head through here," Grace, Charles Mulli's daughter, was saying, her accent reminding us of her sister, Ndondo. Their English is strong, with a hint of a British flavour. "Through the kids' place. Lydia should be in here. We did not tell them you were coming."

My heart skipped a beat. Lydia—I had pulled her across the country on the back of my bike, and now she was back at home. I knew that, though she had journeyed to another country, when she had arrived back home there had been no special treatment. At a young age the kids are taught that this is their family and that they are all brothers and sisters. When we had gone out to dinner to celebrate our arrival in Halifax we'd eaten at East Side Mario's. There, they give the kids candy. When the three Kenyans received theirs there were some words shared in Swahili, and the candies went untouched. We asked why. Ndondo had answered, "They won't eat it unless they have one for each of their brothers and sisters back home."

All 800 of them. When we told the restaurant staff, they were more than happy to oblige. With plastic bags they dug into their candy drawer and scooped it out. Later at the hotel we counted over 900 candies—one for each.

And so Lydia, Paul and Mumina had arrived back and been reintegrated into their home. I was told that they were given some time to share about what had gone on. We were told Lydia commented, "The love that this man has for us as kids that he doesn't know—I will never forget that." Charles once told me that he had never seen any of his kids as taken by something as Lydia was with what we did. Aside from the one evening program, there was no special treatment.

That didn't mean that Lydia didn't remember, however.

From across the room we saw her, sitting on the ground with a little child on her lap. They were clapping together as a larger group sang, their voices resonating beautifully in the metal-walled building. There was a lot of noise as other kids ran around, shrieking and having fun. I watched her from a distance, wondering how long it would take for her to look up and—

She saw us.

Her jaw dropped and her eyes bulged. With no warning, it must have been like two worlds colliding for her. She stood up quickly, making sure the little girl was sitting safely on the ground, and ran towards us.

"Meesta Arvid!" she exclaimed, wrapping me and then Ruth in a hug. I looked to Ruth and saw her crying, realizing that tears were streaming down my face as well.

"It's so good to see you, Lydia," Ruth said. I could hardly speak—the entire experience felt out-of-this-world.

"Come," Lydia said, grabbing us both by the hand. Grace was laughing, smiling at us and the joy that came through our shared experiences. "Come, come!" she exclaimed, pulling so hard her hands slipped out of ours. She got ahead of us and went around the corner.

"We better follow," Grace said. We did, turning the corner to see—

"Meesta Arvid!" Paul Gachoka exclaimed. He had grown—I'm not sure I would have wanted to carry him up the mountains anymore—and had a huge smile on his face. Lydia had gone ahead to tell him we were there, and his excitement was palpable. Nonetheless, he took the more even-keeled emotional approach of a guy, his reaction a little more reserved than Lydia's had been.

"Let's go to see Mumina," Lydia said. "He should be in the high school." Around us, little black kids were taking off in all directions, running past us. A few went to the school ahead of us, and Lydia and Paul laughed. Before we even arrived at the building Mumina had come out, word having reached him. He, like Paul, met us with excitement but a little less emotion than Lydia. Standing there, the five of us together, it felt like we had never been apart.

"Come, meet my friend," Lydia was saying, calling over a girl. She was shy, yet still able to meet our gaze. Paul and Mumina introduced us to some of their friends as well, hardly believing that we had appeared out of the blue.

"Now, now," Grace said. "We'll have time to talk later. You still have things to get done," she indicated. The kids ran off reluctantly and left the three of us standing outside the high school, looking at the buildings. My mind could hardly process what had just happened. Emotionally on a roller-coaster, we looked at Grace as if to ask, *What next?*

"I'd like you to meet Lillian," Grace said. She waved over a young girl, about 12 years old, with a big, beaming smile on her face. She was average height and, like many, looked thinner than kids her age would in North America. Nevertheless, she was healthy, with a spring in her step and a sparkle in her eye. I waited for further explanation as to why Lillian was special, but none came.

I looked to Ruth, then to Grace, then back to Lillian.

"Hi, I'm Lillian." She held out her hand to shake mine. I felt the skin—healthy and vibrant—in my hand.

"It's nice to meet you." I looked back at Grace, wondering when the explanation would come. But she was waiting for it to dawn on me, and then it finally did—

This was Lillian. *No!* my mind wanted to shout out. It didn't make sense. This couldn't be *the* Lillian. We'd heard her story, but I'd assumed she couldn't be the same one. Lillian had been found in a slum a few years back. When they had found her she had been unable to speak, so tiny and shrivelled that they assumed her to be much younger. They couldn't move her without causing pain, and they took her immediately to a hospital. She had been hours away from death, said the doctors. But the biggest shock was her age—and her weight. Already eight years old, she weighed only 14 pounds. *Some babies hit 14 pounds by the time they're a few months old,* I thought.

By all accounts, she should have died. Her body was so emaciated that there was little hope. But the proper combination of love, food, shelter, care and medicine had nursed Lillian back to health. Whereas she should have been dead—she had been only hours away from death—she was now a healthy weight with a happy smile.

I can't describe how odd it was to see her full of life and energy. The contrast was like night and day. We had seen pictures of her—she had been a skeleton. Yet here she was, standing right in front of me. I looked to Ruth and then back at Lillian, taking her in with this new perspective.

"It's amazing to meet you, Lillian," I said that time. I grabbed her hand, and we went for a walk. She stayed by our side, and Grace continued to talk, but I kept missing her words. I was struck by the oddity of this.

Usually you can push away an image of a starving child. But in that moment I realized that I hadn't pushed it away, and things had actually changed. All of our effort was helping God to do this. It reminded me to never, ever dismiss the difference that we can make if we step out of our comfort zones. I couldn't help but hold the image of the picture we had seen in my head, comparing it with the reality holding my hand with warmth and life.

God is good.

On Spoke 2005, I had carried a picture of a little girl named Charity with me. Laminated and waterproofed, it sat in a water bottle that went all 7,000 km across the country. Her life, like many of the MCF kids, started off with difficulty and adversity. Her mom was a teenager and clearly felt that Charity was a drain on her life. On two separate occasions, she tried to take Charity's life, but through the grace of God and the help of people who came to Charity's rescue she survived—and ended up at MCF. God was taking Charity's tragic story and turning it into something miraculous.

As Ruth and I sat down on the bench at the back of the gathering hall, I smiled at all the faces around us. Being white and clearly not young, we stood out like sore thumbs. While the music and singing resounded from the hundreds of voices, echoing back off the walls in a beautiful symphony, the smaller kids played just in front of us. They would laugh, run up to each other and give hugs and smile—so many smiles.

There was a younger girl who was clearly one of the popular ones. Her smile was beautiful and her eyes were brilliant. She seemed to radiate in a way that made the others feel comfortable to be around her. It was obvious that her presence was to them both a joy and a blessing.

I've always loved playing with kids, and now was no different. I got her to smile, blinking her eyes bashfully at me. Around three years old, she was just beginning to explore the world. After a few minutes she came up to me, and I offered for her to sit in my lap. She jumped up with no hesitation and played with my wedding band for nearly half an hour, twisting and turning it. Her black hands were a contrast in my white ones, and the reality of my world came crashing down around me.

I had known it from the moment I saw her, but now it was sinking in. This was Charity. I had carried her picture with me for 7,000 km and talked about it time after time, and now she had stepped off of the bookmark and become a real living and breathing human. I had tears in my eyes as she played with my ring, smiling at me all the while. Ruth, sitting beside me, knew what must be going through my head and gave my leg a squeeze. Though we were in silence, the experience was speaking volumes.

I've come to realize that it's only when we allow God to change us—to take a picture and transform it into a real person—that true change is possible. Up until that point I had been pouring all my energy and efforts into raising funds for the kids "over there," but Charity was suddenly no longer distant. Sitting on my lap, playing with my ring, holding my fingers—this was God's transformative work happening in front of my eyes. This was a life that should have perished but was rescued. This was someone who was born with no chance of becoming anything other than a statistic, but now she had been given a chance, a chance to excel. Who knows what Charity will do in life? She still has many years and many decisions ahead of her. But one thing I do know—without the love of Charles and his family, without the miracles and hope that God brings, Charity would never have been given that chance. But the chance is hers—and ours—for the taking.

The dirt crunched beneath our shoes. Around us were all the kids, formerly orphans but no longer. Now they had an identity and a family. Their feet ran circles around me as we walked.

It was mealtime, and we had front row seats for the process. They mostly ate *ugali*, an ethnic dish with cooked vegetables. Each kid got their own bowl, some eating with a spoon and others without.

"Did you see the shirt?" I asked Ruth.

"Which shirt?" she responded.

"I think that one's from Vancouver." I pointed to a small boy running away from us. I had caught a glimpse of his shirt. Most of their clothing comes to them through the generosity of people from all over the world. It meant an eclectic—and hardly uniform—dress code.

"Decent-sized portions," I said, looking at the food. They weren't allowed to go back for seconds, but it didn't look like any of them would be going hungry.

"Too many of them for tables." Ruth laughed. Though the food was simple and many were sitting on the ground in groups with their friends, there was a joyous spirit about the process. They were thankful for what they had.

"They're not bickering," I said, "about how much they got or their friends got."

I turned around to take in the setting, looking over at the kitchen. The kitchen was an outdoor wood stove, hunkered under a roof. I was about to analyze the setup when I felt something hit my hand. Or, rather, my hand hit something.

I looked down in horror as I realized what had happened. One of the kids had been walking so close behind me that I'd swung out and knocked the nearly full bowl of *ugali* right out of his hands. It smashed into the ground in slow motion, and the *ugali* was spilled and spoiled.

I couldn't get words out of my mouth, and I turned to look to Ruth for help. *What should I do?*

It took all of three seconds for other kids to arrive at the scene. As he picked up his bowl they scooped their hands into theirs, taking a chunk from their meal and dropping it into his bowl. And that was it.

No hesitation, no question. No one needed to rescue him or intervene. The kids took care of it, sacrificing their own meals. Five or six kids stepped in, and he had a full bowl. *What kind of a place is this?* I asked myself. I looked at Ruth, amazed and in awe.

MCF has a few campuses, one of which is the Ndalani campus. Snaking through the corner of Ndalani is the Thika River, a great place for the kids to go down and swim. During the rainy season the river swells and fills up its banks, with crocodiles and hippopotamuses coming with the water. It's here that they bathe, wash and do their laundry. Most of the buildings are stone with metal roofs, designed by Charles himself.

Because MCF has been around for more than 20 years, many of those who began as children have graduated on to careers. Some learn trades at MCF, and it's these young men who build the campus buildings. The dorms are large, with two rooms full of 15 bunk beds. All told, MCF Ndalani houses about 600 kids.

As I learned about the facilities and the setup, I couldn't help but be amazed that everything is done with incredible care, precision and prayer. God's leading is evident in everything that goes on, from the spiritual care to the building of a well. There isn't a corner at MCF that's missing the presence of God's Spirit.

Walking through the campus I realized a few things. There's no garbage anywhere. This is partly due to the fact that nothing they eat is wrapped—it's either grown by them or purchased from a market. Nothing like the prepackaged foods and meals that we experience in the Western world.

Charles' background lies in business, and that fact oozes out of every part of MCF. They own greenhouses and export beans to the European market (the health and safety regulations for this are enormous, and the fact that a non-profit street rescue mission is accredited to this level is a miracle in itself). They also own fish ponds that they stock, maintain and harvest themselves to provide the kids with protein.

With my background and experience in business, I had half expected to be able to offer valuable input to improve their workflow or structure. But I was blown away—their initiatives were bold but done with an incredible level of detail. It was clear to me that they knew what they were doing. Everything was documented, beyond what I had seen where I came from. Charles' biological kids have a huge hand in running the business end of things, and when I talked to them, I realized that they are far more educated than I am. They could easily be profitable running a business over in our end of the world.

This level of proficiency and excellence has led to MCF being a gleaming example to business individuals and non-profits. "See, this is what can be done in this type of organization," they say, taking people for tours of MCF to show just what is possible. They have brought their self-sufficiency up to nearly 50 percent, a level that's unheard of for anything resembling an orphanage—and all with a family the size of a small village (over 1,000 kids).

Blown away.

That's how I felt. I couldn't even begin to put words to the level of professionalism, quality and excellence that the business initiatives of MCF exude. Charles has dreams of making MCF entirely self-sustaining, and I think it would be possible if he didn't have such a big heart. He's incredibly generous, welcoming more and more kids into the home, expanding their walls and reach. Giving back to the community when political nightmares bring the country to bloodshed. But he's not the kind of guy to hang tightly to what he has. If the storerooms are full, it's because people have needs that have to be met. If God gives him something, he turns around and gives it back.

I had gone to MCF to see if the organization was all it was cracked up to be. I came away from our two weeks shaking my head in disbelief, unable to understand how something so miraculous and incredible could exist. It was far more than I had hoped, and I realized that my own perceptions and stereotypes had crumbled. Though I wasn't a street child from Kenya, MCF had just changed my life.

The evening programs at MCF are a taste of heaven. Given that I was told from an early age to keep my mouth shut when music was playing, music hasn't been my forte throughout life. But when several hundred start singing, you can't help but feel the rhythm move through your body. Their voices lift up as one, sending a passionate song of worship up to the God who rescued them.

The first time we joined in the evening program we were surprised by the process. At some point, completely randomly and without anything being prearranged, someone is called up to give his or her testimony. Their stories are often harsh and brutal.

As we continued to listen to countless other stories at the evening programs, I was amazed by what hit me—*This is why they experience such an effective transformation.*

When Quitting Is Not an Option

One day, in a private session with a young woman at MCF, we heard the brutal story of her life. Her mother had attempted to kill her with a machete, and she had wounds running across her back and forearms from the blade as she turned or blocked to protect herself.

"You don't have to tell us," Ruth said, tears forming at the corner of her eye. Sarah, already older than many of the MCF kids, spoke with clarity and a somewhat-removed emotion. For Ruth, it was difficult to listen to.

"You don't have to tell us," Ruth repeated. But Sarah just kept on going, not heeding the allowance.

"It's part of the process," Grace Mulli said, reaching out to touch Ruth's arm. She had sadness in her eyes but a greater understanding of what was going on. We're used to shying away from the dirt and the grime, to sweeping our troubles and our past under the rug. Other than at our baptism, we don't often have times to tell our testimonies. And even there, we're mindful of what we share. But this was entirely different. "She wants to tell you her story because this is part of healing," Grace continued. "We don't hide things. It comes out into the open—and that's how she can move forward."

Sarah continued telling her story, with tears on her face as well as on ours. The pain she experienced was mind-blowing, and to think that it came from her own mother—I felt like we had travelled to a different world, never mind a different continent.

Her story, much like all the others, became a part of the tapestry of MCF. Orphans don't have clean and simple backgrounds. They're messy, especially in a society where alcoholism and AIDS are so rampant. They don't sweep the dirt under the rug, but instead they've learned that it takes a process for kids to be rehabilitated. They are surrounded by a family environment, accepted with similar but different stories, and each gets equal attention. By allowing stories like Sarah's into the open they can begin to experience healing because they get back to the root of the problem and tackle it as a community. They support each other. They learn from each other. They cry with each other. And they heal together.

Seeing the three kids back in their home in Kenya

Meeting Charity for the first time

The Loewens and the Mullis, separated by an ocean but connected by God

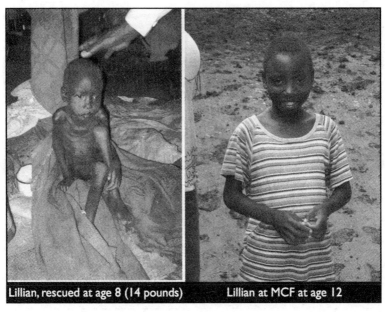

Lillian, rescued at age 8 (14 pounds)   Lillian at MCF at age 12

Lillian, one of many miracles

Giving It Up
Quitting My Day Job

The hum of the airplane's engine cut through the windows and fuselage, but I ignored it. I swallowed back the dryness that was in my throat. We had made it through check-in and boarding and were now sitting in our seats. There was an awkward tension that I hadn't felt in a long time. Whenever I present my crazy ideas for bike rides to Ruth I do it slowly, one element at a time. It gives her time to absorb them and come to grips with what they mean for me, for us. The nerves I was feeling were stronger than when I had come up with the ridiculous idea of hauling three Kenyan orphans across the country.

"So..."

Oh good, I thought, *she broke the moment first.* "So," I agreed, nodding my head. Over the past two weeks we had seen an entirely new world. It was hard to believe that people within a day's travel could live so differently than we did. It felt so strange that in a world as connected as ours we hadn't found the compassion and empathy to make the necessary changes in order to provide the bare essentials for the world's population.

We had taken everything in for two weeks, and with the plane's engines propelling us back to our security, our home, our comfort, it was time to let everything come out. I breathed deeply and then looked at her. There was so much I wanted to say.

"What did you love about MCF?" Ruth asked.

My mind spun with possible answers.

"So, so much," I began. "For one, it is clear that God is present there. They do nothing without seeking God's will and help first. They realize that the road to healing is a long yet powerful process. They depend on God in ways I can't even imagine. I mean, we gave up my job, but having empty cupboards one day and going to sleep with the confidence that they will be full the next, that's,

211

that's just—" I couldn't finish the sentence. I couldn't come up with a word to adequately describe it. It sounded cliché, but when it came to MCF it was the reality.

Charles Mulli had done just that—prayed and let God deal with it. The next morning a truck arrived at the orphanage with food for several days—and money for several months. I may have opened the fridge and left without taking anything before, but that wasn't because it was empty. The last time our fridge was empty was when it arrived at our house to be plugged in.

"And the kids," my voice was full of emotion. "They're incredible. I mean— these are the kids that the world has left out in the cold—literally—to die. Their own families pushed them aside and let them fend for themselves. They have nothing. They were nothing. They had to fight, steal and lie to live. Now they have family, hope, education, food, shelter. It's a transformation that I can't even begin to understand. This gives me hope.

"And then there's the business side of things. MCF blew me away. Most orphanages are giant money-pits—they simply take and take donations without doing anything themselves. But Charles has such a good business head on his shoulders that he's providing income and food and then turning around and sharing it with the neighbourhood.

"What do you think?" I asked Ruth, finally taking a moment to breathe.

"It's incredible." Ruth nodded. "Incredible. I've never seen anything like it."

"I know it's early and we haven't talked about it much," I said, "but I feel like God is calling me to this."

"To what?" Ruth asked.

"I don't know yet," I said, "but I can't get any of it out of my mind."

She was silent. I didn't like this silence. Ruth readily admits that she isn't a dreamer in the same way that I am. Though it has nothing to do with our genders, she has often taken the behind-the-scenes role in many of our ventures. I know that any and all of the things I've done would have been impossible without her help. This tugging that I was feeling, I knew, would be the same. If I had any hopes of it being successful, I would need her on board. Maybe I'd said too much—gone too quickly—but I hadn't been able to control it.

When Charles had begun to take street kids into his house, Esther hadn't been so eager. It ruined their comfort and family dynamics, and it filled their beautiful home with the struggles of the street. Eventually, however, she had come around. And now she's as much a part of MCF as Charles is. I knew it would have to be the same for us. I know that God doesn't always call both individuals of a couple to something, but I am a firm believer that if God calls one of the spouses He will at least enable the other to be okay with it.

"We've got a lot to talk about," Ruth said.

"It's a long flight," I joked, glancing out the window as the clouds below covered up our view of the African tundra.

There was tension. Inevitably there will be tension when you take a year's worth of salary and stretch it out to 29 months and make decisions that will impact the rest of your life. Those 29 months were a huge blessing, because we used them as a process to work out just what was going on. If we were going to go forward with this, we needed to be united. If we wanted to give up income, we needed to be united.

It was not easy.

There was a constant tension.

We've done enough.

There is so much more to do.

These two sides of the battle played themselves out in my mind and in our house over and over. Charles Mulli asked me to be on the board of directors for MCFCF (the Canadian extension of MCF), and work began to pick up. We were raising money, working actively and getting opportunities to speak. Whether or not we wanted to jump in, things were heating up.

Every event was getting bigger. The awareness was growing.

Yet I was getting more and more nervous. The end of our severance was approaching. This included all the benefits that I had had as an employee, like health insurance. It felt like coming to the end of our severance and going back to work would be putting the brakes on a process that was just picking up speed. I had reached the conviction point—where I realized that we needed to find a way to make this continue. It would have been possible to go to those we knew and ask for financial support, but we felt it didn't make sense if we hadn't exhausted everything we had.

It was time for a family meeting, or a "family forum" (as we called them).

Everything about the meeting was awkward. We forced all six of our kids to sit down and then presented them with the fact that I would not be going back to work. Instead, we would continue to work for MCF. In what I would consider the crux of the meeting we told them, "We'll basically be spending your inheritance."

Their concern was palpable, but for us and not their future. While many families would be squabbling over their piece of the pie, our kids wondered how we could possibly take care of ourselves without a salary.

When we had sat down with our financial planner he had told us there was nothing he could do to make it work. Instead, we set up our RRSPs to be able to withdraw them as needed. Still, he cautioned us to set a cap—a marker beyond which we wouldn't let the RRSPs sink.

We left the meeting feeling elated. We had always known our kids supported us, but time and prayers are one thing—money is another. In many ways, it mirrored the step of faith we were taking. We could have left it at Spoke 2005. No one would have questioned us if I had gone back to work, if I had let MCF deal with its own finances.

Most of the time we don't question the selfish decisions we or others make. Living largely for ourselves has become the norm, even in Christian society. Our kids were giving up their future inheritance, just as we were giving up a lifetime of earnings. *Will we be okay?* I asked myself.

God continued to provide for our every need. In one instance, two of our friends came to us and said, "How in the world are you guys living?" We answered them honestly, and they believed so strongly in what we were doing that they wanted to be a part of it, supporting us with a portion of what our income would need to be.

I have found that when you take a risk and step out in trust, God is more than willing to respond with generosity.

Then Christmas came. It's strange to spend money on presents when you don't have an income and stressful when you know the gifts are sitting on a credit card. We experienced emotional stress every time we thought about it. *What if God doesn't come through? What if we are wrong? What if we have misread the signs, the passion, the drive? What are we getting ourselves into?*

The doorbell rang. I walked down the hallway towards the front door and saw the silhouette of a couple through the glass. When I opened it, I smiled— friends from our church were standing there. They looked a little nervous.

"Hi, Arvid," they said. "We're just here to stop by for a minute. We've been asked by a third party to give this envelope to you." They handed it over, a smile on their faces. "Have a good Christmas!" And they left.

I opened it and was blown away—there was $1,000 inside.

Something simple—and huge—instantly gave us the peace that we were walking the road that God wanted us to be on. Though we may only have been able to see a few steps ahead of us, God was looking out for us. We were diving into the deep, about to experience the answer to the question that many Christians ask: *What does life look like when you fully trust in God? When you give up your security?*

It was a good thing we weren't counting on our money for security. Shortly after our decision, the recession hit. People all over the country were gripped with fear as their RRSPs and investments fell. We had committed to live as we were until our RRSPs hit our cap. In the first blow of the recession, half of what we had planned to live on disappeared. It was ironic that we, without an income, slept better than most that night, since we'd already put our future in God's hands.

If this is what it feels like to trust God, I thought, *I'm okay with that.*

We had no idea what more could possibly be in store for us.

The Loewen family with three kids and their spouses, 2007

Planned Adversity
RAAM 2008

I was learning to trust God more and more and was focusing my attention on fundraising for MCF. Cycling across Canada had garnered significant attention, but if we were going to be fully committed to MCF, we needed to take my cycling platform to the next level.

RAAM presented the perfect opportunity. It was a challenge that far outdid any other ride I had accomplished, but with millions of page views during its 12-day journey, I could create international attention for MCF.

As the equivalent to the Tour de France for endurance events, RAAM is well-known, incredibly organized, high-profile and extremely difficult. It is "the world's toughest bike race," a title no one contests. During many of my DNFs I took a distant look at RAAM and thought, *Maybe RAAM is not for me.*

To put RAAM into perspective, RAAM is the length of Furnace Creek times six. And its disqualification time is the Furnace Creek time times six. That's right. RAAM is like biking six Furnace Creek 508s back-to-back-to-back-to-back-to-back-to-back. And if you don't finish each of those within 48 hours, you're out. To top it all off, you have to cross that same terrain from Furnace Creek in the first three days, in the heat of June.

The more I thought about it, I began to wonder if I was insane. *Can I really finish Furnace Creek and then do it five more times?*

This would be the defining moment for me in my support of MCF. I would challenge the world's toughest bike race to raise funds for the orphans in Kenya, create awareness of MCF and establish myself as a legitimate cyclist. Though I was a speaker, I knew that accomplishing something as big as RAAM would create opportunities to share my story and, more importantly, to share MCF's story with others.

When Quitting Is Not an Option

During an interview before the ride, Danny Chew had been intrigued with my cause. He asked me what drove me to bike the way I do, to put so much effort into riding across the country in under 12 days. "I know that the problem is big," I answered, "but if I can make a difference to even one child, it is worth it."

I stood at the starting point, waiting for my name to be called. And I was surrounded by some impressive cyclists.

Jure Robic was a Slovenian soldier and a legend. He had won RAAM three times, more than any other male rider. He was known for starting the ride hard—and finishing harder. He often went the first two nights without sleep to establish a lead over the second-place rider. He would then spend the remaining six days doing everything to defend that lead while his mental capacity diminished to the point where his crew, also Slovenian soldiers, locked the vehicle doors out of fear and refused to let him in. (Sadly, Jure Robic passed away in a cycling accident in 2010. He remains the male RAAM rider with the most wins.)

I shuttled forward to the front of the group, ready to hear my name. I lifted my right foot, gave a nod to the cyclist beside me, and clipped it into the pedal. My nerves were on fire, my heart pumping faster than it usually does when I ride—and I hadn't even started yet.

"Arvid Loewen," the announcer said. They held up fingers in front of me, counting down the seconds.

Three.

Two.

One.

My journey across the country had started. I swallowed back my fear and biked across the bridge.

For the first few hours, there are too many riders in a small stretch to have their crews immediately following. I was already climbing a hill, the first of many. I was reminded that RAAM entailed 170,000 feet of climbing, more than five times the vertical height of Everest.

This was just the beginning.

There was a slight bump and the telltale sound that I feared. I looked down, seeing the rubber around my wheels flatten out as it met the ground. My speed instantly dropped, and I pulled to the side of the road, unclipping my feet. I was alone, barely into the beginning of the ride, and I had just flatted.

I had the tire off, replaced the tube and was already working the wheel on before the next rider passed me. Within a few more riders I was back on the bike, shaking out the nerves.

There was a sound behind me, and I instantly recognized it. It was the clicking of pedal strokes. *Somebody is coming,* I thought to myself. Judging by the sound of it, there was no doubt who was behind me. *Jure.*

I turned to look and stared at the three-time champion of RAAM, barrelling up the hill towards me. I was climbing at about 15 or 16 km/h, a steady but not slow pace. It looked like Jure was dancing on the pedals. His face was focused and set but not in pain. He was doing a minimum of 25 km/h. He looked light, as if his cycling jersey was pumped up with helium.

I was in awe as he passed me with a slight nod that acknowledged my presence but no words or conversation to distract his focus. He couldn't talk with every rider he passed in the first couple hours or he would be out of breath from words. He climbed away from me as if I was standing still.

As he turned the corner in front of me and pulled farther ahead, I realized that it was the last time I would see him. A few hours in and I knew for sure I wasn't going to win—not that I'd ever really considered it. It was an honour to be on the same course as him, even if the gap between us would stretch to hours within the first day.

And then—

Pop!

Not again, I thought. The same tire was deflating in front of my eyes, and now I had a problem. I'd already replaced the tube and didn't have another. With the cause of MCF on my jersey, I felt like I had the weight of the entire organization on my shoulders. They were praying for me, counting on me, and I intended to make it to the finish line for them.

I looked up, hearing another bike's wheels spinning as it approached me.

"Crew 132!" I called. "Let them know I've got a flat." He nodded and wished me luck.

If I remembered the numbers correctly, my crew was only a few kilometres up the road from me, waiting at one of the crew parking lots. Hopefully, it wouldn't take too long for them to hear, pack up and get back to me.

The heat of the day was already washing over my body, and I checked my watch. Three hours in…two flats…I stepped over to the side of the road, where there was a bit of shade. I popped off the wheel, removed the tire and tube and, frustrated, sat down to wait.

Five hours into a 12-day race and I was exhausted. It was hot, not insanely hot, but the sun was bright and beating down on my back. I smelled the air around me. There was something different. *Is it more humid?* I was cresting the hill when—

Is that a forest fire? I thought, a wave of heat hitting me smack in the face. I gasped for air, feeling the immediate difference. My eyes began searching the sights, trying to find the source of the heat.

Where's the fire? I asked.

It took me a few seconds to realize there was no fire. In front of me, dropping down thousands of feet in a gloriously beautiful switchback descent, was what they call the "Glass Elevator." Opening up before me was the expanse of the Mojave Desert, visible all in one glance. I was about to descend into it, every curve and turn visible. I wondered if I'd wear my brake pads out on the way down (on a ride of that length I bring more than one pair along). But more important than the huge descent ahead of me (from thousands of feet to below sea level), was the fact that an unearthly amount of heat was rushing up the mountain at me.

The heat felt like a wall, and I prepared myself to plunge into the desert, afraid of what was ahead of me. Behind me my crew was closing the vehicle windows and blasting the air conditioning.

I started descending, taking the corners carefully. Descending can be a lot of fun, but most people don't realize the strain it actually puts on your body. Gripping the handlebars and brakes tightly, your arms are locked and tensed. Your legs aren't spinning (since you can hardly keep up with the speed anyway), and you're on constant alert for anything that could be in your way, as well as trying to determine the best line to travel for the switchbacks.

By the time I reached the bottom of the Glass Elevator, its incredible beauty had been replaced in my mind by frustration. The town of Borrego Springs, a little oasis in the vastness of the desert, was shortly ahead. I started pedalling and felt pain like fire shoot through my muscles. Everything—my hands, calves, thighs—had cramped from the heat. They were completely locked up, and it hurt to even move them. Looking a lot like a cowboy, I started to pedal bow-legged. I couldn't believe how much pain I was experiencing only a quarter of a day into the race.

I heard the revving of the crew vehicle, and they pulled up beside me. On my crew for RAAM were my wife, Ruth, my son, Paul, his wife, Jeanette, my daughter Stephanie, and her husband, Josh. We were the smallest crew at RAAM, and the only crew made up of only family. Paul looked ready to make a joke about how awkwardly I was biking. The window slid down, then instantly back up. It looked like they didn't want to feel the air either. Yet there I was, stuck in 45 degree temperatures with the sun burning down on me.

Think about the kids, I told myself. *Do it for the kids.*

The second morning dawned bright and early. I had had a relaxing two hours of sleep and was itching to get back onto my bike. I was one of the only riders to sleep any decent amount, so I woke up near the back of the pack—close to second or third from the end. Though I'd had a rough day with the cramping and the heat, I was ready and raring to go.

In the days to follow, I had some great days of biking, pushing myself and regaining some of the positions that we had lost. It felt good to make up ground and pass riders.

A decade ago, in Furnace Creek, I had set my personal best for speed on a downhill: 95 km/h. I was determined to break that. Coming into the town of Mexican Hat, Utah, I had climbed significantly. It was a long and winding descent, and I decided that this would be the time. There was a tailwind, and it was a long downhill.

I pushed it up a gear, spinning my legs and feeling the bike respond. The speedometer climbed past 60, then 70 and 75. I was nowhere near the top of my speed—there was still plenty to go. I was leaning forward, body over the handlebars and hands in the drop bars.

There was a slight shift in the direction of the descent, and what had been a tailwind quickly became a crosswind. That wind decided it was going to ruin my day—it pulled my deep-dish wheel (a wheel with a significantly larger rim) to the side and, since my weight was mostly on the front of the bike, picked the wheel up and set it down a foot over. Since my body hadn't shifted with the wheel, my bike started to whip back and forth underneath me.

It's a terrifying feeling at 75 km/h. I thought my wheel must be broken and was scrambling to regain control. At that speed, in that kind of conditions, there was nowhere to go but down—with the wheels out from under me. I had the mental image of my body scraping along the concrete at 75 km/h go through my head, wondering how far I would slide. To just wrench on the brakes would send my weight careening forward, so I applied pressure gently and slowly, fighting with the handlebars all the way.

Eventually, as my speed decreased, the effect of the wind diminished and I had the bike back under control. My heart was racing even faster than I'd been going. I looked down at my wheel, thinking it would look like a Pringles chip—but it was normal.

I slowed down even more, taking the turns and descents more gradually. I had learned my lesson, and from that point on my need for speed has significantly diminished. I'll still gun it sometimes, but it has to be a smooth, straight road and not my deep-dish wheels (which act like a sail).

Glad that I'd kept my skin from being the new topping of the pavement, I finally got my breath back.

I was exhausted. I guess I shouldn't have been surprised. After all, I had conquered 1,000 miles. But that was only a third of the way. There was a lot more ground to cover.

It was dark, the night stretching on for an eternity.

Ahead of me—way ahead of me—were flashing lights. In the stillness of the night we could see for tens of miles, making it possible to see another rider and crew off in the distance. They seemed so close yet were so incredibly far. Always out of reach.

Waving my hand beside me, I heard the crew instantly respond.

"Can you make me some soup?" I asked. "I'm falling asleep on the bike here."

"Sure," Ruth responded. She grabbed the portable teapot that plugged into the 12V sockets in the vehicle.

"Tell me a joke," I said.

Paul leaned over and laughed. "You think we got one on the spot?" he asked.

"Try me."

"There's a guy biking in the middle of the night in the desert. What's he doing there?"

"I don't know," I answered. "What?"

"We don't know either." He laughed. "We gotta drop back."

With that, they were gone. I was alone again. The darkness crashed in around me and surrounded me. I tried shaking my head back and forth. It didn't clear the fog that had permeated my mind. I closed my eyes for a split second. When you're that tired, you can rationalize anything.

I snapped them back open at the sound of the horn. I jerked the handlebars, realizing that I had drifted into the middle of the lane. I shook my head again, taking water and squirting it over my head. *I need to sleep*, I thought. The water helped only slightly, taking the edge off some of the heat as well.

Waving the vehicle back up, I looked in the window. I had just burned two of my precious conversations for the hour.

"Give me the soup," I said. "I need to eat something to keep me awake."

"Water's not boiling," Ruth responded. "It won't be cooked."

"Doesn't matter," I responded.

Diligently, she poured it into the container and handed it out the vehicle window. I placed it between my aero bars, on a small platform with Velcro. The container had Velcro on the bottom as well, holding it there snugly. When every second counts, you learn to intake while working.

She gave me another spoon.

"Here," Jeanette's voice came from the front window. "Put this in your back pocket." It was a mint Aero bar, something I had taken a liking to. She'd broken the wrapper so it would be easier to open when I wanted it.

"Thanks," I responded. "How soon until we get to the hotel?"

"Soon," Ruth responded. "Ten miles."

I nodded, and the vehicle disappeared back. It was me and the night again.

The spoon dipped into the noodles, and I knew I had made a mistake. My impatience would cost me. I lifted it to my mouth and took a bite. The noodles were still crunchy; the water had hardly any flavour. Frustrated, I grabbed the chocolate bar from my back pocket and bit into it. The sugar gave me a bit of energy, but it remained tough to keep my eyes open.

When Quitting Is Not an Option

My odometer splits distances into 100ths, essentially ten metres. But when you get past 100 km on the odometer it moves the decimal over and only shows 100 m at a time. It is amazing how much you can cheer with each and every track-length that you accomplish. At some point I break it down even further, celebrating mini victories with every line in the road.

Finally, Taos! My heart leapt with joy.

Driving into the town was a remarkable experience, since it's about as Spanish as architecture can be. I felt like I had crossed the border and jumped into Mexico. The route took us around the neighbourhood and back up to the time station. As I neared the station, a man jumped off the side of the road and started waving his arms.

"Stop, stop!" he cried. I recognized him instantly as one of the race organizers. I hit the brakes and stopped in front of him, confused. The crew pulled up beside me, wondering why this strange man had accosted me in the middle of the night.

"Is there something wrong?" I asked.

"Were you planning on sleeping here?" he asked.

"Yes," we said, my eyes agreeing.

"Good," he said. "A rider was attacked by a drunk with a hammer. We're calling a mandatory stop until the night is over. Take four hours off the bike."

Four hours sounded like heaven to me. It didn't even sink in that someone on the ride had been in danger. I had answered his question honestly, and I realized later that those whose intentions were to continue cycling received the four hours back as time docked off their total ride time. But it didn't matter; all I wanted to do was hit the pillow—and I hit it hard.

After the night in Taos, the adventure continued. The countryside, thankfully, had morphed from the mountains of Colorado to the rolling flats of Kansas. This was the kind of terrain I was used to, even though I enjoyed climbing in the mountains.

But then the problem hit: I couldn't hold my own head up.

How are you supposed to bike halfway across the country when you can't even hold your own head up? Had I ever noticed before that my head was heavy? I hadn't ever realized there were muscles that had to hold it up—since I'd never really felt them get tired before.

My mind jumped to Kenya. *What will happen if I quit? What will happen if I give up the cause?* They were praying for me, I knew that. As the darkness enveloped me, the kids in Kenya felt so incredibly far away.

Another jarring impact with a bump in the ground, another struggle to keep my bike in a straight line. I was holding the handlebars with my left hand, my right arm propped in the aerobar elbow pad, my chin resting in my hand. This was it. I couldn't maintain this. Both my wrists were sore—from holding my head or from holding the handlebars.

I pulled to the side of the road, the support vehicle's tires crunching in the gravel behind me. They came to a stop, and Paul climbed out first, joined in a few seconds by Jeanette and Ruth. As they approached, I could see the hopelessness I was feeling reflected in their eyes.

"I can't do this. I can't do this for five more days," I croaked. My voice was dry—it wouldn't fully heal unless I gave it time to rest. We had been chatting, in the few minutes you're allowed to drive beside the rider, about how best to approach the situation.

"Take the top of the aerobars out," I began, "turn it upside down and strap it onto my back and attach it to my head."

"That'll be uncomfortable in ten minutes," Paul countered.

"We could put a Pringles tube taped onto the handlebars—just something to rest my chin on." They seemed to be considering it for a moment, but they wouldn't have that, either.

"The jarring from the road," Ruth suggested. "It could jam into your throat."

I wanted to argue and point out that I was the one with the failing neck, that I was the one who had had countless hours to think about this problem, but I didn't have the heart. There comes a time as the rider when you realize that your role is to pedal the bike and let others make decisions for you. In this case, they quickly overruled my two ideas.

Jeanette suggested that we pray, and we did. We prayed for healing to come back into my neck and for the strength to continue riding even though things were tough. We prayed that the work we were doing would make a tangible difference to those in Kenya.

When Quitting Is Not an Option

As we prayed I heard another vehicle approaching and looked up, expecting to see Stephanie and Josh. Instead, it was a RAAM media vehicle. They had the camera lens sticking out the window and caught the last portion of our prayer. Through the ride they had made a point of talking to me about my faith and the reason behind what I was doing.

Danny Chew, a mathematician and rather vocal atheist, climbed out of the passenger seat. He had repeatedly reminded me, "Do it for the orphans, Arvid!" Out of the other side of the vehicle came Allen Larson, a committed Christian. They had both been RAAM champions in previous years. Allen Larson, in fact, had struggled with the same neck condition that I was currently experiencing and even won RAAM with it.

"Having neck problems?" Allen asked, after waiting for our prayer to be finished.

"I can't hold my head anymore," I described. I felt like a failure. It wasn't my lungs, my legs, my mental toughness that was failing me. It was something that felt entirely out of my control.

"No problem," Danny said. "Here's what you do." He began to describe a contraption that I was supposed to build on my back. Paul was listening intently and would have been taking notes if he had a pen. It didn't take long before Allen had pulled out a pad of paper and was drawing a diagram.

"Arvid." Allen looked me in the eye. Standing upright made it easier to keep my head from bobbing around. "This is no reason to quit. This is just a part of RAAM. Get used to it. Keep going. Deal with it."

I wanted to tell him that it was easy for him to say, but I knew that he spoke from experience. This was a condition called Shermer's neck. It wasn't dangerous and would do no permanent damage.

They left Paul with a pad of paper, even with dimensions and measurements. Josh and Stephanie arrived, and we talked it through with them. I didn't want to stop too long—the race was heating up—but this was crucially important.

Stephanie and Josh took off in the car to head to a hardware store, where they would stock up on PVC piping, glue, strapping and a few other essentials for a Shermer's neck brace.

I got back on the bike, knowing that I was running out of steam but holding out hope that something would work, and kept moving.

We pulled over onto the side of the road, doing our best to hide in the shade. Josh and Paul were already measuring out the PVC piping, getting ready to saw. Based on the diagram and measurements they had from Allen Larson they had soon cobbled together an H-frame. In its raw form the brace was quite simple. But given that I would need to wear it until I reached Annapolis, I needed it to be comfortable.

As they fiddled with it on my back and discussed it (hardly listening to my advice), I could feel the seconds on the clock ticking by. By this point in the race I had been jockeying with a rider named Doug Levy. The official RAAM stats would show that we passed each other a total of 11 times between the beginning and end, but that story only showed which order we came through the time stations. In between those time stations we had jockeyed many more times, passing each other while eating, peeing, sleeping. I knew that Levy would find out about my neck and would be able to put more distance between the two of us. I mentally waved goodbye, not putting him out of mind but realizing that the battle between him and I had been replaced by a much more significant one: the battle to finish.

Finally happy with their design, Paul and Josh let me get back on the bike. I strapped it onto me, feeling unsure about what the next hour, day and week would look like.

It was comfortable and it did the job—it took the weight off my neck and allowed those muscles to recuperate. I didn't want to admit that their design had been good, but it had been.

Within a few hours, the chin cup was sweaty and disgusting. I told them about the problem, and Paul got right back to work. He created another one, using two pieces of plastic and wrapping it in duct tape, designing it to fit to his chin, one of the strong features he inherited from me. Then he poked a hole in the bottom and added a towel to soften the feel against my skin. Once I put it on, it felt a lot more comfortable. Every once in a while the sweat would find its way down to the drain and pour out over my handlebars. The struggle with my neck was far from over, but the issue had been alleviated. I could get back to riding my bike.

Something off to the side would grab my attention, and I'd try to look, only to realize that I couldn't properly turn my head. I would have to sit up and turn my entire torso to get a good look. I felt like a horse with blinders on so that it stayed focused. There was only one direction to look, and that was forward. I couldn't turn right or left, so Annapolis was the only way to go.

Can I do this? I asked myself. I'd been repeating the same question for the last 24 hours. People seem to say, "It's Arvid—of course he can do it." If they knew how many times I struggled with self-doubt, with the question of whether I should bike another kilometre, they would never feel so confident.

This was one of those times. The brace was working. I was biking again. But I needed motivation.

What possible difference can this ride make for the kids at MCF?

"What's up?" Ruth asked, rolling the window down as the van pulled up beside me. She had a water bottle in her hand, just in case.

"I don't think I can do this," I explained.

"You want us to get up on the roof and dance?" Paul asked. He's been known to do that from time to time. He definitely inherited all of his dance moves from me.

"No," I chuckled, "I think I need *real* motivation. Ruth, can you ask my friend Ben Sawatzky to give $5,000 to MCF for every rider I pass from here until the finish line?"

"Are you serious?" she asked.

"Never been more serious." I smiled, then stood up on my pedals, my head still trapped in its PVC cage, and pedalled away from them.

The answer came half an hour later. "You're on. And I expect you to pass five of them."

Five? I thought, *Oh crap, you can't be serious. Why did I do this?*

Just like that my ability to make excuses was gone. I had an opportunity to tangibly make a huge difference in the next few days. Though ups and downs continued to come, I set my will on finishing and finishing strong.

Forty hours, I told myself. *Forty hours.*

In the early days, 40 hours was a long ride. Now it was all that lay between me and Annapolis, if I didn't sleep. *I can do this,* I thought.

Levy was still within range. I had passed another rider, and there were a few more within striking distance.

Fog had rolled in as I went through West Virginia, and it felt like biking through a cloud. The climbs were steep—far steeper than in the west—though not as long. I pushed with everything I had, feeling my neck strengthen and allowing myself to go without the neck brace for brief periods of time. My goal was to regain my strength and ride into Annapolis with my head held high.

As I turned the corner, I saw something through the fog.

Are those…lights?

They were. Jones was just ahead of me, a lot closer than I had thought.

Resolving to raise as much money as possible, I rode through the night with only short naps in the back of the van, getting onto the bike as quickly as possible. With that kind of perseverance, climbing up the mountainous hills became almost enjoyable. I was able to pass Levy and put distance between us, moving ahead of Jones as well. Since I had challenged Ben (or he had challenged me), I had passed three riders.

There is an odd serenity to the final several hours of a ride like RAAM. The finish line is visible on the highway signage as you cycle nearer. You realize that a normal three-hour training ride is all you have left. You start to mentally cycle through all the highs and lows of the ride, celebrating the highs and questioning whether the lows were as low as you thought. Other than completely freak circumstances, you know that you can finish. Suddenly the ride has crossed from the impossible and improbable to the likely and simple.

Even more than that is an immense feeling of relief. All the miles that you've already cycled are done. The question mark that hung in your mind has straightened out and become an exclamation point. Your crew starts acting goofy, staging sprints in the fields on the side of the road, setting up blankets and having picnics, blasting music out the vehicle and climbing trees to get pictures.

Though I had my faith in God pouring through me in emotion, many riders, religious or not, experience a similar feeling of elation. It doesn't matter whether you have a cause or not—that feeling simply overtakes you and you realize that, no matter how ridiculously horrible the nights and low points were, this wasn't so bad. It's this feeling that draws riders back.

When Quitting Is Not an Option

The official race portion of RAAM ends in a rather non-celebratory fashion at a mall in Annapolis. To prevent a mad head-to-head dash through the streets of a city in the case of a close finish, riders simply pull into the parking lot and log their time. RAAM is finished. Riders then bike in an escort to the Atlantic Ocean.

Ruth, Stephanie and Josh had gone ahead to the ocean finish line to capture pictures while Paul and Jeanette followed me in the support vehicle. As I followed the pace car I revelled in what had just happened.

As I approached the finish, there was a crowd cheering and clapping, congratulating me by name. Finally, the pavement ended, and I turned onto the finishing strip, the last 50. Though my head was now brace-free, I didn't notice the jarring of the cobblestone surface.

Behind me, Paul and Jeanette parked the car and jumped out, coming to join in the celebration. Ahead of me I saw Ruth, waiting expectantly. Around me was a crowd of RAAM media, officials, family, other crews and local tourists. They were clapping, cheering and hollering, and I was the centre of attention. After spending 11 days alone on a bike, being stared at was a rather uncomfortable feeling.

The stop at the mall serves another purpose: it's a holding tank for the riders to sit while they give each and every rider their own time at the finish line. Coming to a rest under the finishing banner, I suddenly got nervous. *Don't fall now*, I thought. Thankfully, my feet unclipped properly and I could put them down on the ground. *How do I get off the bike without them seeing how awkward it is?*

Instead of attempting to do something fancy, I stayed on the bike for as long as possible, letting the cameras roll with the bike between my legs. Ruth came over and gave me a hug, the hug I had been waiting 11 days for. I followed that up with hugs from the rest of my family—my crew—and then finally dismounted from the bike. By that point not everyone was looking, and Ruth could help me.

On the podium ahead of me was my name, already written there as an official finisher. Underneath it was the time, 11 days, 3 hours, 19 minutes. It took a moment for it to settle in: *I finished RAAM.*

"Come on up, Arvid," someone was encouraging me. I walked towards the stage, my shoes clacking on the cobblestones. I made it up the stairs—I'm not sure how—and stood there. This year the medals would be handed out by a middle-aged woman, the "mama" of RAAM. We're not quite sure if it was a breach in protocol, but she handed over the medal to my wife, Ruth, to slip over my neck. The strap hit there, and I felt the weight hanging down on my chest.

Every rider is given a chance to stand up there behind a mic and share. I'm not sure whose idea it was that people in the worst possible moment of their lives, when they've slept 20 to 25 hours in the past 11 days, when they've never felt so tired, should be allowed to speak.

"What were some of the most memorable things?" she asked. All the cameras were snapping photos and recording me. This was my moment. With God's grace I was coherent.

"For me it was the fact that we were able to do this as a family. My family has been incredibly supportive in my dreams and desire to do this. God has surrounded us and protected us, and I am so thankful that we were able to make it through safely. For us, as a family, this is a faith-based initiative for a cause. I raise funds on behalf of Mully Children's Family, a street rescue mission in Kenya, Africa."

I would continue, sharing in a brief minute my passion for MCF and for what God is doing there. Emotion ran through my body as I realized what I had accomplished. Finishing RAAM had put me on a stage that would create opportunities. By this point I had raised more money than any other RAAM rider, earning the Lon Haldeman award from RAAM, garnering more attention. Though I hadn't been able to see it before, the effort and pain had been worth it. Helping MCF—helping the world's most desperate—was a cause for which I was willing to sacrifice my energy and time and endure a whole lot of pain. *It was worth it*, I realized, tears flowing freely down my aged cheeks.

I came into RAAM thinking I had a legitimate chance of finishing. It's a daunting race, and it pushes riders to their limit. In order to make it exciting and keep the difficulty a few notches higher than any other ride, the disqualification time is set near most riders' breaking point. Even the most accomplished of riders can come into RAAM and hit obstacles that they cannot overcome. Each ride is unique. Weather, crew, health and navigation can all derail a rider.

I had quit rides and walked away disgruntled. Until RAAM, I had very little experience with hitting rock bottom and recovering. Since rock bottom is, well, rock bottom, most would think that that would be the end. When you hit rock bottom, you pack up the bike, tell the crew it's over and figure out how you're going to get home.

But if that was always the case then I don't think anyone would ever have finished RAAM—ever. In fact, RAAM would probably cease to exist.

In ultra-marathon cycling, you learn to separate the mental understanding of "this is not possible" from the actual act of quitting. I was in RAAM and I was learning—daily—just what it means to push through adversity. Cycling has become, for me, a testing ground for the rest of life. It's all about controlled adversity. I willingly put myself in situations that I know are going to be tough. I know that, more than anything, the time will come when I will want to call it quits.

More often than not, when things get tough we assume that the only logical response is to quit. Since we can no longer see what we are doing as possible we respond by quitting. I was coming to realize that simply because we cannot mentally comprehend what is going on we don't need to quit. Quitting does not always need to be an option.

In fact, the miracle of all dark nights is that the sun always rises.

After every mountain there is a downhill.

After every low point there is an upswing.

By now, some 13 years into ultra-marathon cycling, I had experienced enough upswings to see beyond the low point. Instead of responding with quitting, I removed the connection between "This is impossible" and "I quit." Though it isn't easy, I trained myself to keep riding while I worked through the impossibility. If I kept doing that long enough, eventually things got better— the sun rose, I worked through the mental fog, and a new day dawned.

Life is like that. Things can (and probably will) be tough. Sometimes we want to quit, and sometimes we're pushing ourselves beyond a point from which there is no returning. But if we learn to separate the impossibility from giving up we can push through adversity and experience the joy of the upswing. Because it's coming, it's always coming.

At every major low point it ran through my mind to quit—and believe me, there were plenty of low points. Through a ride like RAAM a rider will experience every high and low point—emotionally, physically, mentally, spiritually. It's essential to never make the decision to quit in the low point. You push through, sleep on it if you have to and wait for the sun to rise.

It always does.

At the start of RAAM 2008

Danny Chew and Allen Larson stop by to offer their advice

First neck-brace chin-sling prototype

Feeling like a horse with blinders, Arvid continues.

Being awarded the finisher's medal by wife, Ruth

The only all-family crew on RAAM

Family
Mully Children's Family

By 2010 I had raised well over a million dollars for MCF, yet the need seemed to be growing, not shrinking. In fact, my regular correspondence with Charles Mulli indicated that MCF had greater needs now than when I first learned of the organization six years before. Something did not seem right, so I decided to return to Kenya and investigate further.

When I arrived, my mind could hardly comprehend what I was seeing.

In 2005, there had been 832 kids at MCF. Now there were over 2,000. It soon became clear why the needs had grown exponentially.

In the past few years, I had fundraised for many specific projects. This visit showed me the incredible success of those initiatives—I was amazed by the fact that my efforts had been put to great use. They had built dams, fishponds, a new kitchen shelter and greenhouses. A lot of the funds for these had come from us. It was humbling to see the real, physical, tangible representation of my work.

I spoke with an agricultural manager, using my background in business to probe beneath the surface into the operations and business structure. Again and again I was blown away at the level to which they had demonstrated remarkable business prowess and knowledge. They were disciplined in record-keeping and well accredited. This level of professionalism had gone leaps and bounds beyond many professional organizations I had dealt with.

At one point I sat down with Charles and we had a chance to talk. *Am I really helping?* I asked myself. *Should I continue? How much more pain should I put myself through for MCF?* Charles shared with me some of the dreams he had. What Charles was and is doing is far more than an orphanage. It's a little taste of heaven on earth—it's working towards God's kingdom. His dreams include continuing to grow things, improving their agricultural footprint and export, moving towards self-sustainability. He has visions of a hospital on campus and even a university.

Pause for a moment and focus on that. Not only has Charles rescued children (the lowest of the low, in many cases), rehabilitated them, loved them and educated them above and beyond standards to be the top in the country, he has visions of taking that a step further. Getting post-secondary education in Kenya is rare. It's a lot more than just paying the tuition. A university takes a high level of accreditation and work—yet that's one of his goals.

Charles doesn't push the schedule; he functions on God's time. He prays and waits until God brings someone into his life that wants to do it—then the project is given momentum and birth, coming off the ground. I do not know when his goals for a university will be realized, but I do know one thing: just like all his other projects, when it happens you can count on it being one of the best in the country.

Though I've gotten to know Charles well over the years, one of the things I've come to realize is that most of us, myself included, have no idea what the grand vision of Charles Mulli is. He's always five steps ahead, envisioning a reality that we couldn't even imagine. God has planted a blueprint in his mind that can radically change his corner of the country—and the world.

And yet, when it comes down to it, he knows that none of the success comes because of him. God has His fingerprints on everything at MCF. One of the most remarkable things you realize when you visit MCF is that it is enveloped in its own little spiritual bubble. You know that the Spirit of God is there. You know that you are protected, that God has established a domain there and isn't budging.

The atmosphere is one of joy, love and depth. Picture an ideal family— that's what MCF feels like. Many who visit MCF describe it as heaven on earth, and if there's anything that can take that title it is their campus.

One of my most moving experiences was taking part in a small gathering: just me, the Mullis and Esther, Grace, Ndondo and Dickson (several of their biological kids). One by one, everyone went around the table and spoke about their relationship with MCF Canada and, more specifically, our relationship with the Mullis. I can't even put into words the emotion I felt as I realized the connection that we had made to this incredible family. I was humbled and blessed to realize that, on the other side, they were thankful for the connection they had made with us.

My relationship with MCF was only half a decade old, but I knew it was being cemented, layer by layer, with everything that was going on.

"We'll be heading to the Kibera slum," Angela said. Angela had grown up in MCF and would be my tour guide. An MCF worker in charge of rescuing kids joined us.

"Okay." I swallowed back some fear. I had asked to see where the kids came from in hopes that seeing their origins would increase my resolve to help them. I hoped I wouldn't regret it—or at least I would live to regret it.

"You'll have to leave all your identification behind," Angela said. "You don't want to take that with you."

I knew the travelling rules. You always have your passport with you, strapped to your body. You don't go anywhere without it. And now I was being very clearly instructed to leave it behind.

"Are you sure you want to do this?" the man asked. I nodded. That was about all the confidence I had.

As I pulled my passport from my pocket, locking it in their office, I caught a glimpse of myself in a mirror.

White, I thought. *I might be the only white face.* I thought back to Ruth, who hadn't been able to join me on this trip. To my kids, back in Canada. To my grandsons who had just been born. I could picture their adorable faces, waiting for their grandpa to come back. Before the first had even been born the second had already been announced. (Though only two had been born, the pattern would continue. From mid-2009 until November of 2013 someone was always pregnant, giving Ruth and me eight grandsons in less than four years.)

What if I don't make it out?

I knew that my grandsons had good parents, that they would be loved. Where I was going it was often the opposite.

Ruth and I had wondered if our determination to do the work we were doing would dissolve when we had our own grandkids. I was afraid we'd be distracted, turning our attention inwards. Yet the opposite happened. Our grandchildren reminded us why we had gotten involved in the first place. Kids across the world are kids—they all need love, care and attention. If, for whatever reason, we wouldn't have been able to love our grandkids, I know that I would have been thankful if someone like Charles Mulli had stepped in. *This is why I'm here,* I thought, *Because of them. Because all kids deserve the kind of love, support and opportunities that they'll receive.*

When Quitting Is Not an Option

As I got into the vehicle to head to the Kibera slum, the question changed from *What if I don't make it out?* to *What if I don't make a difference? What if there's a kid I can't help?*

I don't need to fade gently into retirement, I had realized. I can make a difference. We all can. Though the plans were only in the works, I had grabbed the grandpa theme and run with it. My next ride would be called Grandpas Can, a call to action for those who often head south for retirement and leisure. Standing in opposition to that, I felt like my journey to significance was just beginning.

Bump!

The road jarred my attention back to the present. I could see the buildings disappearing and felt like I had broken through that wall of the bubble. I said a short prayer and hoped that my fears were unfounded.

How can this exist? I asked myself. I had just come from a little slice of heaven on earth, a pocket where the world was perfect and made sense. *But this, this...this just doesn't make sense.*

The Kibera slum stretched before me from left to right, going off into the distance. A square of about three miles by three miles, the slum is home to somewhere around a million of the world's poorest. It's a massive slum, and it was the complete opposite of everything I had seen in MCF. Here, most residents lacked the bare essentials: electricity, water, food. These things that, at MCF, were the mere building blocks from which a further foundation of love and hope could be constructed.

Shanty and sketchy roofs stretched off into the distance, the sea of buildings only broken occasionally by a tree. Everything was brown. The roofs, some of them tin, were mostly rusted. The ground was a combination of dirt, refuse and the leftovers of human waste. The sights, sounds and smells were too much to take in. I felt broken, like even the existence of something like this defied explanation. Though I couldn't put words to it, nothing here made sense. It was so completely and obviously in defiance to the way God had designed the world.

Something like this shouldn't exist, I thought, *How can it exist? How did we let it get like this?* I asked. God had given us something special, and we had let it devolve into human heartache.

"We'll be heading into the slum in that direction." Angela pointed. I didn't see anything particularly different about it than any other direction. Everything looked the same to me, but she seemed to have a reasonably good map in her head. "There's a school there that we'll be going to."

"A school?" I asked, incredulous.

"Yes." Angela smiled. "Though not what you might think. It's a remarkable story, actually. The government doesn't do much to get involved. If you were a police officer or a government official, how far would you wander in? At what point does your authority end?"

I nodded, understanding what she was saying. There comes a point when the sheer numbers are overwhelming and it's easier to let the situation deal with itself—no matter how ugly that might get.

"The school was founded by four ladies from the slum itself. They saw a need for the kids to be educated and for their time to be filled with something other than scavenging or sniffing."

"How many students?"

"About five hundred," she said, "though the number obviously varies depending on whether the kids move, are needed for working or want to be there. It runs to grade 6."

"Is there anywhere to go after that?"

She shook her head.

"We'll head in here," she said. There was a path between shacks. The shacks were tiny, most of them not even tall enough for someone to stand up inside. The path we were following could hardly be called a path. The ground was wet, sticky and a horrible surface for walking. Partially because there was nowhere else to put it and partially because they needed a walking surface, garbage littered the entire street. By stepping on the more solid pieces you could avoid sinking into the mud. Navigation was awkward, as each step needed to be intentional and well-aimed. Even then, the piece of garbage you were stepping on wasn't necessarily solid and could shift beneath your feet.

You live in this...? I couldn't help but wonder. *How?*

On the sides of the street, sheets of plastic serving as their tables, people were selling all kinds of junk. It was stuff that had been thrown out, cleaned and recommissioned for sale. I saw a key, a broken cellphone case, some chipped bowls. They were trying to grab everyone's attention, crying out for someone to buy their wares. They clamoured for my attention as a white face in a black world. I gripped my camera (the only thing I had brought with me) and felt emotion well up inside of me.

We continued walking, my hip giving me trouble. The pain was magnified by the difficult walking, but I figured it was a small concern compared to what surrounded me.

"Here it is," Angela said. I looked to where she was pointing and saw nothing.

The cluster of shacks didn't look different at all from everything else. I'm not sure what I was expecting—a brick school building with a gym? Instead, it was a regular dirt compound of shacks, surrounded by a wall. Though it had a humble exterior, Angela assured me that this collection of buildings was, in fact, a certified school now.

Angela walked into the school, waving at a woman—one of the founders. She came over to us.

"This is Arvid," Angela said, introducing me. I shook the lady's hand, looking into her eyes. There were kids all around, some energetic and excited to be there, others probably not so much. It was clear to me, though, that the passion behind the school meant a love for and commitment to them that the kids could feel. Though this didn't look like much, it was a sort of home for them.

"He's here to see the slum." Angela explained who I was while I took in the sights. The kids had very little, that much was clear. But my suspicions had been right—kids are kids. When I'm at MCF, when I'm at home, when I'm standing in the middle of the Kibera slum. Though their situation may be dire and they may have to scrounge for food, kids are still kids. There's a sparkle in their eyes that tells me they know more about the world than adults ever will, that there's a joy there that, if we don't squash it, can change the world. They laugh, they play, they bug each other.

No kid, whether born into a powerful family in the richest neighbourhood or to a teenage girl in Africa's largest slum, plans to be a drug dealer or prostitute. Even the children in the slums have dreams. *How long will their dreams last? If given the right opportunity, if allowed to flourish instead of being destroyed by the culture around them, who knows what they might be capable of?*

That, I realized, was exactly what MCF was doing—taking those at the bottom of society with no hope or chance of accomplishing those dreams, sometimes fighting through rehabilitation to undo much of the damage the world had done, and empowering them until they were, once again, capable of not only dreaming but accomplishing those dreams.

"Can one of the kids take us to where they live?" Angela was asking the teacher. She nodded, looking out at the kids. She finally pointed to a boy and called him over. There were a few words exchanged and he nodded, looking me up and down. I was nervous—still—but intrigued at the same time. Already I felt like we had gone far into the slum, but we were still near the outskirts.

I followed Angela, keeping silent as the boy led us through the "streets." The farther in we went, the worse things got. People were everywhere, in various states of health and desperation. The streets were covered in anything and everything; the smell of human waste got stronger and fouler.

"What is your name?" Angela asked him. He answered, but it was too quick for me to catch it.

"How old are you?"

"Thirteen."

"Do you have parents?"

"No," he responded. "They died from AIDS when I was young."

"Who do you live with?"

"My older sister," he said. He was moving far more easily than us. I couldn't help but look at every person that I saw, amazed at the pain that they were experiencing. Taking everything in, I was moving slowly. For him, though, it was like a walk down a residential street. This was life—he had never known anything different, so why would he look at it like that? He seemed to skip from dry spot and smooth surface to the next one with ease, as if he knew them by heart. Though to me it seemed like hell, this, to him, was home. "She's married and has five kids. I live with the oldest three and help take care of them."

Family ties are strong. I thought about my own family. I had chosen to live a radical life. Some have expressed concerns with what I'm doing, that I'm squandering my future away. But with my family beside me, I feel like I can face the naysayers head on. If I didn't have their voices supporting me, the other voices would drown out any encouragement I could conjure up for myself. If those who are the closest to you support you, anything is possible.

It reminded me of a conversation with a friend about one of the videos from our ride. I'd been struggling through a rather difficult time about 80 percent of the way through the ride. In the video, I stated my purpose and intent, focusing on what was driving me to do the crazy things I was doing. He told me he watched the video intently, and then he said, "I wasn't watching you."

"What do you mean?" I asked.

"I watched Ruth the entire time," he said. I recalled now that she had been holding a bag of ice against my knee for the duration of the video. "Do you have any idea how fortunate you are?" he asked. "You have a wife that will sit beside you through the toughest time in your life, hold your hand, and encourage you to continue doing what you believe in. That kind of support is incredible—and rare."

In front of me, a woman was sitting with her eyes closed. I wondered if she was alive or dead. *If she's dead, how long will it take for someone to notice?* I asked myself. We had been walking for a few minutes now, and I wondered when we'd be arriving—I wasn't sure how far into the slum I wanted to go.

"Here we are," he said, showing us his home. I wouldn't call it a house—that term would be generous. It was about 7x7 feet. On one side it had a wall of mud, another side was a sheet of metal, and the back was butting into a hill. A roof, patched and pretty weak looking, covered the entire structure. The walls didn't meet the ground, so it was open. The door, a simple piece of wood, jammed into the ground and seemed to only be capable of opening about a foot. The whole structure was about 4.5 feet tall, with no light inside. Around the outside, in an attempt to divert the water, they had dug ridges and trenches.

"My sister runs a restaurant out of this house," he said.

I had to shake off the traditional restaurant image that came to mind. *This?* I wanted to ask. *Four of you live here, and it's a restaurant?*

"Come on in," he said, as he attempted to push the door further open. It didn't budge, so he shuffled through. I ducked down, twisted my body and hoped I'd be able to make it back out after.

It took a few moments for my eyes to adjust to the light. In the corner there was a cooking pot, the fire still burning underneath. The pot was full of lentils, a pretty thick and heavy soup-stew. "Those who want a lunch come and they get some stew," he was saying, pointing at the pot. There didn't seem to be any other options. "They eat outside, at the table." I didn't recall seeing a table, but as I glanced beyond the door I saw a small coffee table off to the side. There was a three-legged stool as well as a stump. "When they're done she wipes the plate and gets it ready for the next person."

It was dark in the house, and I was thankful for that. Tears were starting to form at the corners of my eyes. I pictured our backyard at home, where I was pouring energy into making it a playground for our grandsons.

"Can I see where your sister lives?" I asked.

"Sure," he said, bounding back out the door with energy. Standing up again, Angela and I followed behind him as he navigated his way through the garbage strewn about.

"What about him?" I asked Angela.

There was silence for a moment. She seemed to know what I was talking about. We clearly were going to have to walk a reasonable distance before arriving, so now was as good a time as any to have a conversation.

"He won't be able to go to school after grade 6," Angela said. "His sister's kids will be old enough to go to school, and she won't be able to pay all the school fees."

"So at the end of grade 6 he'll...?"

"Yes," she responded. "Beyond that point his only hope for survival is to steal and to resort to prostitution. To deal with the pain, a boy like him will resort to sniffing glue and get involved in the drug scene. He'll become a typical street child, like thousands of others."

"Is he the kind of kid MCF would rescue?"

"Yes," she answered. "If we can we try to catch those on the brink, we intervene before they hit rock bottom. There are those at the bottom and those that are on their way to the bottom. We take both, but a kid like him—a kid that isn't desperate yet—will have a better chance if he already has a sibling at MCF."

"MCF's schools are among the best in the country, right?" I asked.

"Yes," she said, pride in her voice.

"And this is where the students come from?"

"Yes."

"Amazing." I fell silent for a minute. "How do you choose?"

She paused for a minute. I knew that it would not be a simple answer. I could not imagine the weight on their shoulders—deciding about others to either rescue them or leave them behind. While the joy of rescue would be amazing, the defeat of leaving someone behind would crush me.

"It's not easy, that's for sure," she finally began. Up ahead, the boy was talking with someone on the side of the road. He seemed to be excited to show us his sister's home. "And it's not the same all the time. If we come into a slum blind—not looking for a sibling of someone already at MCF—we take along a few kids who came from that area. That way they can act as a sort of 'reference' for us, in that the kids in the neighbourhood might remember them and they can vouch that we're there to help, not hurt. For most of them they've not only been disappointed by adults but actually abused and hurt. They don't have a lot of trust left. But they see their friends—who have been gone for a few years—healthy, whole and happy and know that something good is happening.

"We hand out food, tell Bible stories, get to know them a little. We search pretty hard because we want to give the most vulnerable in society a chance." I was reminded of Lillian, who was 14 pounds when she was rescued at the age of eight. "Even though the streets are tough, there's still a respect out there. They'll say, 'You can only take two? If that's the case, take that guy and this guy. They won't be alive in six months.' Though they're desperate for help and living in horrible conditions, they can still recognize that there are others out there who need the help more than they do. The kids themselves help us in that way; they identify the most needy.

"And then there's the process. If they still have a parent, Daddy Mulli will get their permission. Officials will be notified, letting them know we've taken them. The government is more than happy to get them off the streets. As soon as they arrive at MCF, they are assigned into a buddy system. It's not just an organization, it's a family environment, and they can feel that the minute they arrive."

"I can't imagine the adjustment is easy," I said.

"Not at all. Think about it this way—you've been fighting your entire life for the last scrap of food, and, suddenly, your needs are taken care of. They'll steal food; almost all of them do at the beginning. It's just in their nature. They've taken the act of survival and completely separated it from the right-wrong question of stealing. In their minds, and rightly so, the need for survival outweighs the conscience. We understand that they'll steal and realize that it takes time for the mindset to change. They'll take the food to their beds and hide it, only to wake up the next day and realize that they're getting more. Eventually they stop taking food.

"Almost no kid is drug-free, no matter the age. When they arrive at MCF they are cut off, 100 percent. There's no gradual approach with drugs like with stealing. But they're given a buddy, surrounded by prayer, and Mom and Dad take one-on-one time with each and every kid. You saw our dad's office, right?"

I laughed. "The desk under the tree by the river?" Mulli's office was just that—a simple desk under a tree. I had marvelled at the genius of it. Having no walls and being in a place with reasonable proximity to traffic, it made him approachable. At any point he could see someone and call out to them to join him. Also, being in the complete open meant that no suspicion could ever arise, especially when dealing with younger women.

"That's the one." She smiled. "He'll sit down with each and every kid, hear their story."

"Do they run away?" I asked, thinking particularly about the drug-free rule.

She laughed. "Yes, all the time. Sometimes they think they're being controlled and they make a break for it. Daddy Mulli—or someone else—will go look for them. They know where they came from, so they're likely to return there. They never force them to come back; they simply give them an opportunity. Some will run away ten times before they become part of the long-term family. Each time they might regress in the drug use or their lifestyle. But we work with them again and again until it sticks."

"Does it always stick?"

"Not quite," she admitted. "Some choose to leave and never come back. There comes a point where they've made their decision and we can no longer pursue them. Help can truly only be offered to those who want to receive it."

"But most do receive it—and gladly! After all, this is quite different from where we were this morning."

Yet it's the same people, I thought. The slum stood in complete contrast to MCF. At MCF I felt safe and at home. Here, well, if I hadn't been with Angela I wouldn't have made it 500 yards into the slum.

"When we rescue," she continued, "we don't discriminate. Though Kenya is rife with political and tribal tensions, we never ask which religion or tribe they come from. The rescue is based solely on need. At our campus we are all one. We are, however, honest that they will be integrated into a Christian humanitarian environment."

"And the kids—many become Christians?"

A young kid ran past me, touching my hand. Others were calling out almost in a sing-song voice. They seemed surprised to see a white person in their slum—which made sense.

"About 95 percent," Angela answered. "The rehabilitation that happens through prayer and spiritual deliverance is more than enough evidence that Jesus Christ is very alive and very real. When God takes you from this to MCF, you know He's real."

"How do they thank you?"

"They come back," she said. "Once they've graduated, there's an unwritten practice of giving back to MCF. Some are waiting for university, but others volunteer simply to work at MCF for a few years while they establish themselves. They work there through their transition into adulthood. Our goal is to reintegrate them with society as strong and contributing members, as well as being a light to their family and those around them."

"Come in!" the boy said, and we entered his sister's house. This shack was larger and in slightly better condition. It was a larger room, divided by a cloth. His sister's husband had a workshop, where he would paint pottery and do woodworking to sell in the market. Bigger however, does not mean big. It was tiny—the size of a typical North American bedroom.

We spent a few minutes there, then retraced our steps to the school. Without them guiding me, I would have been entirely lost.

There was noise—a good, healthy noise—when we arrived back at the school. It was lunchtime, and the kids chattered away as they ate ugali, taking in their only meal for the day. I sat down with one of the women who had founded the school and observed what was going on. It was a simple meal, and I could hardly believe that it was expected to fuel them for an entire day and night—but it was all they had.

I felt a nudge in my side and turned to look. She was looking at me and pointed towards the kids. "Have you noticed the broken plates and bowls? My only wish is to give them all a bowl for Christmas, so they could eat their meal with dignity." Though it was clear that she was asking me for money, it was done with honesty and sincerity—and even a little bit of hesitation. I had no doubt that she had been disappointed by white people before.

I was reminded of the words from the book of James: "If one of you says to them, 'Go in peace; keep warm and well fed,' but does nothing about their physical needs, what good is it?" *What good is it, indeed?*

How many times do we pray for other people when we are the answer?

In this case, I knew the answer: it was me.

It seems there is a lot of doubt in God that is sown when we spend time asking repeatedly for things that don't ever come to fruition. Perhaps instead of looking for answers to questions we should spend our time wondering to what question we are the answer.

It was an odd contrast, thinking of my family at home and then seeing the Kibera slum. *Is this what happens when we don't reach out to others? When we don't help? When we don't love? When we lose what it means to be a family?*

Family: Mully Children's Family

There is something incredibly integral and life changing about having parents, about having a family. At MCF they make up, quite literally, the world's largest family. The kids who are rescued from the Kibera slums and places just like it aren't just placed into an organization. They receive parents, brothers and sisters.

And after all, why shouldn't they? God has taken each and every one of us and adopted us into His family. It would only make sense for us to extend that welcome to others, be they our neighbours or on the other side of the globe.

Children are thankful to be able to go to school in the Kibera slum.

A three-mile square is home to one million people.

A typical home in the slum

Reality hits when you see what a family calls home

Claiming Victory
GrandpasCan 2011

The doctor's office was a place I'd been quite a few times. Over the years, since my soccer era, my left hip had deteriorated. It was already in an advanced stage of osteoarthritis, hurting to even walk. I hobbled up onto the table, waiting for him to examine me.

He knew I was hoping to be the fastest person to cycle coast to coast across Canada, so I was happy when he said, "You have the right thigh of an elite 35-year-old cyclist!" I felt my heart surge, given that I was 20 years older than that.

He looked down at my left leg. It was noticeably shorter when I stood, the years having compacted it until I had a limp. An inch and a half shorter, in fact. He looked back up at me, and I met his gaze. "And the left thigh of a 14-year-old girl. Good luck with that!" He let out a chuckle, and I realized that he was serious. I mean, yes, my thigh was two inches smaller in diameter, but really—

"You also have heart, determination and a cause that is unprecedented. I have no doubts that the Guinness World Record is within your grasp."

Guinness World Record? The words hit me hard. Though Guinness had many shock-and-awe records to grab your attention, there were still some that I would consider pure. Like any real kid, I had always been intrigued by Guinness. But I paid very little attention to it—I was, after all, involved in real sports. I had reached an elite level in soccer but nowhere near world-class.

Whenever a cyclist went across Canada, I paid attention. Early on in my cycling career I had seen Ron Dossenbach go across the country in record time, and I did the math. *Will I ever be in that league?* I wondered. In 2005, when I crossed the country with the kids on the back of my bike, it was a deliberate attempt to see what Canada was like. Though I wouldn't have admitted it at the time, the record of crossing Canada had always been in the back of my mind.

When Quitting Is Not an Option

Am I fast enough to draw attention? I asked myself. *Can I increase awareness and build a nationwide platform for MCF?* I wanted to show others the kind of change and incredible level of success that was possible with MCF, and I knew the best way to increase the attention was to attempt breaking the Guinness World Record.

From coast to coast, Vancouver to Halifax, the Guinness record stood at 13 days, 9 hours, 6 minutes—an average 18.82 km an hour. We created checkpoints across the country, calculating how long this averaged pacer would take to get to each of them. By doing this, we'd know right from the beginning whether I was ahead or behind the record.

If I wanted to beat the Guinness World Record I would have to build myself a "buffer" above the average, then battle it out to the finish line to stay above that average.

I started hard and rode through Western Canada fast. By the time I had arrived in Winnipeg, about one-third of the way across the country, I had built a 22-hour lead, and the label of *Guinness World Record* on my back was attracting the desired attention. There were those who thought I was going to shatter this record.

I had no such illusions.

I left Winnipeg with some serious fear for what I was about to face. I may have had a significant lead, but I knew that was about to change. I was about to experience Middle Third Syndrome (my own term).

Welcome to the dark part of the tunnel.

It doesn't really matter how long a ride is; all rides have a middle third. It's at this point that I realize that I am too far into a ride to turn back, yet the finish is so far away that I can't even conceive of reaching it. This concept applies to everyone. It's the part of the train tunnel where you can't see where you entered and yet you can't see the light at the other end yet either.

What's unique about the middle third is that it provides you with an opportunity to find a way through a situation that does not seem doable. How do you keep going when you can't imagine reaching the finish line? This is the place where the most dropouts in rides happen. The mental challenge overrides the physical abilities and snuffs out any hope. Though it's often the physical difficulties that get focused on, it is the mental challenges that are the true determiners of a ride. It's in the dark tunnel of the middle third that the battles are fought in the mind. Experience has taught me that when I think I have reached the bottom of the barrel of my strength, I still have more to offer. It takes courage to dig that deep, and it is amazing what you will find when you go there.

It will change you forever.

For me, this part of a ride has become a metaphor for our faith journey. It can be very bleak sometimes, yet we keep going. When things get tough, we no longer have the zip we had at the beginning, and we're too far from the finish line to see it clearly, we lean back on what we have been taught and believe, even though we can't feel it or see it. It's in these times that we realize it's not our belief in God that matters; it's whether or not we keep moving forward even though we don't see the beginning or end. It's our loyalty to what we know. It's our ability to push one metaphorical pedal stroke farther, to climb one more hill, to fight through and depend on what we know from before—that at the end there is a purpose, there is a goal, and it is worth it.

When cycling across Canada the middle third is 2,000 km, enough to span about five days. To further perpetuate the problem, each day becomes its own mini-ride, with a beginning, middle and end. Within the drudgery of five days of being in the middle third come further middle thirds lasting anywhere from 100 to 200 km in the middle of the day. It's like the tunnel has a tunnel.

That tunnel can get seriously dark.

I had left Winnipeg with a heavy heart—and for a very good reason. A few hundred kilometres before I hit my hometown, I'd noticed that my legs had started to take on and retain fluid. They were like water balloons, filling up and becoming weighed down. In order to get the fluid back to where it belongs, legs need to be elevated. That's great and all, but there's only one flaw in the plan—

You can't bike upside down.

Well, maybe someone could. But I certainly wasn't about to be the first to try.

I told Ruth about the problem when I arrived in Winnipeg. We kept it quiet, knowing that some people would react more strongly than necessary.

When Quitting Is Not an Option

Ruth brought some compression stockings for me to wear, hoping that the increased pressure on my ballooning legs would force the fluid back up. They were white, and we nicknamed them the "Paris Hilton stockings." Thankfully we didn't have to pay any royalties.

Whenever I would rest I would elevate my legs, taking any second to get the fluid back into the rest of my body. With fluid in your legs it feels like you are biking underwater. It was enormously frustrating, and it was quickly becoming the battle that would define my middle third. The addition of the fluid was like a punch to the gut when I was already down.

I had, however, prepared myself for the middle third. I was riding emotionally light, knowing that I was invested but not feeling the burden of the outcome. It helped that I had asked specific friends to be spiritual intercessors, praying for the mental strength to make it through the middle third. Our entire attempt was to raise awareness for MCF and what God was doing there. That could be achieved without breaking a Guinness World Record.

The fog rolled in over the hill, tracing lines across the pavement. Sometimes it reminded me of snow in a Manitoba blizzard, but I was thankful it was warmer than that. The night was dark, my flashing red tail light and thin white headlight the only thing other than the stars. The support crew was farther behind, leaving me alone for a few minutes.

My legs felt like dead weight, like tanks that had run out of fuel days ago. In order to change it up, I applied pressure on the way up, using my clip pedals to get a little more power out of each stroke. It felt like I was losing a fraction of my power with each rotation of the pedals, and I knew I wouldn't last much longer. If I had had a sense of humour at that moment, I might have laughed that I was hitting the end of my rope near Marathon, Ontario.

A bumpy road sent shockwaves up my arms. It's interesting what body parts start to fail. My wrists get sore if the road's not perfect. My neck can fail (like it did in RAAM), my legs can swell (like they were now), my joints wear down like the overused parts they are.

I was climbing, always climbing—or so it seemed. It was Ontario, so at least the climbs weren't mountains. But the downhills never seemed to compensate enough for the climbs. And with my legs in the condition they were in, I couldn't even boost my speed on the downhills. I simply coasted and spun, picking up speed but not gaining any time back. That 22-hour gap on the pacer for the record was slowly closing, dropping to 18 hours.

In a split second I decided that I needed to stop to pee and moved to the side of the road. Because I'd been biking uphill so slowly, I came to a stop only a moment after I made the decision. There was no coasting but gravity grabbed onto me and held me there. After peeing, I slumped onto my handlebars, putting my weight on them. The gravel under my shoes crunched, and I felt like at any moment I might slip off the bars and tumble to the ground.

I can't do this, I thought. The darkness surrounded me, only my light to point out the next 50 feet of road. In front of me, as the road bent up to the left, was a ravine. I tried to see how far it went, but the darkness swallowed up my vision before I could see even 20 feet down the embankment. *It's steep enough,* I reasoned. *I'd rather be up on the road than down there.*

What's my game plan? I asked. *What's my game plan to GET OUT OF HERE?*

There comes a time when any marathoner gets really creative with excuses. They picture cracks in the pavement that they can trip or crash over. They blow their ailments and pains out of proportion so that, if they randomly decide to quit, there are excuses to fall back on.

I had hit that point.

I looked down at the ravine again. I spun my bike's handlebars to probe the darkness with its light. There were some large rocks, and farther down there were trees. I doubted that anyone would be able to climb down that embankment in the dark.

If my bike falls down, that's a good reason. I looked back, seeing no one around. I could say I was peeing (not a lie) and my bike slid down the embankment.

At 2:30 in the morning, it sounded like a decent story.

I'll be forced to stop. This will all, finally, be over. I can go home, put this craziness of helping others behind me, and rest.

To be honest, I'm not entirely sure how far I was planning on going. Should I give the bike an extra shove or just let it slide? Should I toss it, seeing it flip and tumble? Would I cringe when the bike smashed into the rocks? Should I turn the lights off first, so it would be harder to find?

Adrenaline was pumping through my body as I pondered what I would say. I was picturing it in my head when a bright light pierced my vision.

When Quitting Is Not an Option

My support vehicle was climbing the hill behind me, coming around the corner. Caught in its headlights, I felt like a deer about to be run over. I was still straddling my bike, though it felt like I had been caught red-handed. And in the ghostly silhouette of the flashing orange light that resided on top of the vehicle, I caught sight of something that rendered my entire ponderings useless: my second bike.

It would be hard to convince anyone that, somehow, the bike had fallen from its rack into the very same ravine and that my climbing up the back of the van had nothing to do with it.

I guess I'd better just get back on and ride, I thought.

In the dark of that night, things came crashing down around me. I had been close to sabotaging my own ride. Up until that moment, I had been functioning under the assumption that I could do it. *Arvid can do this,* I would think. *I've done it before. It's no different than last time.* My son, Paul, calls it the Superman Complex. Not that I've got one, but that others have projected one onto me. They don't see all the failures and pains and the countless times that I contemplate quitting (and numerous times I have quit). They assume that I can do everything. It's fine for people to be confident in my ability, but I'd rather they lack the confidence and get down on their knees and pray for me, because prayer is the only thing that can get me through the ravine (and keep the bike out of it) at 2:30 in the morning outside of Marathon, Ontario.

After getting back on my bike, I realized something that everyone needs to realize at some point in their lives: *I can't do this.* The thought hit me like a sack of bricks and became a prayer. *God, I can't do this. I can't do this alone. I can't get to Halifax in record time.* And even more importantly, *I can't make a difference to the kids at MCF.* I realized that I could no longer dictate the outcome. I had hit a point in the craziness of my attempts where my own physical and mental preparation was falling drastically short.

In the dark, on that highway, with two perfectly functional bikes and two non-functional legs, I relinquished control of the outcome to God. It was a very deliberate moment and an extremely freeing half hour. *I don't know what I'm capable of doing, but I will do the best I can.*

That's more or less all we can do. Beyond that, things are in God's control. If I was going to make it through the night, if I was going to make it to Halifax, if I was going to make it there in Guinness World Record time and if I was going to have an impact beyond my own ability, then I would have to trust God to make it possible.

And that's a good thing, because I hadn't exactly proven myself stable that night—I'd been prepared to throw my bike down a ravine, after all.

We arrived in Marathon, and the crew guided me into the parking lot of a hotel.

"It's been a tough night, Arvid; your bed's ready for you." Vic pointed to where the vehicle was parked. It was one of those hotels where the door accesses directly to the outside. I looked at the hotel room and felt my emotions flowing through my veins. The darkness of the night had not left me, even though I'd handed things over. I was extremely vulnerable and emotionally raw.

I looked back at the motorhome, then at Vic. "No," I said. "I'm not taking it. I'll sleep in the motorhome." I handed my bike off to him and opened the motorhome's door and stepped inside. Coming in with me was a swarm of mosquitoes that I knew would make my night less than wonderful.

The cramped motorhome shower was cold, so I only rinsed myself off. I slept fitfully for an hour or two, waking at 5 a.m. to get back on the bike. It was still dark outside, though the earliest signs of the sun rising from its grave were showing.

I was itching to move again, to put more road behind me and shorten the distance to the finish line. A light fog still crept across the ground, reminders of the night before. *Did I really consider throwing my bike into the ravine?* I asked. I hadn't told anyone about the mental war I had waged, so I couldn't corroborate my memory.

As we got onto the road, my head cleared. The vehicle pulled up beside me, and Vic, feeling like I had slighted his efforts and kindness last night, asked, "Why didn't you take the motel?"

"Vic." I had to cough to clear my throat from its morning rumble. "If I would have taken the motel last night I would not have gotten back on the bike."

I had been so down and so despairing that the comforts of a bed and a warm shower and the mental desire to justify that I deserved a rest would have turned it from a nap into a night. I consider it planting hedges, keeping myself away from dangerous situations.

It's a lot easier to get up from an uncomfortable bed. It's a lot easier to get moving if we haven't surrounded ourselves with comfort and pleasures.

When Quitting Is Not an Option

From Winnipeg through my bleak night in Marathon, I struggled on. The fluid retention did not abate. In many ways, it got worse. Though I was still riding my required hours, my speed was slowing and I was starting to lose ground to the invisible pacer. Having him there, behind me, was an exercise in mental toughness.

Though there was no physical person chasing me, I could feel him breathing down my neck. Every time we went through a split, I would ask my crew how far behind he was. There were a few times where I would gain some time on him, but any time I took a break he would jump back up. He was relentless. I began to idolize him in my mind, picturing him as an ultra-fit cyclist who never needed to stop. The distance to Halifax was too great; the goal I'd set myself was unachievable.

We reached Mattawa, and I was forced to take a rest. The fluid retention simply wouldn't let me continue at anything close to record pace. If I didn't take a break, I'd be forced out simply by biking too slow, no matter how hard I tried. It was a calculated rest. I needed to pick up my speed, which meant rest—even if I had to concede the lead to the pacer for the time being. It was a big unknown, but what was known was that what I was doing right now would not work. I decided to take the unknown failure over the known failure.

In my mind, it was a concession of the Guinness World Record. Once I took a significant rest, I would start behind the pacer. I would ride behind him, but I had full intentions of riding all the way to Halifax. Giving up completely was, for me, symbolic of so many people giving up on the kids at MCF. Many of them had been abandoned by their parents, relatives and the society around them. They had been left to fend for themselves, abandoned by the system and country that they called home. They were left to die or even attacked in an attempt on their lives. God had never given up on them, Charles was willing to work in the trenches to give them hope, and I was not going to quit a silly bike ride.

I made up my mind: *I will not give up.*

In Winnipeg I had been 22 hours ahead of the record. When I went for my rest in Mattawa, that lead had dropped to 12 hours. I rested for 17.5 hours. That put me 5.5 hours behind the pacer, well out of range of regaining the pace.

I would have quit if it weren't for that rest. I was about to quit when I took the rest. But I had learned on RAAM to separate the immediate from the long term. I do not make definite decisions while under a lot of stress. What Ruth and I do is make a decision to make a decision later. Our initial decision was a rest. Our second decision was that, after the rest, I was going to get back on the bike and see what it was like to ride again.

Mentally, I was a wreck. But physically I felt hope as I climbed back on the bike. I took my first pedal stroke tentatively. *How long will it take for my legs to balloon out again? Will I feel the fluid rushing back into them?*

Five strokes. Ten strokes. A hundred.

I was cycling. I was cycling! I climbed the first hill, and the first thought that crossed my mind was *Wow, I can climb again.* I had been through the wringer with my emotions, but my body was responding. All my training could never have prepared my body for this. God had done something while I was resting, something that I knew had to do with all the prayers from my friends and family and the family at MCF. Given the level of difficulty I'd been experiencing beforehand, it was hard to find a medical or physical reason for the ease with which I could move my legs now.

I'm back to who I am, I thought. My confidence was growing, even though I was significantly behind record pace and fighting an uphill battle. The mosquitoes of Northern Ontario were atrocious. I'm from Manitoba, and I know mosquitoes, but Ontario can take the title for mosquito-infested land hands down. I made it through Ontario partially because I simply did not want to get eaten.

The SUV was on the right side of the road, waiting for me. As I pedalled closer I thought I glimpsed something—someone—just past it. With the overnight in Mattawa, I hadn't made it to Ottawa when we were initially expecting. Which meant that Charles Mulli had arrived and had to drive back, in the direction of Winnipeg. Just as I passed the vehicle I saw him, pulled my foot out of the pedal, and coasted off the concrete onto the gravel.

I stopped immediately in front of him, and he greeted me with a hug. The emotions of the last days and week washed over me, and I couldn't stop myself from sobbing. He held tight to me as I continued to cry, everything pouring out of me. I had only known this man for a few years, but it felt like a lifetime.

We broke the embrace, and Charles grabbed my shoulder. I put my arm around him and rubbed my eyes, unable to stop the flow of tears.

When Quitting Is Not an Option

"I'm so glad—very proud of you," Charles said. "You have done what men cannot do, but with God, you know, all things are possible. And we are really promised in Isaiah 40:27–31 that even when young people run they will get weary, but those who trust in the Lord will never, never get weary. And this is today the manifestation of the Lord. God is showing His power in you—and you do great things. You are going to finish, in the name of the Lord."

I do not have the type of confidence he has, to claim these things. It's one thing to pray for victory, but Charles was already claiming the victory in a way I'd never heard anyone else pray. And when he speaks to God, you know and feel that it's with a deep-seated love and care, with the confidence through experience that comes from knowing God intimately. I couldn't stop crying, couldn't believe what he was saying and couldn't believe that this might still be possible.

"Father, we thank You so much."

I pulled him closer to me, hoping that his strong faith could rub off on me through osmosis, just hoping that being close to a man of God like Charles could bring me closer to God. "And we come before you with thanksgiving. And I want to pray for my dear brother. We are in the wilderness, we are on the way, oh Lord, to victory. And I pray that, God, You may grant unto him victory in Jesus' name. That, Father, the world will know that You liveth, that You can raise those who are weak to become strong. And, Father, for the cause of the children in Africa, for the cause of the children at MCF, we thank You and we pray that You may use this son of Yours, the man You made, the man You created, the man whom You called upon, and he has sacrificed his body, his spirit, because of Your name. Thank You, Jesus. Amen."

We embraced once more, and I felt my fabricated world collapsing around me. *Is it possible to believe like that, that all things are possible? Is it possible to depend on God for everything, anything, at all times?* I knew Charles's story: his beginnings in poverty, his reliance on God and eventually becoming prosperous. When he fought his way out of poverty, he turned around to help others. I knew that the sincerity and conviction in Charles' prayer was a reflection of the way he had lived his faith. And, time and again, God had honoured his requests. *Is victory still possible?* I had handed the results of this ride over to God; did He still have bigger plans than I did? *Does God have more in store for me than I can even imagine?*

Charles told me that, when I had rested in the hotel, Esther had cancelled all of MCF's classes for the older kids and organized a school-wide prayer and day of fasting. Six hundred of MCF's young people stopped what they were doing, got down on their knees, and petitioned the God of the universe for me. What a humbling moment. What a powerful moment. I got back on my bike, pedalling with the knowledge of the continuing prayers coming my way from all over the globe.

Just like with Ruth's three-point sermon in 2005, I learned three distinct things on my Guinness World Record attempt in 2011.

When I reach the end of my abilities, God is still in control. Many marathoners run for the high they experience both during the run and, particularly, at the end. Finishing a marathon or anything of extreme length is a wonderful and addictive experience. You need to keep pushing further and further in order to find that high again and satisfy that drive. But what most ultra-marathoners have discovered, especially when you push beyond 24 hours and go into multiday events with inadequate sleep, is that you come to a point where you can no longer say you understand why you are on the bike. Those who don't believe in a God may look at it differently, but it is clear to me that ultra-marathon cycling is something that pushes me beyond my own abilities and forces me to rely on God. When we're in moments like that, beyond what we can do, it's then that we can rely on God most fully.

Think about it this way—if we all go about our lives and do nothing that pushes us, we'll never learn what it's like to be at the end of our rope. We'll also learn that we can trust ourselves, that our gifts and our abilities are enough. But they're not. Cycling like I do, pushing myself beyond my own abilities, is a stark reminder of just how amazing God is. It's at moments like Marathon or Mattawa that I realize that I cannot do this on my own and I need someone to not just fill in the gaps but overtake my life. I need to hand it over.

When it comes to cycling, there is one extra ingredient. I absolutely have to continue to do my best. My ideas are sometimes crazy and off-the-wall. They are hard and take a significant amount of effort. God will not pedal the bike for me. Nor will He teleport me to Halifax. I don't think Guinness would accept that anyway. I still need to work and continue to do my best. He can give me the strength, patience, determination and health, but the pedal strokes are mine. It would be ridiculous for me to stand in Vancouver and pray that I could set a record across the country. God won't do what God does best unless I get on my bike and pedal.

When Quitting Is Not an Option

Making a difference does not come easily, and there is a personal cost to it. When Charles Mulli started taking street children into his life, there might have still been a hope (especially from his family) that life would remain somewhat normal. More than 20 years later, their world has been completely turned upside down. They have given up wealth, security, pleasures and their home—but they've gained the title of the world's largest family. They have compounds, greenhouses, dormitories, schools, fishponds, wells and more. They have sacrificed much to gain even more. More often than not, we cannot see beyond the sacrifice—or if we do, it's only a step or two that we can see.

It's like that in most of life. The impact that our choices have is too far removed for us to make a good decision. Whether it be climate change, world poverty, social injustice or our spiritual health, the short term is clear while the long term is foggy or invisible. We might start out with energy at the beginning and experience some immediate changes. The problem is that those plateau over time, and the big, massive, world-altering changes are far off. We feel that we need to see the future results before we are willing to make the sacrifices in our lives.

When I went for my first 30 km (attempted 40 km) bike ride many years ago, I had no idea just what God had in store for me. If I had known how much work it would take, I might not have signed up. But through sacrifices—some easier than others—I find myself in the midst of experiencing unrestrained blessings. When you make that sacrifice, when you step outside yourself and trust God that the end results will one day come (whether here or in heaven), then you can truly move forward in making a difference.

The personal sacrifices I am making are insignificant compared to the personal rewards I am experiencing. We're all capable of making that difference; it's just a matter of being willing to make the sacrifice first. What's incredible about the sacrifice is that the things you'll lose (money, time, security) are second-rate compared to the things you'll gain (love, hope, joy, family). Though none of it has been easy and my body, eyes and heart have been opened to more pain than I would ever have wanted to experience, my soul has also experienced more joy than I thought possible.

Charles had arrived and thanked God for victory. But he wasn't the one who had to pedal the bike. There were 1,700 km to go and I was 5 hours behind record pace. If the pace you're biking doesn't pick up, there's only one thing you can do to get farther: sleep less.

I decided to go down to 90 minutes of sleep. This was, in my cycling career, the first time I dabbled with going under the two-hour mark.

Oddly, the sleep got better. I had had tough times waking up after 2.5 hours, but after 90 minutes I was way more alert. I cycled on for a few nights, still struggling but plodding along. Finally, I had crept up on that dratted pacer and could see him in the distance—he was an hour ahead now. When I was on the bike it was easy to ride faster than his speed, but he never got off.

With about 800 km to go, I caught him!

I had sacrificed my goal of setting the Guinness World Record and turned the ride into a metaphor for taking care of the kids of MCF: *I will not quit.* Through God's amazing intervention I had regained my shot at the record. I was only ahead by a bit, and there were too many factors to cut it close. I wasn't willing to get within half an hour and then be shut down and miss the record by a few minutes. Not after 13 days.

We met as a crew, and I told them simply that I needed to build up a buffer so that whatever the last stretch threw at me could not derail my record attempt. The meeting was interesting, as there were questions.

"How is this supposed to happen?" They had seen me battle back from fluid in the legs and regain my time. I had slogged along and made it to within striking distance. It didn't hit me at the time, but it was strange to think that what I was about to attempt—riding 800 km straight through with almost no sleep—would have possibly forced me to DNF at the beginning of my career.

I laid out my plans—essentially: bike faster, sleep less (the recipe for pretty much any ultra-marathon). Halifax was a short jaunt away, and the Guinness World Record and the exposure that comes with it was within reach. I had thought I had lost it, but it was back. It was time to let the pacer see the back of me again.

After praying for me in Mattawa, Charles had joined the crew. He was, by far, the most excited to be there. The motorhome didn't go ahead to a hotel but leapfrogged for the last 40 hours. I would climb into one of the small vans and lie down for a nap. The door to the van would hardly be closed and my eyes would already be shut, sleep overtaking me. Within five minutes I'd be back up and need someone to open the back door for me. I'd rap on the window and say, "I'm done."

Charles, with his thick accent, would ask, "What do you mean you're done?"

By the time many people would be turning over for their fourth time I was already done my nap. I guess that's what being exhausted does to you.

His enthusiasm was contagious. When I stopped, he was the first to rush out the door and come to ask what I needed. I'm not sure if he was genuinely always that excited to help or if he saw this as an opportunity to show me, an ardent supporter of his, that he would support me equally. That man truly is a gift from God.

Halifax was coming closer. I could smell the salt in the air. The numbers on the distance signs were diminishing, dropping to under 100. *That's two times to Lockport and back*, I told myself. A smile had crept across my face, a smile that I couldn't wipe off. I was ahead, had built a buffer of nearly three hours. Everything was going well, and I could taste the victory that Charles had claimed and God had given me.

Back in Winnipeg, Dave Balzer was scrambling to deal with all the media. Having the name Guinness World Records attached to the ride was garnering the interest we had hoped for, giving MCF the exposure we dreamed of. And now I was within an afternoon's ride of the finish line and I was ahead of the record. Approaching Halifax, I was rehearsing some of the things I would say.

I asked Dave why, since I am outspokenly Christian, they were interested. His answer was simple.

"The media very quickly caught on that you were not preaching, you were living your faith. It's completely different. They've been so turned off by Christians preaching what we should be doing. They looked at your track record, your sacrifices, and said, 'That's this guy's story, living it instead of preaching it.' And they chose to report it as they saw it."

His words cut me to the core. To be recognized, hailed, as living your faith was a pretty big deal.

As I approached the fair and beautiful city of Halifax (it might not look any better than others, but when it's the finish line of a 13-day journey anything can look beautiful), I had no idea just how many media outlets would grab onto the story. CTV and CBC were there with cameras, and it would be covered by almost every major mainstream newspaper in the country. *Maclean's* magazine featured the story, and I was voted "Grandpa of the Week" in *Zoomer* magazine. It set the tone for Canada-wide exposure for MCF.

At the time I wasn't thinking about that. All I was thinking about was Halifax city hall.

Traffic.

The bridge over the river between Dartmouth and Halifax was at a standstill. Was there construction up ahead? I craned my neck to see what was causing the jam. As far as I could see, there was nothing up ahead. We were all stuck waiting to get onto the bridge, and Ruth was in the vehicle behind.

I knew, once I crossed the bridge, that I was within a few minutes of city hall. I had time to spare for breaking the record. But I didn't want to finish without Ruth there. Cars started to inch forward, and we moved through the jam.

Melissa, a crew member courtesy of Crossroads Communication in Ontario, had the iPhone up and pointed out the window. "We're streaming this live back to home!" she said. They gave me the confirmation that Ruth was almost there, and I stepped back on the bike. The streets were slick with rain, and I made sure to take the corners slowly. Though I still had to push to pedal, the strokes felt light now.

Miraculously, against all odds, God had made it possible for me to not only finish but finish under Guinness World Record time. I turned the last corner, heard some screaming and hollering as my crew parked and dashed to get pictures and video of the moment, and pulled up to the small crowd waiting for me. It was Ruth and a few others, including Frank and Agnes DeFehr, who signed a $50,000 cheque for MCF upon my breaking of the record.

Pushing one last time, I slowed my bike to a stop in front of city hall and felt my heart skip a beat.

It's over. I smiled. *I did it—God did it.* Ruth came first, giving me a hug and a kiss. We held our hug for a few moments as I started to cry. She was my rock, smiling and supporting me incredibly through everything.

Frank came forward to present the cheque, cameras whirring. Media was there, filming the whole thing. In a moment I would get to sit down and talk with the cameras, words that would be shown across the country.

When Quitting Is Not an Option

Behind me, city hall was being sprayed with rain from the clouds, joining in with my tears, as if I could feel the jubilation of the heavens. I remembered standing underneath Vancouver city hall, nervous yet energized. Now I was elated and tired.

The previous record had stood at 13 days, 9 hours, 6 minutes for over a decade. I had biked Vancouver to Halifax in 13 days, 6 hours, 13 minutes, establishing a new Guinness World Record and earning attention and funds for MCF.

Passing through Winnipeg, Arvid stops at the legislative to see his grandsons.

A small portion of the MCF Family

Arvid with his three grandsons

Fluid has set in, forcing Arvid to wear compression stockings

Embracing Charles Mulli on the highway

Receiving the cheque for breaking the Guinness World Record

At the finish line in Halifax with the crew

The Beginning
GrandpasCan 2012

When I went to pick up my Guinness World Record plaque from being framed, the man behind the counter smiled at me as I walked in.

"For Arvid Loewen," I said. He removed the frame from the package and double-checked that it looked fine. He looked up at me, then down at it again. He squinted, then looked up at me again. I could see the mental wheels turning.

"Is this…you?" he asked.

"It is." I laughed. Maybe something about my grey hair and my limp set him off.

"It's on the house," he said, handing it to me.

I knew that the press I had garnered with my successful attempt would not go unnoticed by other cyclists. It had been a fantastic platform, and there were good reasons to try it again, hopefully dropping the record to make it more difficult for others to break. Besides, in the off-season I had undergone hip replacement surgery.

"You think you can beat it?" Paul asked me.

"Come on, Paul. The guy who set it was 55 years old and had a bad hip," I answered.

I trained harder, pushing myself to drop the record (hopefully) under 13 days. Once I recovered from the hip surgery, I felt stronger and better. Whenever I did something abnormal, my kids would say, "What? What was that?"

"What?" I answered, looking at them as if nothing was different.

"Did you just climb that wall?" (We have a climbing wall for the grandkids in our yard.)

"Yes," I said, still at the top.

When Quitting Is Not an Option

"You would never have done that before."

I would deny it, but inside I knew it was true. Though my hip being new was just a part of life, I realized that I was doing more than I had done in a decade. A year after my surgery, Paul and I would go for my first jog in about seven or eight years (only a kilometre in distance). In those years I had literally not even done the running motion once.

In 2005, I had carried with me a picture of a little girl from MCF named Charity. There were two more reasons for cycling across Canada again in 2012. First, Paul Boge had written the sequel to Charles Mulli's life story, *Hope for the Hopeless*. The ride across Canada would be the book launch tour. It told the stories of some of the MCF kids, sharing both the atrocities and incredible transformations. Second, this would be my chance to introduce Canada to Charity.

Along with the book launches would come performances from a small crew of MCF beneficiaries. Three young men and two young women would sing and dance their way into the hearts of Canadians, while Charity would share her testimony. Having them along, in a separate vehicle, cheering me on and praying for me, would be the wind in my sails that I needed when things got tough.

I started out from Vancouver just like I had in 2011. This time I had a stacked crew: Ruth, Paul, my nephew Juergen and my son-in-law Bernie. Ruth, Paul and Juergen are ranked first, second and third in total crewing hours and experience. I was in good hands. Unfortunately, good hands can't do anything when the rider makes a ridiculous mistake.

In Regina, setting a good pace, I turned early and headed down the wrong highway. I biked for nearly an hour while my crew searched for me in pouring rain, convinced that I'd ended up in a ditch somehow. The night turned dark, and I felt myself entrenched in a spiritual battle. I knew I was heading in the wrong direction, but I kept ignoring the instinct to stop and continued on. Finally, when I came to my senses, I pulled to the side of the road.

I was able, eventually, to get a car to stop to help me. The driver was a young man who was convinced I was a carjacker or worse. He spent some time screaming and yelling at me. Then his girlfriend did what she could to calm him down, and they eventually returned me to the right road (and allowed me to use their phone). I got back on the bike with only myself to blame for time wasted. My crew was relieved to see me, to say the least.

Though it was only three hours, and one could chalk it up to a stupid mistake, the emotional toll it took on me wore at me throughout the ride. It was more of a setback mentally than physically. I arrived in Winnipeg behind my 2011 pace, though I knew that my 2011 self would be taking a 17.5 hour break in Mattawa. If I could hold on to that hope, I still had a chance.

In Winnipeg, I left that entire crew behind. Though other crews can and always do an amazing job, there is something unique about having your family with you. No one quite gets me like Ruth, and no one is able to tell me to get back on the bike with as much authority (she's quite soft, though, really).

The rocky walls of Ontario's highways surrounded me. I looked down at my feet, pedalling but hardly moving. Was I making forward progress? I looked up and caught a glimpse of a pickup truck, making its way towards me.

Out of nowhere, as if someone had wrenched its steering wheel, it swerved to the right. My mind couldn't even process it at the speed it was happening. Suddenly it was across the miniscule shoulder, scraping the rock wall and bouncing off.

Its momentum carried it forward, and it flipped, the sound of metal being rent and crumpling reaching my ears. It was far enough in front of me that I wasn't worried, but my eyes bulged and my heart pumped quickly in shock. It continued its tumble until friction finally brought it to a stop, a cloud of dust and an even larger cloud of screeching sound coming to a stop. In the silence that followed, my ears seemed to be bursting, waiting for something, anything. But, now that it had stopped, it was eerily quiet.

I surged forward, picking up my pace. *Is the driver alive?* I asked.

Pulling within 20 feet, I felt adrenaline race through my body. What would I find when I looked through the window? The truck had come to a rest on its side, its metal body marred beyond recognition. Behind me, I heard our support vehicle crunch to a stop. Walter jumped out and joined me.

"Is he okay?" he asked.

I looked inside, through the front window. There was blood on the driver's face, though he seemed to be moving. I could see his lips quivering, like he was trying to talk.

"We'll get you out, just wait," I said.

"We have to be fast," Walter said. Neither of us wanted to name it, but we were afraid that, somewhere in the truck's undercarriage, gasoline was leaking. The risk of a fire or an explosion made us work quickly.

We climbed onto the truck and pulled at the door. The handle released, but the metal of the side panel had been so incredibly damaged that we couldn't pull it open. On the highway, a semi truck was slowing down and pulling over. The driver was clambering down, rushing to join us in our attempt. Another semi approached, another driver coming out to help.

"We'll have to flip it back," a truck driver said. "Get at the other door."

Walter and I started rocking the truck, trying to push it onto its wheels. We didn't have the force, but with the two other drivers we got the vehicle into a rhythm. Finally, with all of our combined strength, it tipped over and landed on its wheels. The door that had been pinned to the ground came open with a strong tug, and we could look into the wrecked cab.

Words poured out of the driver's mouth, but they made no sense. I was just thankful that the blood rushing from his head was coming from his mouth and not his skull. Together, carefully, we helped him from the vehicle, the danger and fear of an explosion forcing us to move. Finally, we got him far enough away that we felt safe, and there we let him down onto the ground, waiting for rescue vehicles.

When I got back on my bike later, my legs were shaking—though not from riding.

I was struggling throughout the ride. With about 600 km to go I had started up "race mode" (some call it "beast mode"), where I put my game face on and don't look back. I sleep less and bike harder, knowing that I can leave it all out on the highway, metaphorically speaking. I was close to record pace, though my actual position was unknown. This ride had, once again, the potential to grab major nationwide attention for MCF.

Shortly after I went into race mode there was a traffic jam. The highway came to a standstill because there was an accident up ahead. I sat down in a chair, content to wait out the traffic jam. In many ways, I allowed it to be an excuse for taking a break. Sure, I couldn't do anything about it, but I was content to sit there. No matter how close the record is, there's not much you can do when your brain shuts it off. I had entered race mode, only to be shut down in a few seconds.

As a crew, we had a good time on the side of the highway. With the Kenyans we were near a dozen, and I enjoyed the company. Cycling across the country is a rather solitary activity, so being together like that lifted my spirits.

Unfortunately, the traffic jam didn't clear until near midnight. When we got moving again the rest of the crew, aside from the two in the follow vehicle, went ahead to a hotel. As I climbed back onto my bike, I decided I needed to make an attempt to regain race mode.

As the dark settled around me and the headlights of the follow vehicle were the only thing I could see, I realized something that contrasted sharply with just a few hours before: I was alone.

So alone.

That loneliness cut through me like a knife and exploded in despair. I recalled Regina and getting lost. I thought back to the truck flipping in front of me. All the struggles I had faced built and built and built until the entire trip seemed like it had become impossible. I felt the weight of all the emotions I had carried with me. My mental world came crashing down around me. I completely lost my focus and my purpose. My rookie support crew, through no fault of their own, was not prepared to deal with this. I was in charge, but my thinking was no longer rational.

I'm the current Guinness World Record holder. I've cycled to Halifax before— what's the big deal with finishing anyways? I didn't think it mattered. At that time I saw no value in it. I had carried such a mental burden that all I wanted was for everything to be lifted off my shoulders.

A part of me still longed to fight. I struggled on through most of the night, making hardly any progress. Why had it suddenly become so hard to bike 15 km an hour? Why couldn't I convince myself to stop standing on the side of the road? Why did I need to psych myself up for every pedal stroke, for every minute, for every tick of my odometer? Where had my motivation gone? What had happened to my desire to break the record, to even finish? To make a difference?

And, one would think that perhaps this story ends on a glorious moment. But it doesn't. It ends here, on the side of the highway in New Brunswick, fighting through an impossible night. Why? Because at that moment, something happened. There are no words for it other than the straight truth:

I shut down.

The record, my own record, had slipped through my fingers like grains of sand. I quit. I packed it in. I put my bike in the van, gave up and went to find a hotel—a huge mistake. There, I said it: I gave up.

When Quitting Is Not an Option

I gave up.

It was over. I was done. I had already decided. My old record would stand. *I failed*, I realized. Even though I had recorded another emotional video, stating that giving up was like giving up on the MCF kids, I called it quits.

It was over.

I have taken you to a slum in Africa, the Paraguayan "green hell," the corners of Alaska and Yukon, the desert of California, Cantaloupe Corner in France, the mountains of BC, the prairies of Manitoba, the hills of Ontario and the sandy beaches of both Halifax and Annapolis. We have ventured through dark nights and beautiful sunrises, through desolate valleys and incredible mountain peaks together. The journey has not all been for nothing.

I raise awareness and funds for MCF. But my goal is not to scare anyone or to shock anyone. I do not like it when people say, "Arvid can do anything." I can't. I've shown you time and time again in this story that there are many things I cannot do and have not done. I have quit. I have failed. I have failed because I succeeded poorly.

I want to show people one thing: You can.

My tagline is "Grandpas Can," but that's because I'm a grandpa. In truth, I want everyone to know that they can. On my second RAAM, in 2013, we met three young cyclists in a McDonald's. They were riding the RAAM route at 100 miles a day, about one-third the pace of the racers. They simply wanted to see the scenery. At one point, I was one of them. I was capable of 100 to 200 km in a single ride, no more.

Charles did not adopt 2,000 kids in a single day.

I did not get the Guinness World Record my first year of biking.

Each of us has a starting point, and that point is rather modest and simple. From there it can grow. You may be at your starting point. You might be looking at me or at Charles and saying, "I can't do that."

And you're absolutely right.

You can't go out and adopt 2,000 kids.

You can't break my record.

But I couldn't have done it 15 years ago, 10 years ago or even 5 years ago.

The world is waiting for people who will make a difference. The world is waiting for people like Charles who will step out and realize that they cannot solve the problem of child poverty, but they can make a difference to that child. Charles took it one at a time—he still takes it one at a time.

I don't know what part of your journey you are on. It's possible that you haven't even started. It's possible that you're well on your way. Either way, don't look at Charles or me and think that it is impossible. Look at Charles or me and think, *They started right where I am.* We are not exceptional; it is God who is exceptional. Everything that we have done flows out of that.

The difference wasn't made in a moment and isn't done being made. I do not know what else my story holds, and that's the beauty of it. Each ride, each day, is a unique opportunity to make a difference in this world. To look at the insurmountable problem, realize that in your present situation it's entirely impossible, and take a step in the right direction and start. That's all God asks of you; it's all God asks of me. One step, one pedal stroke, at a time.

That next day was rough. Unbeknownst to me, my kids were arranging (and finding money for) Ruth to fly out so she could be with me at the end. Unfortunately, I had decided that I wasn't even going to go to the end. I recorded two videos: one in which I described the severity of the situation and the other in which I recorded my concession of not only the record but the ride. I wasn't going to bike another kilometre.

We posted only the first video to YouTube and hung on to the second.

One of the crew members drove to Halifax and picked Ruth up, bringing her back to the hotel late in the evening after my day of rest.

It was not an easy reunion.

During the time that she had been on the plane, I had backed out of what I was doing and changed my mind completely. I had been gung-ho about finishing well and making a stand for fighting through adversity, and suddenly I had given up. Our conversation was similar to one that took place eight years before, in another hotel room, about the fact that it was time for me to get back on the bike.

"You need to finish the ride," she said.

"It's over, Ruth. I can't bike anymore."

"You know you can bike to Halifax, no matter how tired you are." It was true, but I wasn't about to admit it.

"The record is gone."

When Quitting Is Not an Option

"You told me the record didn't matter, that you would finish the ride anyway." That was true too. I remained stubborn, but we decided that I would wait for the next morning to make a decision.

Paul, at home, was completely confused about how things had devolved in the last 24 hours. It was like I had hit a wall—which I had. For me, though, the wall wasn't physical. It was entirely mental. From a shaky start in Regina to a difficult time in Ontario, everything about the ride seemed to go off the rails. And here I was, completely out of the running for the record. Even on fresh legs with a ton of rest I would not have made it to Halifax in the time I needed.

I answered the phone call from Paul with Ruth beside me. He started by being sympathetic to my complaints.

"I'm done biking," I said.

"Okay," he agreed. When a rider is this stubborn there's not much merit in directly arguing. Logic goes out the window. There were a few minutes of me detailing all my difficulties and struggles, to which he also politely agreed.

"I'll meet with the crew in the morning, and we'll drive to Halifax to catch our flights."

"Why don't you try riding in the morning?" Paul asked.

"I'm done."

"I know—you said that already. But you also said that you wouldn't quit. You recorded the video for YouTube and compared quitting the ride to society quitting on the kids at MCF. If you quit your ride now, you're opening the option to quitting on the kids, on those that need help." So he'd decided to stop listening politely and argue reality.

"It's true," I said again. I wished I hadn't. "You don't understand, Paul," I argued, "I'm done. I can't bike anymore."

"That doesn't matter," Paul said. "You can make it to Halifax. I don't care about the record. It's just a bit over a day's ride to the finish line. Everyone is wondering what's going on, what happened, and why you're suddenly quitting so close to the end. You can't quit now. You're in sight of the ocean."

"I can't—" I felt severely outnumbered, by two of the most unfortunately honest people in my life.

"What were your goals for the ride?" Paul asked.

"I'm done, Paul, I'm done."

"Just tell me," he demanded.

"I had three goals," I said, doing my best to remember them. Thankfully, the day of rest had cleared a lot of the fog in my brain. "First, to create and raise awareness for MCF. Second, to remain true to my faith in a public setting, no matter the circumstances. Third, to break my own Guinness World Record."

I didn't want to listen to myself talking, but I heard the words coming out of my mind.

"And those were ranked…" Paul started.

"In the order of priority," I finished.

"The way I see it," Paul continued, "you've only failed the third goal. Nothing that has happened has compromised the first two."

"But…" I wanted to argue. I knew he was right. I knew Ruth was right. It had always been critical to surround myself in times of mental weakness with people who could be both truthful and bold. I didn't want to bike. While resting, I had eaten at a table, spent time with the MCF kids and sat on surfaces with a square area larger than a cup. I didn't want to give that up.

"Listen," Paul said, "look at this as a story. It would have been great to end the story with you breaking your own record. That ending is out the window. But it would seriously suck to end this story with you quitting—that sends the wrong message, too. You said you wouldn't quit on those kids, and you can't."

"What's the ending supposed to be?" I asked, knowing what he would say.

"You said the record was a means to an end and making a difference for MCF by getting to Halifax was what was important. If you quit now, you prove that the record was the point. But you need to show that it's okay to fail as long as you finish. Ending the story with you leaving the record behind and getting back on the bike and making it to Halifax—that's a much better ending. It shows courage and determination, even in the face of adversity and disappointment. It shows that even though the task is impossible, you still have hope that what you can do can make a difference. After all, isn't that what you want to show? That people can make a difference, even if it's difficult? That when you surrender the outcome to God and refuse to quit, amazing things can happen? That you're not a superhero, but each person has the ability to do what God has called them to do?"

Beside me, Ruth was nodding her head. It was a humbling experience to have my son point out my goals in clearly stated terms. For what I did to make sense, for what I wanted to accomplish, finishing was far more important than setting a record.

I went to bed, unsettled with the reality of which I'd been reminded.

When Quitting Is Not an Option

I had quit the day before. It had been the end, but in the morning, I realized that it was only the beginning. The beginning of the rest of my ride, the beginning of the rest of my life. No matter what stage of your life you're in—be you a kid, teen, young adult, adult, middle-aged or a senior citizen—this day can be the beginning; it can be your beginning. Don't let the darkness of last night bog you down. Get back up, forget about the record, get on your bike, get to the finish line and write the rest of your story.

So that's what I did. I got back on my bike and set my sights on Halifax, a full 24 hours behind my previous record. But the record didn't matter; all that mattered was not giving up. It can be the same for you as for me.

Thinking back to our conversation the night before, I was forced to ask myself, *Can I script the end of my story? Isn't that what I have the chance to do every day?* My story's not finished. Your story's not finished. The story's not finished—this is only the beginning.

Looking back at all the challenges, at all the accomplishments and disappointments, I realized that God was telling me something. It's amazing what incredible things can happen in cycling, life and making a difference in the world when quitting is not an option.

Click.   Click.   Click.
Click.   Click.   Click.   Click.   Click.   Click. Click.
Click.Click.ClicClicClicCliCliClClClCCC.

The water bottle of Spoke 2005: the waters of the Pacific and Atlantic Oceans merging, symbolizing the partnership that was formed between the Loewen and the Mulli families.

As a result, formerly destitute children have hope and a future full of opportunities. When quitting is not an option, God will do amazing things.

Arvid and Ruth and family, Christmas 2013

Author's Note

When my dad was taking his second attempt at Furnace Creek 508, I couldn't believe the adversity he was willing to put himself through. I was a part of the crew, though quite young. We had a cameraman along, getting footage that would be used to promote Spoke '99 (Vancouver to Winnipeg). At one point, he turned the camera on me and asked what I thought about it. I said something along the lines of "He's crazy."

"Would you do this when you're older?"

I haven't done an ultra-marathon ride in cycling, but I've done my fair share of running. What my dad does has been an inspiration for me. When I struggle to finish whatever I'm doing, I think back to what I've seen and know that he's struggled a hundred times more.

The same is true for my faith. It has been incredible to watch him take his faith and the calling he has from God so seriously. If he wasn't following God's call, he wouldn't even be in cycling. If he wasn't continually listening to God's voice, he wouldn't be anywhere near as successful.

This book was a joy to write. In 2005, when Dad did Spoke 2005, I had been writing for about three years. I sat down at my laptop and started to write out the first chapter for what I planned would become a book about the ride. I never made it any further. I didn't tell him about my efforts, because I'd given up only 4,000 words in. I had thought that Spoke 2005 would be his greatest cycling achievement, but it wasn't. His story wasn't ready to be told yet.

In 2012, we sat down together and realized that it was time. The journey for him is certainly not over, and his dreams are only getting bigger, but it was time to put his story down on paper and allow it to be read. We didn't take that task lightly. We didn't want it to be a chronological summary of events. We wanted to tell a story, not a biography. Through interview after interview, changes, conversations, additions and subtractions, we worked together to bring this story to you.

Though the words on the pages were typed and written by me, the stories, events and many of the exact phrases come from him. And everything, all of it, comes from his life and is his story. I have been privileged to not only be a spectator to his story but join in as a participant for most of it.

How often does a son get to write his father's story?

Not often.

I take this experience as a blessing like none other.

His story has challenged me, and I hoped it has challenged you. Instead of putting my dad on a pedestal, my hope is that you can see that my dad can do amazing things, and you can too. It is meant not to intimidate but to inspire. Seeing what he does challenges me to push harder, live better and seek God with all my heart and all my actions. I pray that it has done the same for you.

Paul Loewen

Appendix 1
Riding Accomplishments

This riding resume includes rides of more than 500 km and/or 24 hours. Although I do not have complete stats, I have cycled approximately 400,000 km in the 19 years since I started.

NAME	DATE	DISTANCE	TIME
1994			
First ride	March	40 km	DNF after 30 km
Manitoba Randonneurs	August	1000 km	59h 26m
1995			
Manitoba Randonneurs	June	600 km	31h 15m
Paris-Brest-Paris (PBP)	August	1200 km	DNF after 900 km
1996			
Training Ride	May	500 km	17h 32m
Manitoba Randonneurs	July	600 km	28h
Manitoba Randonneurs	August	1000 km	52h 50m
Training Ride: Vancouver —Hinton	August	1200 km	77h
Furnace Creek 508	October	825 km	DNF after 650 km

When Quitting Is Not an Option

1997

Midnight Sun (Alaska)	June	600 km	DNF after 480 km
Boston-Montreal-Boston	August	1200 km	67h 56m

1998

Manitoba Randonneurs	June	600 km	26h 30m
Firecracker 500	July	877 km	40h 25m Qualified for RAAM
Boston-Montreal-Boston	August	1200 km	63h 6m
Furnace Creek 508	October	825 km	DNF after 600 km

1999

Manitoba Randonneurs	May	600 km	24h 58m
Spoke '99: Vancouver —Winnipeg	June	2370 km	5d 11h 30m
Paris-Brest-Paris	August	1200 km	62h 15m

2000

Race Across Oregon	June	900 km	40h 6m
Rocky Mountain 1200	July	1200 km	59h 55m
Boston-Montreal-Boston	August	1200 km	65h 35m
UMCA 24-Hour Championship	September	674 km	24h
Furnace Creek 508	October	825 km	41h 31m

2001

Training Ride: Wisconsin —Winnipeg	April	1200 km	77h
Race Across Oregon	June	900 km	42h 25m

Appendix 1: Riding Accomplishments

24-Hour Training Ride	June	635 km	24h
Spoke 2001: Inuvik —Point Pelee	June	7200 km	DNF after 5.5 days
2002			
Training Ride: London —Winnipeg	July	2294 km	8d
2003			
Training Ride: Thompson —Winnipeg	June	800 km	34h
"Can You Beat the Old Man?" Bike-a-thon (24 hours)	June	602 km	24h
2004			
Training Ride: Edmonton —Winnipeg	April	1450 km	3d 12h
Training Ride: Fairbanks —Winnipeg	July	4500 km	13d 8h
2005			
Spoke 2005, The Canadian Safari: Vancouver—Halifax	June	7000 km	30d
2007			
Food Drive for Orphans	June/July	15000 km	45d
UMCA 24-Hour Championship	September	687 km	24h Qualified for RAAM

2008			
Training Ride: Vancouver—Winnipeg	May	2370 km	5d 4h
RAAM 2008	June	4900 km	11d 3h 19m
2009			
Training Ride: Winnipeg —Maple Creek	May	950 km	3d
Training Ride: Abbotsford —Winnipeg	June	2300 km	7d
Tour for Life	July	8500 km	23d
24-Hour Time Trial	July	711 km	24h
2010			
Training Ride: Abbotsford —Winnipeg	May	2300 km	6d 12h
24-Hour Time Trial	June	692 km	24h
Hot Pursuit: Vancouver —Winnipeg	July	2370 km	4d 3h 43m
2011			
Training Ride: Abbotsford —Winnipeg	May	2300 km	6d 18h
GrandpasCan 2011: Vancouver—Halifax	July	6040 km	13d 6h 13m Broke previous GWR by 2h 53m
2012			
Training Ride: Calgary —Abbotsford	June	1200 km	4d

Appendix 1: Riding Accomplishments

Training Ride: Abbotsford —Winnipeg	June	2300 km	6d 11h
GrandpasCan 2012: Vancouver—Halifax	July	6040 km	14d 5h GWR attempt
2013			
Training ride: Abbotsford— Grande Prairie—Winnipeg	May	2800 km	8d
RAAM 2013	June	4900 km	11d 20h 8m

Appendix 2

Life Timeline

I used dates rarely throughout the story. Below is a timeline of major events, so you can keep the story in order.

November 25, 1956	Born in Paraguay, South America
August 1970	Moved to Canada
1974 to 1981	Tatra Soccer Club, Premiere Division, goalkeeper
June 1975	Grade 12 graduation
December 1975	Began 30 year career at Palliser Furniture, starting as a general labourer
December 1979	Baptized into membership at NKMB Church
May 2, 1981	Married Ruth Olfert
June 2, 1983	Daughter Jodi Rae born
March 7, 1985	Daughter Stephanie Jane born
August 6, 1986	Son Paul David born
1993–2000	Many good family and friend memories with Winter Wonderland in our backyard
March 1994	First bike ride of 40 km
August 1995	First international bike race of 1200 km (Paris-Brest-Paris)

When Quitting Is Not an Option

June 1999	Spoke '99: first bike ride for purpose of fundraising for a charity
December 1999	Sharing our story for the first time at Steinbach MB Church Women's Christmas event. This would be the first of many speaking opportunities.
1999–2013	Involved in Family Life Team at NKMB Church ministering to young families
June 2005	Spoke 2005: first event on behalf of MCF This event would change the course of our life
December 2005, June 2006, April 2007	Three family weddings in 16 months. A new stage: Empty nesters.
May 2006	25th anniversary trip to Vancouver Island with our three couples
May 2006	Completed 30-plus year career with Palliser Furniture, the last several years in the role of VP of Operations, in order to commit my time and energies to MCF. Palliser provides a one-year severance package.
November 2006	First visit to MCF in Kenya, Africa
June 2008	RAAM 2008
September 2008	Decision made to continue working on behalf of MCF without an income. Family forum called. Significant lifestyle changes made to allow us to do this.
May 2009	Ruth's father passed away. He was our last surviving parent.
September 2009	Ruth begins part-time job after being a stay-at-home mom and homemaker for the past 26 years.

Appendix 2: Life Timeline

January 2010	Became a grandfather to Grandson #1! Little did we know then that they would continue to arrive approximately every 6 months for the next 4 years!
July 2010	Grandson #2!
January 2011	Grandson #3!
July 2011	GrandpasCan 2011: new GWR established
August 2011	Grandson #4!
September 2011	Hip replacement
April 2012	Grandson #5!
August 2012	Begin writing of book
September 2012	Grandson #6!
October 2012	Recipient of Queen's Diamond Jubilee Award
May 2013	Grandson #7!
June 2013	RAAM 2013
October 2013	Grandson #8!

Appendix 3

Fun Facts

Distances, times, food and everything else—my records and notable moments from over the years.

PERSONAL BESTS	
Fastest lap at Birds Hill Park (11.1 km)	16m 45s (June 2007)
Fastest ride to Lockport and back (49.5 km)	1h 19m 30s (August 9, 2007)
Fastest 50 km	1h 21m 10s (August 10, 2007)
Fastest 100 km	2h 49m 4s (August 12, 2007)
Fastest 200 km	5h 59m 12s (August 25, 2007)
Fastest 300 km	9h 16m (July 18, 2007)
Fastest 400 km	12h 45m (July 26, 2009)
Fastest 500 km	16h 17m (July 26, 2009)
Fastest 600 km	19h 59m (July 26, 2009)
Most kilometres in 24 hours	711 km (July 26–27, 2009)
Fastest 1200 km	59h 55m (July 2000)
Fastest Vancouver to Winnipeg (2370 km)	4d 3h 43m (July 2010)

Fastest RAAM (Oceanside, CA to Annapolis, MD) (4800 km)	11d 3h 19m (June 2008)
Fastest crossing of Canada (6040 km)	13d 6h 13m (July 2011)
Fastest Vancouver to Calgary (1005 km)	42h 15m (July 2010)
Fastest speed (downhill)	95 km/h (October 1996)
Most time on bike (in 24 hours)	23h 57m (July 2009)
Longest unsupported ride	Fairbanks-Winnipeg (July 2004)
Best finish in a UMCA race	1st in age category (RAAM 2008) 1st in rookie category (Firecracker 500, 1998) 2nd overall (Race Across Oregon, June 2000)
Quickest DNF	16 hours (Midnight Sun, Alaska)

FOOD

Largest meals	1) $30 was supposed to buy supper for Ruth and me. She ran out of money on my A & W order alone and came back to get more. (Spoke 2005) 2) Three large servings of farmer sausage with scalloped potatoes, followed by a salad bowl with 2 litres of ice cream and 4 cups of strawberries. (Food Drive for Orphans, July 2007) 3) Family-size bag of ripple chips with a soup bowl of onion dip. (Food Drive for Orphans, July 2007)
Unhealthiest bike diet	Ripple chips with dip (Food Drive for Orphans 2007) Big Mac with extra sauce (RAAM 2013)
Most KFC consumed in a ride	40 to 50 pieces in 4 days (Hot Pursuit 2010)

Grossest thing I've eaten	Licking instant pudding off my bike seat. I clearly wasn't thinking. I needed to clean up the mess I had made. (MB Randonneurs)
Quickest vomit into a ride	8 hours (Hot Pursuit 2010)
Most vomits in a single ride	3 (Hot Pursuit 2010)
Grossest food-related experience (rider)	I was cramping badly, so my crew added salt to my powdered Spiz drink while giving leapfrog support. The crew was out of sight when everything came back. Legs, shoes, clothes, face, bike were all covered. They meant well. I have never told them about this. (Furnace Creek 508, 1996)
Grossest experience (crew)	Retrieving my dentures out of ditch due to the same problem as above. (Midnight Sun, Alaska, 1996)
Longest without proper food intake	600 km (PBP 1995)
Favourite snack food while biking	Almonds
Most water consumed in 24 hours	16 litres
Most weight lost on a ride	15 pounds (PBP 1995)
SOCCER	
Least goals against in soccer season	10 in regular season (18 games)
Highest level achieved (soccer)	Premiere Division, (Winnipeg) Canada's top amateur level

When Quitting Is Not an Option

INJURY & RECOVERY

Worst biking injury	Touched the back tire of cyclist in front of me, resulting in landing on the ground. Right hip badly bruised, grapefruit-sized hematoma. (MB Randonneur ride)
Longest recovery time from a ride	Two months due to numbness in hands/fingers. (RAAM 2008)
Longest time off bike (since 1994)	12 months (after Spoke 2001)

WEATHER & SCENERY

Hottest temperature biked through	Approx. 50 degrees Celsius (RAAM 2013)
Worst headwind	Moose Jaw to Winnipeg, 50 to 70 km/hr head-cross winds (Spoke '99)
Best tailwind	Thief River Falls-Winnipeg training ride, 70 km/hr tailwind for 320 km. Rode 320 km in less than 8 hours!
Coolest place to bike through	Rural France with its many small towns
Coolest city to bike through	Jerome, Arizona
Hardest climb	Townes Pass through Death Valley, 10-mile climb up to 5,000 feet (Furnace Creek 508)
Best descent	"Glass Elevator" in California (RAAM)
Favourite stretch of road	The last mile before home/finish
Memorable scenery	St. Lawrence Seaway (northern route)
Most fun I've ever had on a bike	The "black holes" on Furnace Creek 508
Worst navigational blunder	My own wrong turn in Regina (GrandpasCan 2012)

Most wildlife spotted on a ride	Herd of wild horses, herd of buffalo, dozens of mountain goats, black bears, coyotes, foxes, grizzly bears (Fairbanks-Winnipeg, 2004)
Approximate number of times North Henderson has been biked	1000
Approximate number of laps around Birds Hill Park	2000 to 3000
Number of states biked in	23
Number of provinces/ territories biked in	9 provinces, 2 territories
Number of times biked BC-Winnipeg	11
Most desolate stretch of road	Mojave Desert
SLEEP	
First time biking through the night	1994, first organized ride with MB Randonneurs
Softest bed during bike ride	Back of the van
Worst night during bike ride	The 7th night on RAAM 2008. Unable to wake up and tried everything: wet washcloths applied to eyelids and extra-extra strength coffee, jokes, etc.
Longest without sleep	65 hours (BMB, August 2000)
Most bizarre post-ride experience	First night after RAAM 2008, ready to ride again in the middle of the night when I had already completed the race

When Quitting Is Not an Option

RANDOM

Funniest tan line	Helmet head stripes
First time wearing spandex	Paris-Brest-Paris (1995)
Scariest thing I've encountered	First upon the scene of an accident (Race Across Oregon, 2001)
Most hopeless moment	Furnace Creek 1996 Spoke 2001
Easiest moment	Getting off the bike after a successful event

WORDS

Best comment I've received	"Can I touch your legs?" (by a very dear 70-year-old lady)
Most common comment I've received	"Did you come by bike?" (everyone thinks it's original)
Best response to what I do	"I could do that if I only wanted to."
Most common thoughts while riding	What would have made me start this thing?
Largest media reach	GrandpasCan 2011
Largest speaking audience	Fundraising banquet, approx. 450 (2005)

MEANINGFUL

Best music to listen to	Praise & worship
Times visited MCF	3
Amount fundraised for MCF	$3 million
Most meaningful award/trophy	Yellow jersey (Spoke 2005)
Greatest physical accomplishment	GrandpasCan 2011, GWR

Personal quotes/statements	1. The things we do for ourselves will be forgotten when we are gone. The things we do for others will live on. 2. Everyone has a right to speak. The right to be heard must be earned. 3. The only thing that gets easier with age is napping.
A meaningful moment	While I was straddling the bike while vomiting, my MCF passenger tapped me on the back and said, "Meesta Avid, I am praying for you." (Spoke 2005, Day One)
Miraculous sobering moment	The truck incident (Spoke 2005)
Most rewarding accomplishment	Making a difference

Appendix 4
Behind the Scenes

I may be the one pedalling, but it often takes an army of people to keep me on the bike. These people sacrifice their time, energy, sleep, comfort, and much more as they help me accomplish the rides I set out for myself. They do far more than get me from the start line to the finish line—they share a common vision and work with me for a cause. A crew can do everything short of physically moving the bike forward, and they have done absolutely everything else to keep me on the road. To them I say one enormous THANK YOU!

Name	Date	Crew
Furnace Creek 508	October 1996	Frank & Agnes DeFehr Dave & Ester DeFehr Graham McMillan
Midnight Sun	June 1997	Ruth Loewen Juergen Loewen
Firecracker 500	July 1998	Ruth Loewen Jodi Loewen Stephanie Loewen Paul Loewen Harvey Rempel

When Quitting Is Not an Option

Furnace Creek 508	October 1998	Ruth Loewen
		Jodi Loewen
		Stephanie Loewen
		Paul Loewen
		Juergen Loewen
		Burton Buller
Spoke '99	June 1999	Ruth Loewen
		Delbert Enns
		David Balzer
		Miroslav Peyter
Paris-Brest-Paris	August 1999	Ruth Loewen
		Juergen Loewen
Race Across Oregon	June 2000	Ruth Loewen
		Juergen Loewen
UMCA 24-Hour Championship	September 2000	Ruth Loewen
		Paul Loewen
Furnace Creek 508	October 2000	Ruth Loewen
		Juergen Loewen
Race Across Oregon	June 2001	Ruth Loewen
		Jodi Loewen
		Stephanie Klassen
Spoke 2001	June 2001	Ruth Loewen
		Paul Loewen
		Jeff Derksen
		Harv Sawatzky
		Henry & Bettie Bergen
Training Ride: Thompson, MB —Winnipeg, MB	June 2003	Stephanie Loewen
		Jeanette Dyck

"Can You Beat the Old Man?" Bike-a-thon (24 hours)	June 2003	Ruth Loewen Henry & Brigitte Penner
Spoke 2005, The Canadian Safari: Vancouver, BC —Halifax, NS	June 2005	Ruth Loewen Paul Boge Josh Ruby Stephanie Loewen David & Hermine Olfert Ndondo Mutua Lydia Akinyi Mumina Ndumi Paul Gachoka Paul Loewen Kevin Pauls Bob & Donna Koslowsky Jodi Loewen George & Erika Klassen Laura Klassen
Food Drive for Orphans	June/July 2007	Ruth Loewen Bernie & Jodi Friesen Josh & Stephanie Ruby Paul & Jeanette Loewen
UMCA 24-Hour Championship	September 2007	Ruth Loewen Josh & Stephanie Ruby
Training Ride: Vancouver, BC —Winnipeg, MB	May 2008	Bernie & Jodi Friesen
RAAM 2008	June 2008	Ruth Loewen Josh & Stephanie Ruby Paul & Jeanette Loewen
Tour for Life	July 2009	Ruth Loewen Bernie & Jodi Friesen Josh & Stephanie Ruby Paul & Jeanette Loewen

When Quitting Is Not an Option

24-Hour Time Trial	July 2009	Ruth Loewen
		Bernie & Jodi Friesen
		Josh & Stephanie Ruby
		Paul & Jeanette Loewen
24-Hour Time Trial	June 2010	Ruth Loewen
		Bernie & Jodi Friesen
		Josh & Stephanie Ruby
		Paul & Jeanette Loewen
Hot Pursuit: Vancouver, BC —Winnipeg, MB	July 2010	Juergen Loewen
		Ron Malech
		Paul & Jeanette Loewen
		Ruth Loewen
		Henry & Bettie Bergen
		Henry Penner
GrandpasCan 2011: Vancouver, BC—Halifax, NS	July 2011	Juergen Loewen
		Wesley Loewen
		Kevin Pauls
		Ruth Loewen
		Josh Ruby
		Henry Bergen
		Victor Neufeld
		Stephen Redekopp
		Henry & Brigitte Penner
		David Balzer
		Evan Balzer
		Melissa McEachern
		Charles Mulli

GrandpasCan 2012 Vancouver, BC—Halifax, NS	July 2012	Ruth Loewen Paul Loewen Bernie Friesen Juergen Loewen Walter & Ruth Ewert Ed & Vi Siemens Weldon & Arlene Neufeld Ernie & Fritz Warkentin Dylan Watson Paul & Beth Smith Harry Dahl Paul Boge Mueni Guggemos Charity Mueni Joseph Rama Randu Benedict Mukwata John Matiku Lydia Akinyi Mary Kivuva Frank Tilley
RAAM 2013	June 2013	Ruth Loewen Henry & Brigitte Penner Weldon & Arlene Neufeld Matthew Veith

If you like this book, you'll like...

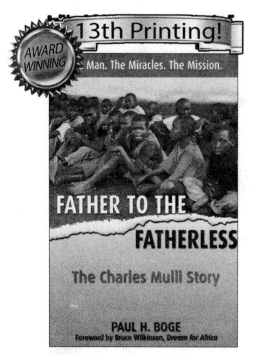

Father to the Fatherless: The Charles Mulli Story
by Paul H. Boge
foreword by Bruce Wilkinson
ISBN 9781897213025

Six-year-old Charles Mulli wakes up in his Kenyan hut to discover his parents have abandoned him. Forced to beg from hut to hut in search of food, Charles scrapes out a meagre existence while trying to come to terms with his abusive past and seemingly hopeless future. As a teenager, Charles is invited by a friend to a crusade where he commits his life to Christ. That act begins a unique adventure of faith, miracles, and a passion for reaching street children.

Hope for the Hopeless: The Charles Mulli mission
by Paul H. Boge
ISBN 9781927355039

Charles Mulli's journey of faith challenges him to trust Christ in desperate times, confront evil forces and believe God for even greater miracles of healing and deliverance. It takes him into the heart of the most devastating event in recent Kenyan history, where in the wake of the post-election violence that shook Kenya to its core, while the nation stands in fear and desperation, Mulli risks everything to follow the call of Christ on his life to bring hope to the hopeless. You will be greatly moved by these amazing true stories of tragedy turned miraculous.

CASTLE QUAY BOOKS
WWW.CASTLEQUAYBOOKS.COM

If you like this book, you'll like...

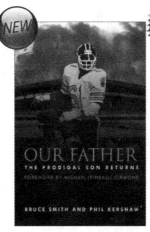

Living Beyond My
Circumstances
by Deborah L. Willows
with Steph Beth Nickel
foreword: Joni Eareckson Tada
ISBN 9781927355183

Our Father: The Prodigal Son
Returns
by Bruce Smith &
Phil Kershaw
foreword: "Pinball" Clemons
ISBN 9781927355305

Bent Hope: A Street Journal
by Tim Huff
foreword by Michael Frost
benediction by Steve Bell
ISBN 9781894860369

COMPASSION SERIES FOR CHILDREN

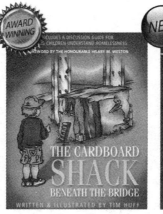

Dancing With Dynamite:
Celebrating Against the Odds
by Tim Huff
ISBN 9781894860499

The Cardboard Shack
Beneath the Bridge
by Tim Huff
foreword Hon. Hilary M. Weston
ISBN 9781897186091

It's Hard Not To Stare: Helping
Children Understand Disabilities
by Tim Huff
foreword Hon. David C. Onley
ISBN 9781927355282